CONCISE COURSE **TEXTS**

EDDEY ON
THE ENGLISH
LEGAL SYSTEM

OTHER BOOKS IN THE SERIES

AUSTRALIA
LBC Information Services
Sydney

CANADA and USA
Carswell
Toronto: Ontario

NEW ZEALAND
Brooker's
Auckland

SINGAPORE and MALAYSIA
Thomson Information (S.E. Asia)
Singapore

CONCISE COURSE TEXTS

EDDEY ON
THE ENGLISH
LEGAL SYSTEM

By

PENNY DARBYSHIRE PH.D., M.A.
Senior Lecturer in Law,
Kingston Law School,
Kingston University

SIXTH EDITION

LONDON
SWEET & MAXWELL
1996

First Edition 1971
Second Edition 1977
Third Edition 1982
Fourth Edition 1987
Reprinted 1990
Fifth Edition 1992
Sixth Edition 1996

Published in 1996 by
Sweet & Maxwell Ltd of
100 Avenue Road,
London NW3 3PF
Typeset by
Mendip Communications Ltd,
Frome, Somerset
Printed in England by
Clays Ltd, St. Ives plc

A CIP catalogue
record for this book
is available from
the British Library

ISBN 0–421–555009

Preface

Hectic Times in the ELS

The pace of change in the ELS has not slowed since the last edition. On the contrary, civil justice has been under scrutiny yet again, by the Heilbron Committee and Lord Woolf, even so soon after the upheaval caused by Part One of the Courts and Legal Services Act 1990. The 1995 practice directions resulting from these two, with their requirements for skeleton arguments in civil cases and introduction of case management by the judge have already transformed the shape of civil trials in the High Court, from a demonstration of traditional oral advocacy, lead by the parties, to a discussion of the contents of the pre-read "bundle", more tightly controlled by the judge. The Royal Commission on Criminal Justice 1993 has resulted in several legislative outcomes, including the Criminal Appeal Act 1995, the controversial Criminal Justice and Public Order Act 1994, with its massive qualification to the right of silence and the astonishing but unopposed Criminal Procedure and Investigations Bill 1996, which is hurtling towards royal assent even as I write. This Bill changes the shape of criminal procedure just as radically as the changes in the civil process, requiring unprecedented pre-trial disclosure on the part of the defendant. These two measures can be said to dramatically shift the burden of proof and must give the lie to the rhetoric that, in English law, the defendant benefits from a presumption of innocence. If we enjoyed the entrenchment of our rights in a written constitution, we might begin to grasp the scale of these changes in our constitutional rights and might even give some thought to their desirability.

New EC case law, especially the later *Factortame* cases, and the Maastricht Treaty have, since the last edition, impacted on another area of our unwritten constitution, parliamentary sovereignty.

The less dramatic changes in the English legal system explained in this book are too many to outline here but they include: the Civil

Evidence Act 1995, abolishing the hearsay rule in civil cases; the consolidating Arbitration Act 1996; the Defamation Act 1996, introducing a new "fast track" procedure for defamation cases; the Family Law Act 1996, with its emphasis on mediation; the opening up of the system of appointments for the inferior judiciary, providing job specs., advertising to recruit new judges and interviewing candidates and the case of *Pepper v. Hart*, which has been applied broadly by judges as an opportunity to go quite far and quite frequently behind the face of legislation, in an endeavour to discover parliamentary intent.

As if all this were not enough, we can expect yet another radical restructuring of the funding and organisation of legal aid and legal services, as a white paper is to be published imminently (Summer 1996), following the consultative 1995 Green Paper *Legal Aid – Targeting Need*.

Lots to keep up with! Have a good read and don't stop here. By the time you read this book, or any law book, it will be out of date.

Kingston Law School   Penny Darbyshire
July 1996

Contents

Table of Cases

4

Table of Statutes

Table of European Conventions and Legislation

CHAPTER 1

THE LEGAL PROFESSION

1. BARRISTERS AND SOLICITORS

In the English legal system a practising lawyer must hold one of two professional qualifications; she must either have been admitted to practise as a solicitor or have been called to the Bar as a barrister. This division of the legal profession is of long standing and each branch has its own characteristic functions as well as a separate governing body and professional rules.

The barrister is usually thought of primarily as an advocate, since this is the work in which she is most often engaged. Until 1990, barristers had the virtually exclusive right of audience as advocates before all the superior courts, and could also appear in the inferior courts. When acting professionally, barristers are known as "counsel". In total there were, in 1995, 8,498 barristers in practice, a number which is just about small enough to make this branch of the profession a closely-knit unit. This point is significant, bearing in mind that the senior judges in the English legal system have, until now, been drawn exclusively from the ranks of experienced counsel.

The solicitor can be an advocate in the inferior courts and may, since the Courts and Legal Services Act 1990 (hereinafter CLSA), apply for rights of audience at all levels but she is more familiar to the public in her role as a general legal adviser. There are approximately 80,000 solicitors of whom around 63,000 hold practising certificates and their offices are a familiar feature in the business centres of cities and towns throughout England and Wales.

A significant difference between the two professions is that members of the public are able to call at a solicitor's office and seek advice in a personal interview, whereas a barrister can at present only be consulted indirectly through a solicitor, except by other professionals, such as accountants. It can be seen that there is a possible analogy in these circumstances to the medical profession, with the solicitor being regarded as a general practitioner and the barrister as a consultant.

1

The analogy must not be taken too far, however, since the legal knowledge of the newly qualified barrister is not to be compared with that of the senior partners of a firm of solicitors, whose legal experience may extend over many years and cover diverse fields of law. In many instances too the solicitor is more of a specialist than the barrister. A 1991 survey showed that most solicitors consider themselves specialists.

Apart from the barristers and solicitors who are involved in the private practice of the law, it is necessary to remember that a large number of professionally qualified lawyers are employed in central and local government, in commerce and industry and in education. Many of these, because they are not engaged in the practice of the law, would not be included in the figures given above.

2. TRAINING

(i) Barristers

A would-be barrister must first register as a student member of one of the four Inns of Court. The Inns of Court are Gray's Inn, Lincoln's Inn, Inner Temple and Middle Temple. All these institutions are to be found in close proximity to the Royal Courts of Justice in London. These four establishments, to one of which every barrister must belong, have a long history as the original homes of the earliest advocates to practise as a profession.

Detailed regulations govern entry to the profession. The general pattern is for the student to obtain a law degree and thereafter to undergo the one year Bar Vocational Course. This training is provided by the Council of Legal Education and will be provided by several universities, from 1997. On satisfactory completion of the vocational course, students are called to the Bar by their Inn of Court. Graduates who do not have a law degree have to take and pass a one-year course, before proceeding to the vocational course. Whilst studying to become a barrister, the students are required to attend their Inn of Court to obtain an awareness of the ways of the profession which they are intending to join. Their attendance is enforced by the requirement that they be present for a number of dinners each legal term. However brilliant the student, she cannot be called to the Bar unless she has eaten all her 18 dinners.

Even after call to the Bar, the student's training is not complete, because if she intends to practise as a barrister she has to undergo a process known as pupillage. This involves understudying a junior counsel in day-to-day practice for a period of 12 months. To balance the picture it is necessary to stress that many individuals who qualify as barristers do not intend to enter practice after their call. This is especially so in the case of many students from overseas. No pupillage requirement applies to these students. Barristers entering practice after 1997 will be required to undergo continuing education.

(ii) Solicitors

Training for the would-be solicitor has long been a combination of examinations in law and the understudying of a solicitor in practice. This latter process involves the student serving "a term of articles" as a trainee solicitor.

The usual method of entry is by the student obtaining a law degree and then proceeding to a one-year Legal Practice Course. Provision is made, however, for non-law graduates and mature students to qualify as solicitors by undergoing an educational stage to be completed before the vocational stage can be attempted. For all students a period in articles will be compulsory. All newly admitted solicitors must now undergo regular "continuing education" by attending non-examined training.

When the student has completed articles satisfactorily, and passed all the examinations to which he is subject, he may then apply to the Law Society to be "admitted". This process is effected by the Master of the Rolls formally adding the name of the new solicitor to the roll of officers of the Supreme Court. From the date of admission, the student becomes a solicitor of the Supreme Court and, as such, an officer of the court, but he may not practise until he has taken out an annual practising certificate individually issued by the Law Society. There is a substantial annual fee payable to the Law Society for the practising certificate and an additional payment to the compensation fund is also required. This is the fund from which payments are made by the Law Society to clients who have suffered financial loss through the misconduct of a solicitor. In order to obtain a practising certificate the solicitor also has to comply with very detailed regulations governing solicitors' accounts and pay a substantial annual premium through the Law Society for indemnity insurance against negligence claims.

Reforms proposed in 1996

The Lord Chancellor's Advisory Committee on Legal Education and Conduct this year published their *First Report on Legal Education and Training*, in which they have recommended a fairly radical change in legal education. The consider that a law degree should be recognised as an independent liberal education so that its contents should cease to be dictated by the two sides of the profession. (At the moment, all qualifying law degrees must contain seven core subjects to a required standard.) Provided the law graduate has studied two years' law, this should be sufficient. There should be an increase in the time spent studying legal subjects by those non-law graduates on conversion courses. There should be a period of common professional legal studies of at least 18 weeks for all intending lawyers, who would receive a Licentiate in Professional Legal Studies. Licentiates would then spend a further 18 weeks in specialist training as a solicitor or barrister, either preceding or following a period of in-service training.

3. ORGANISATION

The organisation of the two branches of the legal profession is the responsibility of two quite independent sets of governing bodies.

BARRISTERS

(i) The Inns of Court

The four Inns of Court are administered by their respective senior members who are called the Benchers. The Inn of Court which registers the student is also responsible for calling her to the Bar. The Inns, historically, had a collegiate function in training new barristers. They now provide the dining system and own and administer valuable property in the Temple area from which most of London's practising barristers rent their chambers.

(ii) The General Council of the Bar (known as "the Bar Council")

This is the professional governing body of the Bar. It comprises elected barristers and was created in 1987. The Bar Council performs similar professional functions to the Law Society. It lays down the Bar's Code of Conduct and administers the system for disciplining errant barristers and it represents the Bar as a trade union. In addition, the six court circuits have their own Bar Associations, as do specialist barristers.

(iii) The Council of Legal Education

As the name indicates, this body deals with the arrangements for the admission, examination and training of students in their preparation for call to the Bar.

(iv) Junior Counsel and Queen's Counsel

All practising barristers are junior counsel unless they have been designated Queen's Counsel (Q.C.). There are some 891 Queen's Counsel in practice, of whom 57 are women. The status is bestowed on about 45 counsel a year by the Queen on the advice of the Lord Chancellor. Annually, the Lord Chancellor's office issues an invitation to junior counsel, who may wish to be considered for designation, to apply. Before a junior counsel can hope to achieve the status she must be able to point to at least 10 years' successful practice as a barrister (or, from 1995, solicitor advocate: see below) and applicants are normally aged 38–50. The strange system of inviting applications results from the fact that the change of status is, financially, something of a speculation. Once appointed, the Queen's Counsel is barred from much routine work and is expected to appear only in the most important cases, for which briefs may not be so readily available. She is known as a "Leader" because she is often accompanied in a court case by one, and sometimes two, junior counsel. There used to be a rule called the Two Counsel Rule whereby a Q.C. had to pay a junior to appear as an assistant in court. This was abolished in 1977, following criticism by the Monopolies and Mergers Commission, but it is still widely followed in practice. The practice has been the subject of repeated criticism and scrutiny and regulations inspired by the Lord Chancellor's Efficiency Commission on Criminal Practice have made serious inroads into the practice from November 1988. The process of becoming a Queen's Counsel is called "taking silk", referring to the fact that the new status involves a change from a stuff gown to a silk gown.

The Lord Chancellor has set out details of the eligibility criteria for Q.C.'s in *Silk* (1996) (current at the time of writing). Candidates should appear regularly before the courts of England and Wales. They will normally have been barristers or solicitors for 10–15 years, with at least five years' advocacy experience in the higher courts and are normally aged 38–50. This means that, although solicitor advocates objected that the Lord Chancellor forgot to invite them to apply for silk in 1995, none of them is likely to be considered suitable until about 1999. The Lord Chancellor grants silk only to practitioners "who have reached the appropriate level of professional eminence and distinction", who display these attributes: intellectual ability; outstanding ability as an advocate; high professional standing and respect; maturity of judgment and balance; a high quality practice based on demanding cases (paraphrased).

(v) The barrister's clerk

It is common practice for a group of barristers in chambers to share a clerk. Clerks play a major part in each set of chambers as business managers and it is said that the clerk can make, or break, the barrister. The barrister's clerk arranges the work of the barrister and negotiates the fee to be marked on the brief by the solicitor unless it is a legal aid case when the taxing officer of the court will assess the fee. There is an Institute of Barristers' Clerks, which represents clerks' interests.

SOLICITORS

(i) The Law Society

Solicitors are subject to the Law Society which is controlled by an elected body consisting of a Council and an annually elected President, and they are assisted by a full-time Secretary and a large Secretariat. The Law Society is recognised for certain purposes in Acts of Parliament and in this way it has control over all solicitors. For other non-statutory purposes membership of the Law Society is voluntary. The Society publishes the *Law Society's Gazette* for its voluntary members. The Solicitors' Complaints Bureau and Solicitors' Disciplinary Tribunal deal with alleged professional misconduct by solicitors. The Tribunal is made up of solicitors and lay members appointed by the Master of the Rolls. The Tribunal has power to strike the name of the offending solicitor off the Roll, or they may suspend a solicitor from practice, or administer a reprimand, order payment of a penalty of up to £5,000 or order the solicitor to pay certain costs.

(ii) The Institute of Legal Executives

The body which represents the senior persons employed in solicitors' offices is the Institute of Legal Executives, which has its own examination system for admission as an Associate or a Fellow of the Institute. The routine work of a solicitor's office is largely carried out by legal executives, and they are significant fee earners in many solicitors' practices.

4. HISTORY

The division of the legal profession into advocates on the one hand, and those who prepare the case for the advocate on the other hand, has been traced back to about 1340.

The barristers seem to have been known originally as "apprentices-at-law" and those who were given the right of audience before the superior law courts were known as serjeants-at-law. This rank was abolished by one of the provisions of the Judicature Act 1873.

Those who were concerned with the paperwork preparation of cases were called "attorneys" in the common law courts, "proctors" in the ecclesiastical and admiralty courts and "solicitors" in the chancery courts. As the Inns of Court developed their exclusiveness in the field of advocacy in the sixteenth century, so in 1739 an organisation was set up called "The Society of Gentlemen Practisers in the Courts of Law and Equity", which grouped together the non-advocates. It was this same society which ultimately was to give way to the Law Society, incorporated in 1831 and granted a royal charter in 1845. At the same time the term "solicitor" came to be the accepted description for the non-barrister lawyer, as the term "barrister" also became accepted as the descriptive term for the professional advocate.

5. WORK OF BARRISTERS AND SOLICITORS

(i) Barristers

Most barristers are professional advocates earning their living by the presentation of civil and criminal cases in court. As such, a barrister must be capable of prosecuting in a criminal case one day and defending an accused person the next; or of preparing a skeleton argument and taking the case for a plaintiff in a civil action one day and doing the same for a defendant the next. In this way the barrister attains a real degree of objectivity and of independence of mind, becoming a specialist in advocacy.

At the same time, it is a mistake to regard the barrister entirely as an advocate. In practice there is a great deal of paperwork involved in the pre-trial stages of a case, particularly so where a civil action is in question and pleadings and skeleton arguments have to be prepared. Again, barristers will often be asked, by solicitors or other professionals, to give written advice on a particular legal matter. This is known as "taking counsel's opinion". It can be said, then, that all barristers do spend a lot of time on paperwork, apart from their actual appearances in court in their capacity as advocates. Indeed, some barristers who have specialised in a particular branch of the law as, for example, planning law, tax law or employment law, may do most of their work from their rooms or chambers, or home, in documentary form and only occasionally appear in the courts as advocates.

Two-thirds of practising barristers work in London. The remainder operate from one of 30 provincial centres.

Barristers are not allowed to form partnerships, other than overseas, or with overseas lawyers, but may share the same set of chambers and also frequently share a clerk, so that there are very close links between them. By the very way in which their work comes to hand, it often happens that cases overlap or are fixed for the same day, and then another barrister has to take the case at short notice. This is called a "late brief". In such instances the chambers system does prove useful. The ability to grasp the point of a case quickly and the adaptability to move from court to court, and case to case, at short notice is the mark of the experienced barrister, but critics complain that the client is ill-served by the late brief. Often, legally aided defendants in criminal cases will not see their counsel until the day of the hearing. Late briefs were a subject of Michael Zander's 1992 Crown Court Survey for the Royal Commission on Criminal Justice, who were heavily critical of their prevalence in their 1993 Report.

The remuneration of a barrister is negotiated on her behalf by her clerk and the fee is then marked on the brief, *i.e.* the instructions in the case. Traditionally and at common law, barristers were not engaged under a contract for services. They could neither sue nor be sued in contract. The CLSA s.61 permits a barrister to enter into a contract, subject to professional rules. Under an agreement by the Bar Council and the Law Society, Law Society rules make non-payment of fees by solicitors a disciplinary offence.

(ii) Solicitors

The name-plates of firms of solicitors are an everyday sight in cities and towns in England and Wales; and although a one-person practice is by no means rare, the trend is towards having several solicitors in partnership and towards ever larger firms or consortia of firms. This gives them the opportunity to specialise to some extent, so that whilst one partner may spend all his time on matrimonial work, another will deal with litigation, another with probate and trusts and so on. In some of the larger London firms there are more than 100 partners and this means that each can really specialise in a branch of the law in which they have an interest.

The 8,500 firms of solicitors in England and Wales will deal with a very wide variety of legal problems. A traditionally significant area of solicitors' work, prior to the recession, was the transfer of property, whether by way of sale or lease, and this particular skill is known as conveyancing. A solicitor, acting for a client who is selling property, guarantees that he will transfer the legal title to the property effectively and will obtain and pay to the client the purchase money which the client has agreed to accept. A solicitor acting for a purchaser guarantees that the client is getting a valid legal title to the property which they have agreed to buy. The Law Society administers an indemnity fund, which is available to compensate any person who suffers financial loss as a result of dishonest conduct on the part of a solicitor in the course of professional obligations. Solicitors may also be sued in the courts for negligence by a client who alleges that the solicitor is in breach of the duty to take proper care in the handling of the client's business.

Another traditional, but now declining part of a typical solicitors practice, is probate work, which is concerned with the obtaining of legal title to a deceased person's estate and then with the actual winding up and distribution of that estate. The CLSA 1990 abolished solicitors' monopoly over probate work (s.54). Litigation, including family disputes, is a fruitful source of work for a large number of solicitors since, as has been seen, the solicitor is responsible for preparing the whole of the case, and the barrister receives this in the form of a "brief" from which she plans her argument in the case. Solicitors used to hold a monopoly over the conduct of litigation but this too was abolished by the CLSA (see below). In addition to preparing litigation, it must be remembered that solicitors have a right of audience, regardless of the CLSA, as advocates in the county court, in magistrates' courts and, for certain cases, in the Crown Court and the High Court.

There is no limit to the topics involving legal considerations which may find their way to a solicitor's office. Family law, tax law, company law, financial services, the activities of local authorities in such matters as compulsory purchase and planning are other major areas of work but obviously, solicitors, as a body, deal with every aspect of the law.

The remuneration of solicitors is to some extent controlled. In litigation the costs claimed by the solicitors are examined—or more correctly "taxed"—by the appropriate officer of the court concerned. This is known as "contentious business". Even where solicitors are engaged in "non-contentious business" the costs are still controlled in the sense that the charge made must be fair and reasonable having regard to all the circumstances of the case. It is possible for a client to challenge a charge by forcing the solicitor to obtain a certificate from the Law Society to the effect that the charge is fair and reasonable.

6. PROFESSIONAL ETIQUETTE

Both barristers and solicitors are closely restricted in their professional conduct by the supervision of their respective governing bodies. The former rigorous prohibition on advertising has been relaxed sufficiently to enable a solicitor to advertise the work he does in newspapers and on radio and television. Barristers were precluded from advertising until the 1990s. Currently a barrister only meets the lay client when the solicitor, or solicitor's representative, is present, so building up the isolation, as well as the objectivity, of the barrister. In order to prevent barristers gaining unfair advantage by cultivating the friendship of solicitors, there used to be a rule which prevented a solicitor and barrister in a case from having lunch together.

Barristers and solicitors are required to dress formally when appearing in a court case; for a barrister this involves wearing wig and gown, since without these he cannot be "seen" or "heard" by the judge. Solicitors appearing in the county, Crown or High Court must wear a gown but no wig. The wearing of wigs has become more controversial since the emergence of solicitor-advocates' full rights of audience, granted under the CLSA 1990. Solicitor-advocates want to wear wigs but by 1996, the Lord Chancellor has not permitted this.

Although solicitors have long been able to form partnerships, the barrister is not permitted to share responsibilities in this way except in partnership with overseas lawyers. She does have the benefit of contact with other barristers in the chambers of which she is a member, but she remains an independent unit, standing or falling entirely by her own efforts. Barristers cannot be sued by their clients for negligence in court or in preparation of court work: *Rondel v. Worsley* [1969] H.L. and *Saif Ali v. Sydney Mitchell* [1978] H.L. but the opposing client may sue for breach of duty: *Kelly v. L.T.E.* [1982] C.A. and the immunity does not extend to negligent advice. Barristers' common law immunity is extended to other advocates by the CLSA 1990, s.62, which also provides immunity from breach of contract suits in the same context.

The rule in *Rondel v. Worsley* is being challenged in a case scheduled for 1996. An individual whose conviction was quashed by the Court of Appeal is suing his barrister for negligent conduct of his criminal defence.

Finally, one result of the division of the legal profession is that no one can practise as both a barrister and a solicitor at the same time although it is now possible to be doubly qualified. Provision has, however, been made for transfer from one profession to the other and it has become easier over the years.

7. CHANGE AND THE LEGAL PROFESSION

THE ABOLITION OF THE CONVEYANCING MONOPOLY

Perhaps the best-known professional monopoly was that of solicitors over property conveyancing. It was the main driving force of controversy behind the establishment of the Royal Commission on Legal Services in 1976. Conveyancing had long been known as the "bread-and-butter" fee earner for solicitors. The public complaint was that the monopoly allowed overcharging. Solicitors defended themselves by saying the monopoly protected the public from charlatans.

The RCLS disappointed all critics by recommending in favour of the monopoly but the Thatcher government established the Farrand Committee, to examine the English system of conveyancing, including the solicitors' monopoly. In 1984, they recommended a system of licensed conveyancers which was effected by the Administration of Justice Act 1985.

Solicitors perceive the threat of conveyancing by employed solicitors, by banks and building societies, to be much more serious to their livelihood, however. The Building Societies Act 1986 gave the Lord Chancellor power to permit this, although he never exercised it.

Instead, Lord Mackay produced new proposals for legislation regulating conveyancing in one of his famous 1989 pack of three green papers on reforming legal services. It was entitled *Conveyancing by Authorised Practitioners* (Cm. 572) and proposed:

— to scrap the framework for authorising conveyancing institutions and individuals contained in the Building Societies Act as being too elaborate;

— to provide a simplified authorisation procedure operated by the Lord Chancellor under the existing regulatory statutes of banks or building societies;

— to require compliance with a code of conduct.

The green paper denied there would be a danger of conflicts of interest in "one-stop shopping" by house buyers obtaining their new

13

home, conveyancing and mortgage under one roof, as lending institutions would only be permitted to do conveyancing by using employed solicitors or licensed conveyancers. Thus, the government were rejecting one of the main points of solicitors' opposition to the plan to open up conveyancing to banks and building societies. Solicitors continued to argue that the public would be insufficiently protected and, worse, that the "unfair competition" from banks and building societies would extinguish most firms of high street solicitors, thus denying the public easy access to legal services.

There swiftly followed the government's refined plans in the 1989 white paper, entitled *Legal Services: A Framework for the Future* (Cm. 740). They proposed to add further safeguards for the public, notably a ban on "tying-in" one service to another, a personal interview by the conveyancer and greater protection against conflicts of interest. The plan also offered greater protection to solicitors by preventing unfair competition, in requiring institutions to demonstrate that they were not offering conveyancing as a "loss leader".

What follows is extraordinary. The end product, in the CLSA 1990, ss.34–53, provides as complex and unwieldy a regulatory machine as it is possible to devise: the opposite of the simple framework proposed in the green paper. It makes difficult reading, so here is a summary:

Section 17 sets out *the statutory objective and the general principle* of providing for new or better ways of providing legal services (including conveyancing services) and a wider choice of persons providing them.

Sections 34 and 35 establish *The Authorised Conveyancing Practitioners Board*, with the general duty to seek to develop competition in the provision of conveyancing services, to supervise the activities of authorised conveyancing practitioners and to consider and report on any matter referred to it by the Lord Chancellor. The Board is empowered to impose an annual levy.

Section 37 provides that the Board shall authorise applicants as practitioners, provided they are satisfied that their business will be carried on by a fit and proper person and that they comply with a list of requirements, for example being insured; maintaining a complaints procedure.

Section 40 empowers the Lord Chancellor to make regulations to secure competence and fair competition among practitioners.

Section 41 establishes *conveyancing appeals tribunals* to hear appeals from people aggrieved by the Board's decision.

Section 43 requires the Board to set up a *conveyancing ombudsman scheme* to hear complaints about authorised practitioners and **section 44** empowers the Board to set up a compensation scheme.

Section 45 requires the Director General of Fair Trading to advise the Lord Chancellor on draft rules and regulations under the Act, with the aim of warning against their potential for restricting, distorting or preventing competition and **section 46** gives the Director investigatory powers.

Sections 46–50 provide investigatory powers for the Board and **sections 51–52** permit it to intervene in authorised practices, to protect clients.

Section 53 allows the *Council for Licensed Conveyancers* to become an authorised body under the Act, which would be entitled to grant rights of audience to licensed conveyancers and enable them to conduct litigation, etc.

REPERCUSSIONS OF THE ABOLITION

1. Advertising

The ban on solicitors' advertising was relaxed in 1984, and further so in 1986 and 1987. Solicitors now advertise on radio, television and in newspapers.

2. Conveyancing costs

Conveyancing costs fell, probably as a result of internal competition (the public habit of "shopping around" rather than remaining faithful to "the family solicitor"). In 1990 solicitors launched a nationwide conveyancing protocol, *Transaction*, designed to streamline conveyancing and by 1991 some firms started to form networks, preparing to offer attractive conveyancing packages to banks and building societies. By 1996, conveyancing costs fell so low that some solicitors petitioned the Law Society to withdraw indemnity from cut price conveyancers and to reintroduce scale fees for conveyancing. They have been warned, however, that this would be illegal.

3. Property shops

Solicitors began selling houses, allowing the client to obtain estate agency and conveyancing services under one roof. The National Association of Solicitors' Property Centres was formed in 1984. The foray of solicitors into estate agency is particularly ironic, in view of the fact that solicitors argue that permitting building societies and estate agents to do conveyancing will lead to conflicts of interest. With the recession, from 1989, the number of solicitors selling property has declined significantly, however and conveyancing is a much less significant proportion of solicitors' work than it was in the 1970s.

4. Legal Practices Directorate

A Legal Practices Directorate was established, in 1987, by the Law Society to identify areas where solicitors could expand their work. *The Law Society Strategy for the Decade* (1991) emphasises potential new work in: advocacy; financial services; the single European market; multinational partnerships; networking and specialising in personal injury work, disaster litigation, social security, etc.

5. Multi-disciplinary partnerships and Multi-national partnerships

Multi-disciplinary partnerships, *i.e.* the possibility of solicitors joining other professional partners, such as accountants, surveyors or tax advisers, was the subject of a 1987 Law Society consultation paper and a matter of ongoing discussion. The Law Society concluded against this development but the Lord Chancellor in his 1989 green papers recommended that the prohibition in M.D.P.s and M.N.P.s should be removed, to enhance public choice. **Section 66** of the CLSA enacted this recommendation and the Lord Chancellor urged the Law Society to look more favourably on M.D.P.s but they have still not been permitted by the Law Society.

6. International Standards

The Law Society has recently been concerned with launching a scheme whereby solicitors' firms can apply for I.S.O. 9000 for the quality of their services. This is part of their present emphasis on client care and quality.

ABOLITION OF THE PROBATE AND LITIGATION MONOPOLIES

As well as enjoying a monopoly over conveyancing, for most of this century solicitors have also held monopolies over *probate work* and the *conduct of litigation*, similarly protected by the Solicitors Act. In his 1989 green papers and white paper, the Lord Chancellor announced that the time had come to abolish these. Accordingly, CLSA, s.28 permits appropriate "authorised bodies" (*i.e.* professional bodies, notably the Law Society) to grant the right to conduct litigation, in a broadly similar way to the granting of rights of audience. Sections 54 and 55, CLSA open up probate services to banks, building societies, insurance companies and legal executives who are permitted to do so by an approved body and who comply with certain safeguards. Of course, all this makes it even more imperative for the high street solicitor to seek new work, in order to survive.

ABOLISHING THE BAR'S MONOPOLY OVER RIGHTS OF AUDIENCE

Solicitors have long held a statutory right to appear in magistrates' courts, county courts and (in a very few localities), in the Crown Court. Barristers have enjoyed a customary monopoly, fixed by a committee of judges, over rights of audience in the High Court, the Court of Appeal and the House of Lords. Most significant in terms of the work it provided was their monopoly over the right to appear in most areas of the Crown Court.

In 1984, as an immediate response to the threat to its conveyancing monopoly, the Law Society launched a campaign for rights of audience in all higher courts.

By 1986, they had crystallised details of their campaign in a document called "Lawyers and The Courts: Time for Some Changes". It proposed a new career structure, with every lawyer receiving a common education and a period in general practice, with all enjoying the same rights of audience in all courts. The Bar would be reserved for specialists, upon completion of further examinations. Direct access to the Bar would be permitted.

This was just the latest in a long series of attacks made by solicitors on the Bar's monopoly. To the Bar's relief, the Royal Commission on Legal Services had, in 1979, rejected solicitors' arguments, concluding that such an extension would be against the public interest because:

(i) If solicitors were permitted rights of audience only in the Crown Court, this would destroy the livelihood of new junior barristers, who derived 50 per cent of their income from such work.

(ii) Jury advocacy involves special skills, only to be maintained with practice, which most solicitors could not spare the time to keep up.

(iii) Since it is up to the solicitor, under the present system, to select a barrister, the solicitor can make a more informed selection than the client could under a system where a client could choose amongst all barristers and all those solicitors specialising in advocacy.

In 1986, in order to take the heat out of their dispute, the two sides of the profession established the Committee on the Future of The Legal Profession (The Marre Committee), to examine legal education, the legal profession and legal services. It reported in July 1988, recommending that solicitors should have extended rights of audience in the Crown Court and should be eligible for appointment as High Court judges.

Government proposals for change

It soon became clear that the Lord Chancellor, Lord Mackay, was keen to extend the Thatcherite approach to monopolies to the Bar's work. In 1989, he published his three green papers and his white paper, *Legal Service: A Framework for the Future*, making it clear that the government view was that the best possible access to legal services was achieved by giving clients the widest possible choice within a free and efficient market. This philosophy was to be applied to the right to appear in court, in the same way as to conveyancing, probate, etc. (see above) and all legal services.

In the main green paper, *The Work and Organisation of the Legal Profession* (Cm. 570), the government set out their views on advocacy. Our adversarial system meant that the court and the client were heavily reliant on the efficient and effective preparation and presentation of a case and the maintenance of high ethical standards. Rights of audience should be restricted to those who are properly trained, experienced and subject to codes of conduct. The basic premise was that satisfaction of those requirements should, alone, be the test for granting rights of audience, not whether an advocate happened to be a barrister or solicitor. Rights of audience would depend on the granting of advocacy certificates by professional bodies, empowered to do so by the Lord Chancellor, following advice from a reconstituted Advisory Committee.

Reactions to the green papers

These were too numerous to summarise, as there were 2,000 responses but the main ones were these:

The Bar

The Bar responded in *Quality of Justice* with its predictable insistence that the public were best served by the continuation of an independent Bar. The government's plans would destroy this and would lead to the concentration of solicitors in fewer, larger firms, reducing consumer choice.

The Law Society

The Law Society in *Striking the Balance*, rejected the proposals as "a potentially dangerous accumulation of power in the hands of the government", although it supported the extension of rights of audience.

The Judges' Council

The Judges' Council condemned the proposals as dangerous, representing "a grave breach of the doctrine of the separation of powers", likely to "impair the competence, integrity and trustworthiness of advocates and, as a result, significantly damage the quality of justice in this country". Increased government control over rights of advocacy and supervision of the legal profession would undermine the role of the judiciary. The Lord Chief Justice even called the green paper "one of the most sinister documents ever to emanate from government".

The Legal Action Group

The Legal Action Group complained that the green papers failed to look at the role of lawyers in the legal aid scheme or in their public service role and failed to examine the role of advice agencies.

The judiciary and the Bar, seeing they were fighting a losing battle, began to make their comments more specific, insisting, for instance, that solicitors should be made subject to the cab-rank rule, in the same way as barristers.

The Lord Chancellor's concessions

The white paper proposals showed that the government had taken some notice of the main responses to the green papers, notably greater judicial involvement in approving change.

The white paper proposals on rights of audience were enacted in the Courts and Legal Services Act 1990.

Section 27 provides the statutory framework for granting *rights of audience*. It provides that rights to appear can only be granted by the "appropriate authorised body" approved under that Act, except in proceedings where there was no restriction on rights to appear.

Section 28 makes similar provision for the *right to conduct litigation*, thus destroying solicitors' virtual monopoly, held under the Solicitors' Act.

Section 29 requires bodies wishing to be authorised under the Act to apply to the Lord Chancellor who may recommend an Order in Council designating the body as an "authorised body". (Schedule 4 details the machinery for approval under this part of the Act. It is designed to ensure that the body's rules further the statutory objective and the general principle and do not inhibit competition, etc. The machinery gives the Lord Chancellor, the Director General of Fair Trading, the Advisory Committee and the "designated judges" a role in authorising a new body).

Sections 31 and 32 preserve barristers' and solicitors' existing audience rights and their governing bodies are accordingly deemed authorised bodies under the Act. Should either of them change their rules of conduct, however, they will have to re-apply for approval.

REPERCUSSIONS OF THE ABOLITION

As with solicitors, the threat of having to compete for work in an open market has already had an important impact on the Bar, and this started even in advance of the passage of the Act. In some respects it has relaxed a number of its practice rules and has even had to acquaint itself with twentieth century business practice and marketing methods, a real shock to the system for this pre-Dickensian profession:

1. Relaxing advertising rules

Sets of chambers now commonly list their members in national newspaper advertisements, and the Bar is providing a new market for P.R. consultants.

2. Devising "A Strategy for the Bar" and "A Blueprint for the Bar"

Devising "A Strategy for the Bar" and promoting new areas of work: for example marketing to those professions who may now access them directly, such as accountants, architects; promoting themselves as specialist advocates and merging chambers to provide stronger units. The Bar Standards Review body published "A Blueprint for the Bar" in 1994. This aims to tighten professional standards, especially in response to criticism of shoddy work by The Royal Commission on Criminal Justice, 1993. For instance, judges will be encouraged to advise and criticise barristers appearing before them, the Bar Council is devising a new complaints mechanism and barristers entering practice after 1997 will be subject to continuing education.

3. Relaxing the chambers rule; setting up the Bar Library

Until recently, barristers were very restricted in where they could establish sets of chambers. Those restrictions have now been abolished. In the 1990s, the Bar attempted to establish a Library, from which barristers could practice without a tenancy in chambers. This innovation failed, however. Barristers are now permitted to practice outside chambers, as sole practitioners, after three years in independent practice but very few do so.

4. Permitting direct access

Permitting direct access to non-practising, employed barristers by their employers' clients. This is important, since there are now nearly as many employed barristers as practising ones. The Bar continues to discuss whether to permit direct access to normal clients but has, so far, voted against it.

5. Paying pupils

Paying pupils and reforming training. For instance, 1995 saw the creation of a new clearing house for pupillage applications to be centrally processed (PACH).

OTHER IMPORTANT ASPECTS OF THE CLSA

1. The statutory objective and the general principle

Section 17 of the statute states that the general objective of this part of the Act is the development of legal services "by making provision for new or better ways of providing such services and a wider choice of persons providing them, while maintaining the proper and efficient administration of justice" and subsection (3) goes on to set out the general principle that rights of audience and litigation should only be determined by reference to education, training and membership of a professional body with an effective set of rules. Most importantly, subsection (3)(c) sets out a *principle of non-discrimination*. It is an explicit version of the Bar's car-rank rule but, of course, it applies to all advocates. This is the Bar's import into the Act, through the medium of their ex-chairman, Lord Alexander: the famous "Alexander amendment". After a ferocious battle between the two sides of the profession, this is a compromise. The Bar would really like to see it applied to the provision of all legal services. Solicitors argue that this would be unreasonable. How could they maintain a reputation for representing victims of domestic violence, for instance, if they were obliged to represent the perpetrators? In any event, they respond, the Bar's cab-rank is more honoured in the breach than the observance. This argument is still running in 1995–96. The Bar in its "Blueprint" has amended the rule to permit barristers to refuse to do legally aided work.

2. The Lord Chancellor's Advisory Committee on Legal Education and Conduct

Its membership is set out in section 19 and section 20 charges it with the general duty of advising the Lord Chancellor, having especial regard to the practices of other EU Member States and the desirability of equality of opportunity. In 1996, it produced its *First Report on Legal Education and Training* (see above).

3. The Legal Services Ombudsman

The Legal Services Ombudsman is created by sections 21–26 to investigate and report on complaints against, broadly speaking, the providers of legal services.

4. Contingency fees

Contingency fees, which were the subject of an individual green paper, have been illegal in England and Wales but permissible in Scotland as *conditional fees*. Conditional fees are provided for under section 58, subject to the Lord Chancellor's requirements. They have eventually been permitted, for certain legal services, from 1995. *Conditional fees* involve a no win, no fee deal between lawyer and client but the fee may not be a percentage of the damages involved, as is common in the United States. The fee must be the normal fee, possibly with a percentage uplift.

LIFE AFTER THE COURTS AND LEGAL SERVICES ACT

At the time of writing, it is still too early to predict the effects of the Act. The next few years will be an exciting time for students of E.L.S. and we will all need to keep a close track on its effects. The more hysterical opponents of the Act, notably the legal profession, have argued that it will lead to the demise of their side of the profession as we know it, thus causing a great loss to the public. More restrained observers point out that surveys have shown that the vast majority of solicitors have no intention of competing with the Bar for advocacy work, to the destruction of the Bar, while the more efficient solicitors will survive by diversifying their activities. Indeed by June 1996, there were only 409 solicitor advocates licensed under the Act to appear in the higher courts. There are complaints that they suffer some prejudice from certain judges and barristers. They do not wear wigs and they had to remind the Lord Chancellor that he should have invited them, as well as barristers, to take silk. He corrected this position in 1995 but, since he requires Q.C.s to be advocates of 10 years standing, solicitors will take years to filter through. The Lord Chancellor's Advisory Committee has refused rights of audience to employed lawyers, including the Crown Prosecution Service.

CHAPTER 2

JUDGES

1. APPOINTMENT

The historical common law proposition, that the monarch is "the fountain of justice", is still nominally effective in the context of the appointment of judges. The courts of law remain the Queen's Courts and the judges remain Her Majesty's judges.

Change in the monarch's constitutional role has, however, meant that, whereas, originally, the power of appointment vested in the monarch was entirely personal, at the present time all judicial appointments are made by the monarch on the advice of representatives of the government. Throughout the 1990s the Lord Chancellor has been making the system of judicial appointments more visible and open, in response to criticism. This has resulted in the publication of *Judicial Appointments*, 1995, in which he describes the criteria for and methods of selecting all judges.

Thus the Lord Chancellor, the Lord Chief Justice, the Master of the Rolls, the President of the Family Division, the Vice-Chancellor, the Lords of Appeal in Ordinary (colloquially known as "Law Lords") and the Lords Justices of Appeal are all appointed by the Queen on the advice of the Prime Minister. The Prime Minister, having selected the Lord Chancellor, will consult with him about these appointments, as vacancies occur, before furnishing his advice to the Queen. The new booklet discloses that the Lord Chancellor customarily consults senior members of the judiciary and, in the case of Law Lords, the existing Law Lords.

The puisne judges of the High Court, circuit judges, recorders, metropolitan and stipendiary magistrates and the vast numbers of lay magistrates are all appointed on the advice of the Lord Chancellor. A qualification of this statement is that for the area of the Duchy of Lancaster recommendations are made by the Chancellor of the Duchy of Lancaster.

The sole qualification for a senior judicial appointment is practical experience as an advocate with audience rights under the Courts and Legal Services Act. A minimum period of experience is required, increasing from 10 years for a High Court judge, to 15 years for a Law Lord. The system of appointing judges from the ranks of practising advocates, predominantly counsel, is in complete contrast to systems elsewhere, where a civil service career as a judge is a common feature. An even greater contrast is with the system in certain American states, where some appointments to judicial office are made by the process of democratic election by the local electorate.

Most English judges are male, although there are at present six female High Court judges and one in the Court of Appeal. Women lawyers argue that this rate of progress is far too slow. A 1991 report for the Law Society by Sally Hughes showed that women who were called to the Bar in the 1970s were significantly under-represented in judicial appointments made in the last five years. Throughout the period, only 6 per cent of the barristers who became recorders were women and, of the 51 recorders who became full-time circuit judges, only two were women. Of the 176 circuit judges appointed, only eight were women. The report found that women appointees were more experienced than their male counterparts. It argued that the appointments system militates against women, as they are less visible than men in, for instance, the social life of the Bar or as Q.C.s in court. Thus, it is alleged that the appointments system discriminates against women, despite the Lord Chancellor's desire, articulated in his 1990 *Judicial Appointments* handbook (and repeated in the 1995 edition), to appoint more women.

The Law Society has been seen as expressing a similar concern that the judicial appointments system discriminates against those of Asian or Afro-Caribbean origin. A report to them by Geoffrey Bindman, published in 1991, suggested that the system, which relies heavily on word-of-mouth observations by colleagues and others of potential candidates, is discriminatory. Bindman argued from statute and case law that a word-of-mouth system of subjective judgments, operated by white people, could discriminate against blacks.

Lord Mackay, the Lord Chancellor, reacted sharply to both criticisms. He released to the press an open letter to the Society, containing a strong rebuff. He even cited counsel's opinion to the effect that the appointment system was not illegal. He also pointed to the fact that he had just established an ethnic minorities advisory committee to advise the Judicial Studies Board on race issues affecting the justice system.

The Courts Act 1971 broke, to a minor extent, the monopoly of the Bar in judicial appointments. It allowed solicitors to be appointed as recorders. The CLSA 1990 goes further, by basing judicial qualification upon advocacy experience. It thus permits a solicitor-advocate to qualify, eventually, for appointment to the highest judicial offices. Thus, there is a potential for opening up the judiciary to a much wider pool of candidates, in terms of class, gender and race.

The fact that judges are drawn from the ranks of advocates has, however, been the subject of constant criticism, notably by The Law Society and JUSTICE. They make the point that the qualities of a good advocate are not the same as those of a good judge and that limiting judicial eligibility in this way deprives us of the chance to appoint lawyers who would be good judges, who do not happen to be advocates. In its 1992 report, *The Judiciary*, JUSTICE, repeating a point they had made in 1972, said:

"The best drama producers may not be the best critics; the best players do not necessarily become the best referees. In particular the strong combative or competitive streak present in many successful advocates is out of place on the Bench."

Thus JUSTICE would like to see this part of the CLSA repealed.

They were also, along with other groups, heavily critical of the system of appointment which effectively rests in the gift of one person, the Lord Chancellor, advised by just two civil servants who have gathered opinions on potential candidates from their colleagues and existing judges. Their report expressed concern over the lack of openness, lay involvement and public accountability in selection and the lack of a formal selection procedure. They said they wanted to see judicial appointments advertised and they repeated the ongoing criticism of the lack of women and ethnic minorities on the Bench.

In 1993, the Lord Chancellor announced a seven point plan to radically reform the system of judicial appointments *below High Court level* which bears a remarkable similarity to most of the JUSTICE recommendations. This plan is set out in his 1994 consultation paper, *Developments in Judicial Appointments Procedures*. It comprises:

(a) improving the forecasting of numbers and expertise of judges required;
(b) job descriptions and statements of the qualities required;
(c) open advertisements;
(d) specific competitions for vacancies;
(e) measures to encourage applications from women and black and Asian practitioners;
(f) a review of application forms and a more structured basis for consultation with the judiciary; and
(g) the involvement of suitable lay people in the selection process.

The job descriptions and criteria for selection of a circuit judge and district judge were set out in great detail for all the world to see in the consultation paper. They have now been refined and republished in November 1995 in the *Judicial Appointments* series, along with those for recorders, masters, stipendiary magistrates and tribunal members. Criteria sought in selecting a circuit judge, for example, are professed to be:

legal knowledge and experience;	integrity;
intellectual and analytical ability;	fairness;
sound judgment;	understanding of people and society;
decisiveness;	sound temperament;
communication skills;	courtesy and humanity;
authority;	commitment to public service.

Detailed job specifications are available from the Judicial Appointments Group of the Lord Chancellor's Department.

The Lord Chancellor started publicly advertising these jobs, exposing the candidates to open competition and interviews by lay people in 1994 and 1995.

All this is quite revolutionary. The system of appointing and selecting the inferior judiciary seems to have gone from the covert influence of an old boy network to an astonishing exercise in open government in one move. There are no plans, however, to extend this system to the appointment of High Court judges. They are still selected in the traditional way, spelled out in *Judicial Appointments*, 1995. High Court judges' jobs are not advertised and candidates do not apply. The

Lord Chancellor invites a suitable individual to fill a vacancy, after gathering information on potential appointees from judges and senior members of the profession who know the candidate. Traditionally, new recruits are drawn from the ranks of silks and will normally have been "tried out" by the Lord Chancellor in the capacity of deputy High Court Judge. This system is criticised as being far too subjective and biased against lawyers who are not regularly visible in the right courts. JUSTICE and other groups want to remove the appointment of all judges from the gift of the all powerful Lord Chancellor and place it in the hands of a Judicial Commission, a group of 13 persons, seven of them lay. The Lord Chancellor is resisting this suggestion.

Throughout 1995 and ongoing in 1996, the House of Commons Select Committee on Home Affairs has been investigating the system of judicial appointments.

2. REMOVAL

(a) Superior Judges

The security in office of superior judges is an important constitutional guarantee of independence from interference by the executive. For centuries, appointment and dismissal were personal to the monarch, so that judges held office "*durante bene placito nostro*"—at pleasure. One result of this state of affairs was that decisions, in cases in which the monarch had an interest, tended to be satisfactory from his standpoint. The dangers became increasingly apparent in the seventeenth century in the reigns of James I and Charles I, so that in the Commonwealth period, which followed the Civil War and the execution of Charles I, the judges were given security in office whilst of good behaviour. The Restoration of Charles II in 1660 saw a return to the former practice, and it was not until the Act of Settlement was passed in 1701 that it was finally established that judges were not to be dismissible at the pleasure of the Crown. That statute provided that judges were to hold office, "*quamdiu se bene gesserint*"—whilst of good behaviour—and that they were to be removed only following an address to the monarch from both Houses of Parliament requesting dismissal. This provision is now to be found in the Supreme Court Act 1981. This method of dismissal has not been used, since its original enactment in 1701, to remove an

English judge but one Irish judge was dismissed under similar provisions in 1830 for embezzlement.

(b) Inferior Judges

The provisions requiring an address from both Houses of Parliament before dismissal only apply to the "superior" judges, by which is meant judges of the High Court, the Court of Appeal and the House of Lords.

The statutes which deal with the system of county courts, the Crown Court and the work of the lay magistrates, make provision for the dismissal of judges and magistrates. In the case of the circuit judges or recorders, the Lord Chancellor may remove them for incapacity or for misbehaviour and can remove the name of a magistrate from the Commission without showing cause.

In 1983 a circuit judge was removed after being convicted of smuggling large quantities of whisky and cigarettes.

In July 1994, the Lord Chancellor wrote to the Lord Chief Justice, elaborating on what conduct he would regard as amounting to "misbehaviour". He included convictions for drink driving and offences involving violence, dishonesty or moral turpitude, as well as sexual harrassment and behaviour likely to offend on racial or religious grounds.

There has long been criticism on the fact that there is no formal system for dealing with complaints against judges. *The Royal Commission on Criminal Justice* report, 1993, suggested a system of performance appraisal, as did JUSTICE, in 1992, as well as suggesting that its proposed Judicial Commission should provide a system for reviewing professional conduct and supervising the consideration of complaints.

(c) Resignation

The status and salary of judgeship are such that, other than on grounds of ill-health or retirement, resignation has not been a phenomenon to be reckoned with. Consequently the announcement in 1970, that Mr Justice Fisher, at the age of 52 and after only two years' service as a High Court judge, was to give up his judicial office to follow a career in the business world came as a substantial break with convention. In 1992, JUSTICE suggested the introduction of fixed term appointments permitting individuals to return to legal practice at the end of their term.

The Supreme Court Act 1981 permits the Lord Chancellor, after consultation with specified members of the judiciary, to declare vacant the office of any judge of High Court or Appeal Court status who is, through ill-health, no longer capable of carrying on working as who is incapable of taking the decision to resign.

(d) Retirement

Until Parliament passed the Judicial Pensions Act 1959, judges were appointed for their lifetime unless they chose to give up office. Since that Act new judges of the High Court and the Appeal Courts were required to retire from office on reaching the age of 75. The Judicial Pensions and Retirement Act 1993 lowered the normal retirement age of all judges to 70, but inferior judges may be permitted to work until 75 if it is considered to be in the public interest. Their appointment may be renewed on a year by year basis by the Lord Chancellor. As for Supreme Court judges appointed from 1995 and Law Lords who were not High Court judges by 1995, they *must* retire at 70.

3. THE INDEPENDENCE OF THE JUDICIARY

The constitutional doctrine of the separation of powers, stated in its best known form by Montesquieu in "*L'Esprit des Lois*" (1748) and translated into action in the constitution of the United States of America, laid great stress on the need for the judiciary to be kept apart from the legislative and executive functions of government. Montesquieu's view was that if there should be, at any time, a combination of the judicial function with the executive or legislative function then tyranny would result.

In the English system judges are, supposedly, independent of politics. By a well understood convention, judges do not take part in politics, nor do they allow their political sympathies to affect their judgment. A judge cannot, by statute, also be a Member of Parliament and, although it was formerly common to appoint judges who had been M.P.s or candidates, this practice has declined massively this century. By convention, Law Lords do not take part in political debates in the House of Lords. In return, lay peers do not attend hearings of the Appellate Committee, although in law there appears to be nothing to stop them from doing so. Another convention is that members of the House of Commons do not attack a judge on a personal basis, except by moving an address for removal. Instead, criticism is directed at the legal principle laid down in the case.

One outstanding anomally, in the attempt to separate judges from political considerations, is that new appointments are made on the recommendation of the Prime Minister, or the Lord Chancellor, both of whom hold political appointments, but perhaps the strangest anomaly in the system is the position of the Lord Chancellor himself. His appointment is a political one and, consequently, he has no security of tenure; he is the head of a government department and member of the Cabinet, and he plays a major role in the work of the House of Lords as a legislative assembly. He is, supposedly, guided by the convention that his political activities must be kept completely apart from the judicial responsibilities of his office but his peculiar position in all three branches of governmental power inevitably leads to accusations of conflicts of interest, accusations of political appointments to the superior judiciary and calls for a new broader-based selection panel and process. The late 1980s and 1990s have seen a remarkable number of outspoken critiques of the present Lord Chancellor and administration by members of the superior judiciary. The repeated allegation is that the Government is eroding judicial independence by diluting the judges' control over judicial business and by over using deputy High Court judges (who are often county court judges) to hear High Court cases. The latest judicial outbursts against the Government have come from Sir Thomas Bingham M.R., who complained, in November 1995, that lack of Court of Appeal Judges was causing "intolerable delays" and from innumerable judges in 1996 most notably, the Lord Chief Justice, objecting to Home Secretary Michael Howard's plans to introduce more minimum sentences. Lord Chief Justice Taylor, who retired in May 1966, on discovering that he had cancer, has been unique in the degree to which he has courted media attention. He established a press office, held press conferences in which he readily attacked the Government and even appeared on the BBC television programme, *Question Time*. He and other outspoken judges have taken advantage of Lod Mackay L.C.'s suspension of the Kilmuir Rules, which had previously prevented judges from voicing out-of-court opinions of this political nature.

To the end that judges shall be independent, the removal of a superior judge from office is made a difficult process. They thus enjoy considerable security of tenure. The fact that no English judge has yet been removed by the monarch on an address from both Houses of Parliament is proof positive that their security in office is well founded. Equally, the substantial salary which is paid annually to High Court and Court of Appeal judges was meant to place judges above political influence or corruption. Now, the rationale articulated by the Review Body on Senior Salaries is that salaries should be high enough to attract sufficient high calibre candidates and to maintain judges' status in the community. Again, as a gesture, the salaries of judges are paid out of the Consolidated Fund and are thus not subject to an annual vote by Parliament.

As a result of the seventeenth century struggle between the monarch and Parliament, the judiciary accepted the constitutional doctrine of the supremacy of Parliament and, consequently, no judge will ever refuse to give effect to legislation properly enacted which does not contravene E.C. law. In return, the legal profession is left substantially free to regulate its own affairs and to make rules of court for the purposes of legal process.

4. JUDICIAL IMMUNITY

An extension of the principle that the judiciary must be independent is the common law concept of judicial immunity, which lays down that a judge may not be sued in a civil action for things said or acts done in the exercise of judicial office, provided they are within jurisdiction or honestly believed to be so. Even malicious statements, made within jurisdiction, do not give rise to an action. Nor do defamatory statements. In *Sirros v. Moore* (1975), Lord Denning said this was so that the judge "should be able to do his work in complete independence and free from fear".

The immunity given to judges is also extended to the lawyers, the jury, the parties and witnesses in respect of anything said in the course of a trial. It is felt that this freedom will lead to the easier discovery of the truth and will also stop further civil actions being brought, thus possibly preventing endless litigation. Even the press has the benefit of immunity, in that newspaper and broadcast reports of judicial proceedings, provided they are fair and accurate and contemporaneous, are absolutely privileged from an action for defamation. As a result of the principle of judicial immunity, there is no formal mechanism for dealing with complaints about judges. In its 1992 report, JUSTICE reiterated their concern about this and recommended a Judicial Standards Committee "to provide an independent mechanism for reviewing the professional conduct of judges". In 1993, the Royal Commission on Criminal Justice recommended a system of performance appraisal involving presiding and resident judges. In evidence to the Home Affairs Select Committee in 1995, the Lord Chancellor said this was "under consideration".

5. TRAINING

Compared with their European counterparts, who receive lengthy training for their judicial careers, English judges receive very little, or none. The Judicial Studies Board supervises some "seminars" for inferior judges and stipendiary magistrates. For example, they are required, before sitting in the Crown Court, to attend an induction seminar on trial and sentence, to visit penal establishments and to sit with a circuit judge for one or two weeks.

After three to five years, the recorder or district judge will be summoned to attend a three day seminar with specialist speakers and sentencing exercises. Thereafter she will attend such refresher seminars every three to five years plus an annual circuit-based sentencing conference. Circuit judges are normally recruited from the ranks of recorders and are subject to the same regime. From time to time, the Judicial Studies Board undertakes broad training exercises in specific topics for all judges at circuit level and all stipendiary magistrates. Since 1989, it has undertaken such projects in relation to The Children Act 1989, ethnic minority awareness training and "human awareness training", to teach judges, for example, not to use speech and behaviour offensive to minorities such as homosexuals (see *Judicial Studies Board Report* (1991–95)).

New High Court judges, however, receive no training and are not the responsibility of the Judicial Studies Board. It is often the case that, at both levels, the appointee's experience as an advocate may be in an entirely different area of law from that applied in her judicial role. For example, a commercial Q.C. may suddenly find herself invited by the Lord Chancellor to sit as a Crown Court recorder, decades after her last involvement with criminal law, or a specialist Q.C. may be appointed as a generalist "Jack-of-all-trades" in the Queen's Bench Division. Furthermore, it is sometimes said, especially by newly appointed judges, that practice as an advocate in the English tradition of adversarial, oral argument is the antithesis of training for the English judge's job, the job of sitting, listening, quietly and impartially, to both sides, without undue interruption.

The traditional objection to judicial training is that it could undermine judicial independence (*Report of the Working Party on Judicial Studies & Information* (1978)). This objection should not apply however, to the Civil Justice Review's suggestion that judges be trained in civil case-management techniques. The lack of thorough-going training for new inferior judges raises serious issues over the quality of justice dispensed in the Crown Court and county courts. Richard Prior, at [1996] N.L.J. 312 paints a horrific picture of the depths of judicial ignorance at this level.

6. JUDICIAL OFFICES

Lord Chancellor

The senior appointment in the judicial system of England and Wales is the Lord Chancellor. Paradoxically, in view of the emphasis which is placed on the independence of the judiciary, the person appointed receives the honour for political reasons, being invited to accept the office by the Prime Minister in the same way as any other member of the administration is selected. It thus follows that, if a Labour government replaces the Conservatives during the lifetime of this edition of this book, a Labour peer will be appointed Lord Chancellor. The Labour shadow is currently Lord Irvine of Lairg. The Lord Chancellor is a prominent member of the government and invariably has a seat in the Cabinet. The appointee will have achieved considerable eminence in both legal and political roles before attaining the office, and once appointed his duties cause him to be the complete denial of the constitutional doctrine of the separation of powers. As well as heading a department of the executive with substantial responsibilities—the Lord Chancellor's Department consists of over 10,000 staff—he is also the Speaker of the House of Lords sitting there on the Woolsack in full ceremonial dress. In the judicial sphere, he is the senior judge of both the House of Lords and the Court of Appeal, and President of the Chancery Division. He seldom sits as a judge and, when he does so, sits in the House of Lords. Recently, only Lord Hailsham and Lord Mackay have done this. Nonetheless, tenure in office depends upon the Prime Minister. He can be replaced at any time and, if the government resigns, the Lord Chancellor, like all government Ministers, goes out of office forthwith. The present Lord Chancellor, Lord Mackay, is the first one not to have been a member of the English Bar. He is Scottish. This could explain why his reforming zeal has effected some of the greatest changes in the English legal system since the Judicature Acts of 1873–75. In December 1995, he became the longest serving Lord Chancellor this century. His present salary (1995) is £132,906.

Lord Chief Justice

The Lord Chief Justice is the second senior judge, after the Lord Chancellor and the senior judge of the Queen's Bench Division of the High Court. He can take part in the ordinary work of the division but more often he is engaged in presiding over the Court of Appeal (Criminal Division), of which he is President, He is made a peer on appointment. The 1996 salary is £127,217.

Master of the Rolls

The Master of the Rolls is the title of the judge who organises the work of and is President of the Court of Appeal (Civil Division). He formally admits newly qualified solicitors to the Roll of the court so enabling them to practise. The salary is £114,874.

The President of the Family Division of the High Court of Justice

The President of the Family Division of the High Court is the senior judge in that division. He organises the work of the division, taking part in it himself, and also sitting to hear appeals in the Divisional Court of the Family Division. The salary is £117,642.

The Office of Vice-Chancellor

The Vice-Chancellor, under the Lord Chancellor, is the senior judge of the Chancery Division. He is responsible for the organisation and management of the business of the Division. The salary is £112,791.

The Lords of Appeal in Ordinary

There are now 12 Lords of Appeal in Ordinary. They are appointed under section 6 of the Appellate Jurisdiction Act 1876, as amended by section 71 of the Courts and Legal Services Act 1990 and form, as the House of Lords in its judicial capacity, the final appeal court for all cases heard in England, Wales, Scotland and Northern Ireland, except Scottish criminal cases. More often called "the Law Lords", they are made peers on appointment, but by convention they take only a limited part in the legislative work of the House of Lords and they do not engage in political controversy. At least two of the Law Lords will be from Scotland and one will be from Northern Ireland. The hearing of cases takes place in a committee room of the Houses of Parliament at Westminster. Their Lordships wear lounge suits on these occasions. The basic qualification for appointment is a 15-year Supreme Court qualification, under the CLSA 1990, or two years in high judicial office. Virtually all English appointments follow experience in the Court of Appeal. The annual salary is £117,642.

Lords Justice of Appeal

The judges who sit in the Court of Appeal are called Lords Justices of Appeal. The one woman, Butler-Sloss, is now referred to as Lord Justice Butler-Sloss. As of March 1996, there are 35 Lords Justices of Appeal and appointments to this office are normally made from High Court judges. The alternative qualification is a 10-year High Court qualification, under the CLSA. As they are already knighted, on appointment they are made privy councillors. Appeal cases which they try are heard at the Royal Courts of Justice in the Strand. The annual salary is £112,791.

Presiding judges

The Courts and Legal Services Act 1990 gave statutory recognition to the system of Presiding Judges set up in 1970. Section 72 requires the appointment of at least two High Court judges as presiding judges in each of the six circuits in England and Wales, and one Senior Presiding Judge for England and Wales from among Lords Justices of Appeal. They have general responsibility for their circuit and for all matters affecting the judiciary there. Under the CLSA, the Senior Presiding Judge is one of the people the Lord Chancellor must consult before making an order on the allocation of court business.

High Court judges

The maximum number of High Court judges is now 95. New judges are allocated to one of the three Divisions of the High Court but theoretically such a judge can be asked to serve in any Division. At present there are 63 in the Queen's Bench Division, 17 in the Chancery Division and 15 in the Family Division. High Court judges are selected either from circuit judges of two years' standing or much more commonly, those with a 10-year High Court qualification, under the CLSA, and are knighted on appointment or made a Dame of The British Empire. High Court judges are addressed as "Your Lordship" and are known as puisne judges. They operate from the Royal Courts of Justice in the Strand or from the provincial district registries of the High Court. They also hear the most serious Crown Court cases. The annual salary is £100,511.

Circuit judges

The Courts Act 1971 divided England and Wales into six regions called "circuits", based on their historic predecessors, and made arrangements for each region to be staffed by High Court judges, circuit judges and recorders. There are 504 circuit judges. A circuit judge must have a 10-year county court or Crown Court qualification or have been a recorder. They are addressed as "Your Honour" and the salary is £73,837. Circuit judges, as well as their Crown Court responsibilities, can also preside in county courts; they thus have a mixed civil and criminal role.

Recorders

Part-time appointments from legal professionals with a 10-year county court or High Court qualification assist in the least serious work of the Crown Court. The main obligation is to serve as a recorder for not less than 20 days in the year. There are over 1,200 recorders and assistant recorders.

District judges

The Courts and Legal Services Act, s.74 renamed county court registrars as district judges. They are appointed from persons with a seven-year general qualification, under the Courts and Legal Services Act. They are usually practising lawyers and sit part-time in the county court. There are over 300.

Deputy judges

Lord Mackay, the Lord Chancellor, has deliberately perpetuated his predecessor's practice of appointing new judges as deputies, testing them out as part-timers, before appointing them to full-time office. Thus there are, in addition to those listed above, hundreds of assistant recorders, deputy district judges, deputy circuit judges and deputy High Court judges. In 1991, the Lord Chancellor came under a public attack from the Lord Chief Justice, who complained that, because of an "acute shortage" of judges, the court system was relying on these part-timers, with an "inordinate number" of deputy judges hearing serious cases.

Magistrates

A full account of the part played in the legal system by magistrates is given in Chapter 3.

Chairmen of tribunals

In Chapter 9 the importance of tribunals in the English legal system is examined. In most tribunals, the Chairman will be a lawyer presiding either full-time or part-time. Some full-time appointments, for example, as some chairmen of Industrial Tribunals, are paid the same salary as a district judge or stipendiary magistrate.

Holders of other important legal offices

The Attorney-General is, like the Lord Chancellor, a political appointment, chosen by the Prime Minister from government members of the House of Commons. Normally the person selected is a Queen's Counsel who has been elected an M.P. and his main task is to act as legal adviser to the government departments. He also appears for the Crown in important cases. He is the titular head of the English Bar. His deputy is the Solicitor-General, also a government member of the House of Commons and an eminent barrister. They are called the Law Officers.

The Director of Public Prosecutions was originally appointed in 1879 to ensure that cases of major importance are dealt with consistently and effectively, and that advice about criminal law matters should be available to chief constables. The Director must have a 10-year general qualification, under the CLSA but she is not a politician. She has a staff of lawyers to assist her and she can employ counsel and solicitors to handle cases on her behalf. Under the Prosecution of Offences Act 1985, the Director of Public Prosecutions heads the national Crown Prosecution Service. The Attorney-General answers in Parliament for the work of the Director's office and the Serious Fraud Office. Barbara Mills Q.C. is the first female D.P.P.

Terminology

When law reports refer to the judge giving judgment in a case, a system of abbreviations is used. These a student will need to recognise. Although current holders of offices are shown, this is by way of example.

Lord Chancellor	Lord Mackay L.C.
Lord Chief Justice	Lord Bingham C.J.
Master of the Rolls	Lord Woolf M.R.
President of the Family Division	Sir Stephen Brown P.
Vice-Chancellor	Sir Richard Scott V.-C.
Lords of Appeal in Ordinary	Lord Slynn of Hadley
Lord Justices of Appeal	Millett L.J.
High Court judges	Bracewell J.

CHAPTER 3

MAGISTRATES

1. THE LAY PRINCIPLE

The preceding chapters have been mainly concerned with the part played by the professional in the administration of justice, from the initial difficulty of obtaining entry to the legal profession as a practising barrister or solicitor, to the invitation ultimately extended to the experienced advocate to become a judge. In this and the next chapter attention is directed to the contribution made by lay people to the English legal system; first, in the form of the lay magistrate, making a major contribution to the work of the courts, and then as a juror, taking the responsibility for decisions of fact in the most serious criminal, and some civil, trials.

The combination of professional and lay people in the system is supposedly felt to be a desirable arrangement, since it ensures that the law, and in particular criminal law, is kept in close contact with representatives of the public who are affected by it. It is argued that this helps to preserve a respect for law throughout the community. As there are over 30,000 lay magistrates at the present time, their share in the administration of justice is undeniably of major importance.

2. APPOINTMENT

Magistrates, properly entitled Justices of the Peace, are appointed by the Crown on the advice of the Lord Chancellor (or the Chancellor of the Duchy of Lancaster for that area). Each area which has a separate body of justices has a Commission from the Crown, and the names of new justices are added to the Schedule attached to the Commission. The magistrate so appointed can carry out her functions only within the area covered by the Commission, and it is a requirement that the magistrate must continue to live within 15 miles of the boundaries of that area.

Inevitably, the Lord Chancellor in recommending names for appointment has to seek local guidance. This is done by 94 advisory committees covering England and Wales. The membership of the committees was secret, to prevent canvassing by aspiring justices but Lord Mackay abolished this rule in the 1990s. Advisory committees occasionally advertise in local newspapers, inviting applications or nominations to the Bench. They also circulate local political and community organisations.

The great difficulty in obtaining a suitable balance in the composition of the local magistracy is that there is a natural tendency for candidates to be chosen from individuals prominent in local public life. Consequently, over the years many appointments have been made from members of the local party political organisations, with the inevitable criticism following that this is akin to a "spoils" system. It is a difficult problem and one which is never likely to be resolved to everyone's satisfaction.

Research has also demonstrated a class bias towards the middle and upper classes on the Bench and that non-whites are under-represented. Aware of the latter, the present Lord Chancellor has announced that he is appointing a higher number of non-whites among new magistrates, to right the balance.

The persons who are selected are chosen as responsible and respected members of their local community, capable of deciding cases without bias and possessed of sound common sense and who can fulfil the requirement to sit, on average, one day per fortnight.

Lay justices receive no remuneration. They are, however, entitled to travelling expenses and to certain subsistence payments and a loss of earnings allowance but this allowance by no means compensates those who operate small businesses.

3. TRAINING

Because magistrates are not legally trained, there used to be considerable criticism that people were taking part in the administration of justice without knowing anything about legal principles or court procedure. Present practice requires every magistrate on appointment to undergo a training course arranged on a local part-time basis. In

1991, this was strengthened substantially, to require induction training and a two-stage basic training course in the first three years from appointment. After three years, magistrates must undergo further training every three years. The further training includes chairmanship training and, since 1996, is a pre-condition for those justices wishing to chair court proceedings. Additional training courses are arranged for magistrates wishing to participate in the youth court or family proceedings.

4. REMOVAL

Dismissal

The Lord Chancellor retains a discretion to remove the name of any magistrate from the Commission for any reason he thinks fit. On the rare occasion when this drastic step is taken, it will usually be because the magistrate has either been guilty of some serious personal misconduct or has failed to carry out her duties as a magistrate in some important respect. The magistrate who announces that she will not enforce an Act of Parliament because she disagrees with its provisions is certain to find that her name will be promptly removed from the Commission.

Retirement

Magistrates retire at the age of 70 when their names are placed on a supplemental list. This means that the magistrate may no longer sit on the Bench but she can still deal with certain paperwork and so retain the status of a Justice of the Peace.

5. ORGANISATION

Every county has a separate Commission of the Peace, as have the London Commission areas and the City of London. Consequently, magistrates are appointed on a local basis and they may only sit, therefore, to try cases within their locality. In total there are now 367 magistrates' benches.

There are 105 magistrates' courts committees. This is the representative body which speaks for the individual magistrate as well as appointing court staff and financing training for staff and magistrates. Since magistrates' courts have long been locally organised, outside the ambit of centralised departmental control over all other courts, one of their hallmarks has long been their individual, sometimes idiosyncratic, differences in practice, procedure and interpretation of the law. An Inspectorate was recently established. In 1994, it started an assessment of quality of service at magistrates' courts and it aims to identify and disseminate good practice. The Inspectorate was put on a statutory footing by The Police And Magistrates' Courts Act 1994, ss.86–88. The Act also provided for the appointment, by each committee, of a "justices' chief executive", a qualified justices clerk who is the line manager of all the other local justices' clerks and staff.

Nationally the Magistrates' Association speaks for the magistrates as a collective body. It publishes a magazine called *The Magistrate*.

6. "THE BENCH"

For the hearing of a case in the magistrates' court, lay justices sit in pairs or groups of three (maximum since 1996). Collectively, they are known as "the bench" and they are addressed as "Your Worships". An annual election of a chairman of the Bench as a whole is held, the choice being made by the justices by a secret ballot. When magistrates sit as a Youth Court, statutory provisions govern its organisation. It is usual for three magistrates to sit, all of whom are drawn from a special panel and the bench will be of mixed gender. The same is true when the court sits to deal with family proceedings.

7. STIPENDIARY MAGISTRATES

The pressure of business in the great cities has meant that as well as having lay magistrates it has been thought desirable to employ full-time salaried lawyers to assist with the work of magistrates. These are called stipendiary magistrates and, in London, metropolitan stipendiary magistrates. Stipendiary magistrates can be appointed on the recommendation of or by the Lord Chancellor from persons with a seven-year general qualification, as defined by the CLSA, s.71.

There are, in 1996, 91 stipendiary magistrates in England and Wales and 95 acting stipendiaries so that the power to appoint stipendiaries is not widely used. The Royal Commission on Criminal Justice, 1993, recommended that there should be a more systematic approach to the role of stipendiaries. In 1994, the Lord Chancellor established a working party to produce guidelines to "identifying more clearly the respective roles of the Stipendiary Magistracy and the lay Bench". It has reported in 1996, making no recommendations of any consequence.

8. MAGISTRATES' CLERKS

Both lay justices and stipendiary magistrates are advised and have their courts administered by magistrates' clerks. The chief clerk at each court is called the justices' clerk, or, in Inner London, the chief clerk. A justices' clerk may be in charge of more than one Bench and the nationwide trend of the last two decades has been to amalgamate Benches under one clerkship. In 1995, there were 214 justices' clerks, all of whom professionally qualified. The service was only pro-fessionalised in the Justices of the Peace Act 1949, which permitted the appointment of justices' clerks with 10 years' experience before 1960. The clerks' staff are called justices' clerks assistants and, like the justices' clerks, they are appointed and paid by the magistrates' courts committees and under the supervision of the justices' chief executive.

Of course, since many justices' clerks are in charge of more than one court and since most courts have more than one courtroom in session at a time, the justices' clerk necessarily delegates both administrative and advisory functions to her assistants. The staff whose job includes advising magistrates in court are called court clerks, of whom there are over 1,900, and they need not be professionally qualified, although some are. Delegated legislation requires that, if not professionally qualified, court clerks should be law graduates or equivalent, or

49

possess a special clerks' Home Office diploma in magisterial law, or be qualified by five years' experience before 1980. A 1985 survey of court clerks' qualifications showed that only about 28 per cent of them were professionally qualified and about half were diploma holders. The Home Secretary has since pronounced that he will not effect a policy of requiring all court clerks to be professionally qualified, contrary to the aims of the Justices' Clerks' Society.

This leads to the curious situation where, in most provincial courtrooms, the court clerk advising the lay justices is not professionally qualified. More anomalous is the fact that in Inner London, where most cases are heard by metropolitan stipendiary magistrates, they are usually advised by deputy chief clerks who are all professionally qualified, or by the chief clerk. (Additionally, there are under 100 court clerks in Inner London.)

The nationwide situation remains patchy, dependent on whether the local magistrates' courts committees pursue a policy of recruiting professionals.

Magistrates are dependent on their clerks for legal advice, in court. Section 78 of the Police and Magistrates' Courts Act 1994 provides that, in doing so, the justices' clerks and court clerks are independent and not subject to the direction of the magistrates' courts committee or the new breed of "super clerks", the justices' chief executive.

9. HISTORY

The justice of the peace has a very long history as an institution in the legal system. It has been claimed that a royal proclamation in 1195, which set up keepers of the peace to assist the sheriff in the maintenance of law and order, was the origin of the justice of the peace. Clearer evidence comes from statutes in 1327 and 1361 under which "good and lawful men" were to be "assigned to keep the peace", holding administrative rather than judicial authority, and like the present-day justice, not legally qualified and acting part-time. The title Justice of the Peace was first used in the 1361 statute. In 1363, a statute required four quarter sessions to be held annually, and gradually the power to deal with criminal cases was added to the administrative work. From 1496, justices were pemitted to try the minor—summary—

criminal cases locally at petty sessions, instead of at quarter sessions, so giving rise to the major jurisdiction of magistrates in their courts of summary jurisdiction at the present time. The administrative responsibility of magistrates for many local government functions remained with them until the setting up of the modern elected authorities under the Local Government Acts of 1888 and 1894. Traces of it are still to be seen in the statutory one-third membership of magistrates on local police authorities, and in their membership of the Crown Court, which replaced quarter sessions.

10. FUNCTIONS OF MAGISTRATES

Magistrates have an important role in the hearing of both criminal and civil cases. This section considers the part played by magistrates in the courts but leaves to Chapter 7 the procedure which operates in those courts.

Criminal

Criminal offences fall into four categories; they are summary, summary triable on indictment, triable either way and indictable. The least serious are the summary offences and these are the offences which Parliament has decreed that magistrates shall determine. They extend from such criminal conduct as drunkenness in a public place to most road traffic offences and minor assault. Such cases are heard and determined by magistrates in what is formally known as a court of summary jurisdiction.

Additionally, magistrates try the vast bulk of offences "triable either way", that is the middle category of offences, triable summarily or on indictment.

In many instances, the statute defining the offence will set out the maximum punishment which can be awarded. In general, magistrates' sentencing powers are limited to six months' imprisonment and/or a

£5,000 fine. If the same person is convicted of two or more offences at the one hearing the power to imprison is increased to 12 months. If the magistrates decide that their powers are not adequate for an appropriate sentence in a particular case, they can send the person concerned to the Crown Court for sentence since that court has much greater sentencing powers.

Ninety-eight per cent of all criminal cases heard in England and Wales are heard by magistrates. From time to time proposals are made seeking to increase the number of cases triable by magistrates by transferring into the summary category certain offences, such as minor cases of theft, where at present the accused may choose to be tried by a jury, in other words, which are "triable either way." Such proposals were considered, yet again, in the 1995 Home Office discussion paper *Mode of Trial*, discussed latter.

In indictable cases, which are the more serious criminal offences, covering such matters as rape, burglary and homicide, magistrates do not have the power to try the case themselves and in cases "triable either way", the magistrates or defence may opt for trial by the Crown Court. Here, the trial will be by judge and jury.

The Crown Court

The Courts Act 1971 replaced assizes and quarter sessions with the Crown Court. Magistrates have a significant part to play in the operation of the Crown Court, since they are called upon to sit, as judges, with the circuit judge or the recorder in the hearing of certain cases. For example, in the hearing of an appeal from the decision of a magistrates' court in a summary case, or where magistrates have committed a defendant for sentence to the Crown Court, not less than two nor more than four magistrates must sit with the judge. The magistrates must accept the judge's ruling on points of law but otherwise the decision of the court is by a majority. If necessary, the presiding judge has a casting vote.

Civil

Although magistrates have an enormous workload of criminal cases, dealing with most in their entirety, they have also been given a substantial jurisdiction by Parliament over a number of civil matters.

Some of these matters remain with the magistrates as a result of their history. The responsibility which the justices of the peace had from the time of Elizabeth I in administering the poor law in the locality led to their having a special concern for the maintenance of the illegitimate child. One result has been that magistrates have always been empowered to make certain civil orders relating to children and now have a significant jurisdiction, under the Children Act 1989, exercised by specialist family panels in family proceedings courts.

From legislation in the later years of the nineteenth century, magistrates derived a responsibility in the making of separation and maintenance orders in matrimonial disputes. Because of the highly personal nature of the evidence, the public is excluded from these hearings.

Magistrates have also long been responsible under licensing law for determining applications by pubs, clubs, etc. for liquor licences and music and dancing licences. This is the last relic of the magistrates' local government functions, which otherwise disappeared in 1888.

CHAPTER 4

THE JURY

1. "THE BULWARK OF OUR LIBERTIES"

The introduction of laypeople as the arbiters on matters of fact in judicial hearings is of long standing in the English legal system. Criticism has been directed at the use of juries. It is argued that the 12 laypeople are easily swayed by the eloquence of a barrister against the weight of the evidence, and that the average intelligence of such a group of citizens, called to attend against their wishes, leaves them ill-equipped to cope with the complexity of many of the cases in which they have to give a verdict. Against this view are many judicial pronouncements in praise of the jury, one of the more striking being Lord Devlin's view that "the jury is the lamp that shows that freedom lives", and another is Blackstone's statement that it is "the bulwark of our liberties".

The report of The Roskill Committee on Fraud Trials (1986) has renewed the debate by calling for the use of "assessors" instead of juries in certain complicated fraud cases. This debate has been revived in 1992, following the Guinness trial and the Blue Arrow fraud trial, the longest trial in legal history, lasting over a year and again in 1996, following the acquittals after the Maxwell trial. It is also being suggested that more offences should be designated summary offences, so that trial by jury would be available only for the most serious criminal cases.

2. SELECTION OF JURORS

The Juries Act 1974, as amended, specifies that every person between the ages of 18 and 70, who is registered on the annual electoral register as an elector and who has lived in this country for at least five years, is qualified to serve as a juror. The Act goes on to detail certain disqualifications and exemptions. For example, members of the legal profession and clergymen are ineligible. Persons convicted of criminal offences, and who are serving or have served in the last 10 years sentences of imprisonment, detention or youth custody of three months or more or have been to Borstal are disqualified as are those currently on bail (added by the Criminal Justice and Public Order Act (1994)). A suspended sentence of imprisonment or detention or the making of community service order, all within the 10-year period, act as a disqualification, as does being placed on probation within a five-year period. A person who has been sentenced to imprisonment or youth custody for five years or more is permanently disqualified. Certain members of the community, such as members of the armed forces, doctors and those over 65, may be excused from jury service if they so wish as may members of religious organisations, whose tenets or beliefs are incompatible with jury service (added by the 1994 Act). The court has a discretion to release a person called for jury service, or defer service if proper cause is shown.

Selection from the electoral register is now done manually on a random number basis approved by the Royal Statistical Society except for two computerised areas (Manchester and Stoke-on-Trent). Before the 1980s, jury summoning officers were given the freedom to select jurors from the electoral register, as they chose, and this led to some selecting alphabetically whilst others selected street by street. Even now there remain several factors destroying randomness. Most obviously, the electoral register is not accurately representative of the populations because of population mobility, house moves, death and, latterly, because of people declining to register, in an attempt to evade the Council Tax and it is up to the summoning officer which electoral register she uses and thus which area the jurors will come from. In the 1980s, there were complaints from black defendants that jurors have been summoned from white areas. Judges have resisted most attempts to artificially construct mixed race juries but in one trial the judge ordered an adjournment and, in another, ordered a jury be summoned from a different district, in the hope of selecting a mixed jury. The Royal Commission on Criminal Justice 1993, recommended that prosecution or defence be enabled to apply to the judge, pre-trial, for the selection of a jury containing up to three people from minority communities.

The group summoned to attend at a particular Crown Court location is called "the panel", from which juries are selected for trials over a certain period (usually two weeks) and the prosecution at this stage may exercise a problematic form of scrutiny known as "vetting."

3. RIGHTS OF JURORS

Legislation permits a juror to receive reimbursement of her travelling expenses, a subsistence allowance and, where appropriate, a financial loss allowance. This is intended to compensate the juror who has had, for example, to employ additional labour in her business because she has had to serve on the jury and has thus suffered a direct loss of earnings. The low allowance (£44.80 per day in 1996) by no means compensates many employed people.

Jury service is obligatory and personal inconvenience, such as having to cancel a holiday, may be no excuse. Medical evidence, or compelling business reasons, are possible methods of escape. The excusal rate probably varies greatly from court to court, depending on the policies of the summoning officers. The complexity of modern crime, which can lead to cases continuing over a number of weeks, is another factor which may present difficulties in finding 12 persons able to give up sufficient of their time. For the 1995–96 Maxwell brothers' fraud trial, scheduled to last six months, some 800 people were summoned. Seven hundred were excused on the ground of unavailability.

An interesting historical survival is the rule that jurors cannot be punished if they bring in a perverse acquittal contrary to the direction of the judge. This was laid down in *Bushell's* Case in 1670 where two Quakers were charged with tumultuous assembly. The jury were ordered to convict, but instead returned a verdict of "not guilty". The judge sent the jury to prison until they should pay a fine by way of punishment. On appeal, it was held that the fine and imprisonment could not be allowed to stand. The Ponting trial of 1985 saw a jury bring in a verdict of "not guilty" in an Official Secrets Act case where a conviction had been expected.

4. VETTING

Controversy arose during the highly publicised Official Secrets Act trial in 1978, known as the "ABC Trial" (because of the three defendants' surnames: Aubrey, Berry and Campbell). It became known that successive Attorneys-General had been secretly vetting jurors in this and other politically sensitive trials and trials involving professional gangs. *The Times* discovered and published the Attorney-General's vetting guidelines which disclosed that the panels' names were checked against Special Branch records, the national police computer and local CID records in trials involving, for example, the IRA. In the ABC trial, prosecuting counsel implied that vetting was carried out in order to eliminate "disloyal" elements from the jury. From then on, disclosures of vetting were rife and it transpired that much information of marginal relevance was revealed by vetting (for example in one trial that a juror had been a member of a squat and that other jurors had reported crimes to the police or complained about them) and that a number of circuit judges were informally sanctioning police vetting.

In 1980 the two divisions of the Court of Appeal gave rather conflicting rulings on the legality of jury vetting. In *R. v. Sheffield Crown Court, ex p. Brownlow*, the Civil Division, led by Lord Denning, unanimously ruled jury vetting by the police to be unconstitutional, although they appeared to accept vetting sanctioned by the Attorney-General.

The case was closely followed, in the Criminal Division of the Court of Appeal, by *R. v. Mason*, in which police vetting had taken place, although it had not been sanctioned by the judge. Indeed, it was revealed that it was the practice of the constabulary concerned (Northamptonshire) to vet all the county's juries. Lawton L.J., leading the court, held vetting practice was supportable as common sense. Previously convicted jurors should be excluded, as they might be prejudiced. He distinguished *Brownlow* on the grounds that his court had to consider jury vetting in greater depth.

In response, the Attorney-General amended the guidelines immediately, enhancing controls over vetting and distinguishing between (a) vetting carried out by the police and (b) "authorised checks", requiring his personal consent:

(a) Police may make checks against criminal records, following guidelines set down by the Association of Chief Police Officers, to establish that jurors are not disqualified.

(b) "Authorised checks" are now to be carried out only with the Attorney-General's permission, following a recommendation by the D.P.P. The D.P.P. decides what part of the information disclosed should be forwarded to the prosecution (*note: not* the defence). Except in terrorism cases, such checks will not now be carried out in politically motivated cases, or those involving criminal gangs and in, for example, Official Secrets trials, vetting will only be permitted where national security is involved and the hearing is likely to be *in camera.*

(c) Additionally, in cases falling under the guidelines, after an "authorised check", the Attorney-General will consider and, in other cases, the Chief Constable may consider, defence requests for information revealed on jurors. The Royal Commission On Criminal Justice 1993, recommended the routine screening of jurors for criminal convictions.

5. CHALLENGES TO THE ARRAY

Once the panel has been assembled, all parties have a common law right, preserved by section 12(6) of the Juries Act 1974, to challenge the whole panel, on the grounds that the summoning officer is biased or has acted improperly. For example this was attempted in *Danvers* (Crown Court 1982) by a black defendant, on the grounds that the all-white jury did not reflect the ethnic composition of the community.

6. CHALLENGES BY THE PROSECUTION

Whether or not checks have been made on the panel, the prosecution may exclude any of them from a particular jury by asking them to "stand by for the Crown" without reasons, until the whole panel, except for the last 12, is exhausted. Reasons, "cause", must be given for any further challenges but, with panels often consisting of 100 or more, the prosecution rarely needs to explain its challenges. The Roskill

Committee recommended the abolition of this right but the Government declined to include it in the Criminal Justice Bill 1986.

The Attorney-General announced, in 1988, that the prosecution's right to stand a juror by without giving reasons would now be limited to two instances:

    (i)   to remove a "manifestly unsuitable" juror;

    (ii) to remove a juror in a terrorist or security trial where the Attorney-General has authorised vetting.

This goes some way towards responding to complaints over the imbalance between prosecution and defence rights of challenge.

7. CHALLENGES BY THE DEFENCE

Once the jury are assembled in court, the defence may challenge any number of potential jurors *for cause* (*i.e.* good reason acceptable to the judge) but what is an acceptable "cause" has been qualified by a 1973 Practice Note issued by the Lord Chief Justice, who stated it was contrary to established practice for jurors to be excused on grounds such as race, religion, political beliefs or occupation. This followed a trial of alleged anarchists called "The Angry Brigade", where the defence had requested the judge to ask people to exclude themselves if, for example, they were members of the Conservative Party or if they had relatives in the police force or serving in the forces in Northern Ireland.

It is also clear that the reasons must be those known to the defence and should not normally be ascertained by examining the potential juror in court. In other words, no practice exists such as the "voir dire" system in the United States, where potential jurors are examined by psychologists and other professionals to discover any prejudices. There have been occasional, well publicised exceptions, however, in the 1980s, where the judge has permitted examination of jurors on their affiliations or beliefs, notably in cases involving black defendants. In the 1995–96 Maxwell brothers' fraud trial, potential jurors were questioned on their views of the evidence because of prejudicial pre-trial publicity.

Until recently, the defence could make a certain number of peremptory challenges, that is, challenges without reasons. This number was reduced from seven to three in the Criminal Law Act 1977 and has now been abolished, amidst great controversy, by the Criminal Justice Act 1988. This resulted from unsupported but widespread public allegations that the right to peremptory challenge was being abused by defence lawyers, deliberately trying to skew the jury and from the recommendation of the Roskill Committee on fraud trials (1986) that it be abolished. This leaves a gross imbalance between prosecution and defence rights of challenge, which the Criminal Bar Association argues is a breach of Article 6 of the European Convention on Human Rights.

8. EXCUSAL BY THE JUDGE

Under the Juries Act, section 10, the judge may discharge from service any juror about whom there is doubt as to "his capacity to act effectively as a juror" because of physical disability or insufficient understanding of English. Additionally, judges have a common law discretion to discharge jurors and they occasionally interpret this quite broadly. For example, the whole panel was discharged in the controversial 1979 anarchists trial and the eventual jury at the trial were discharged for life, after acquitting most of the defendants.

9. FUNCTION OF THE JURY

The purpose of having the jury is to enable the decision on fact in a case to be taken by a small group from the community, rather than for it to be left entirely in the hands of the lawyers. Thus, in criminal cases tried on indictment at the Crown Court, the guilt of the person accused has to be established to the satisfaction of the 12 jurors in the case beyond all reasonable doubt (but a majority verdict may be permissible, see below). At the conclusion of the case it is for the jury, after hearing the judge's "summing up" of the prosecution and defence case, to retire and consider their verdict in private. On the pronouncement of that verdict by the foreman of the jury the accused is found either "guilty" or "not guilty". If "not guilty" the defendant is acquitted and is free to leave the court; if "guilty" he is convicted, and the sentence of the court is the responsibility of the judge. The judge will first hear the criminal record of the prisoner and then a plea in mitigation of sentence, which is made by defence counsel. The jury has no part to play in the decision as to sentence. Equally the jury has no part in decisions which are concerned with law or legal procedure. In practice, the judge at a trial will, on occasions, have to ask the jury to retire, so that she can decide on a point of law which has arisen and which will be argued by counsel in the case. In criminal cases this is most often about the admissibility of evidence, in the form of statements or confessions alleged to have been made by the accused on arrest.

As will be seen in Chapter 7, criminal offences are for trial purposes designated as (1) triable on indictment only, (2) triable summarily only, (3) triable either way and (4) summary, triable on indictment (a category added in 1988). Jury trial in criminal cases is obligatory to those charged with an offence triable on indictment only and available to those who so qualify under the triable either way provisions.

In civil cases the jury has declined massively, this century. Although under court rules a jury of eight may be called in the county court at the discretion of the judge, in practice the use of such a jury is not common. Jury trial is also available in certain trials in the Queen's Bench Division but jury trials here and in the county court only amount to a few hundred per year. In the following types of case there is, by section 69 of the Supreme Court Act 1981, a right to jury trial: libel, slander, malicious prosecution, false imprisonment and fraud. Even here jury trial can be refused if a prolonged examination of documents, or accounts, or a scientific or local investigation, or other complex material is involved. In all other cases, the judge has a discretion to allow a jury trial. The trend away from jury trial in civil cases has been comparatively rapid since, as recently as 1933, 50 per cent of cases involved a jury. In *Ward v. James* (1966) a five-judge Court of Appeal decided that trial by judge alone should be the usual mode of trial, save where statute provided otherwise, or where a judge decided that the exceptional circumstances warranted it. This decline in the use of jury trials in civil cases can be accounted for on two grounds: one is the inconsistency in the award of damages, and the other is the exorbitant figures for damages which sometimes resulted. Recent examples of this include the award of £600,000 libel damages to Sonia Sutcliffe, ex-wife of the "Yorkshire Ripper", against the publishers of *Private Eye*. This was reduced, on appeal, to £60,000. The CLSA, s.8 provided a new rule-making power to empower the Court of Appeal to substitute its own award of damages. It has obviously been easier to achieve consistency in the scale of damages for personal injuries because that matter is left to the judges. Throughout the 1990s, however, juries have continued to make outlandishly high damages awards in the defamation actions of the rich and famous, much to the exasperation of the judiciary. Notice the disgust expressed in the words of the Master of the Rolls, in December 1995, in *John v. Mirror Group Newspapers*, an appeal in which the Mirror group succeeded in getting the Court of Appeal to reduce to £75,000 the jury's award of £350,000 to Elton John, for alleging that he displayed symptoms of an eating disorder at a Hollywood party:

> "It is in our view offensive to public opinion, and rightly so, that a defamation plaintiff should recover damages for injury to reputation greater, perhaps by a significant factor, than if that same plaintiff had been rendered a helpless cripple or an insensate vegetable. The time has in our view come when judges, and counsel, should be free to draw the attention of juries to these comparisons."

Also in 1995, a jury award of £750,000 damages made to Graeme Souness, against his ex-wife for calling him a "dirty rat" in *The People*, was settled, pending appeal to the Court of Appeal for £100,000. In 1996, four large awards of damages against the Metropolitan Police in jury trials for action such as false imprisonment provoked the Metropolitan Police Commissioner to call for judicial guidelines to be set down for juries in these cases, similar to those in defamation cases.

The coroner, whose task it is to inquire into the cause of death whenever a person dies other than from natural causes, can, and in some circumstances must, call a jury for the inquest. The coroner's jury can number from seven to 11 and it will, after hearing the evidence, return a verdict as to the cause of death and the coroner must record this verdict. The general intention is to ensure that deaths are thoroughly investigated, and, where the death is the result of an accident, to try and prevent a recurrence.

10. MAJORITY VERDICTS

For centuries, the English legal system required that the verdict of the jury in both civil and criminal trials should be unanimous. If unanimity could not be achieved then a re-trial was necessary.

In the 1960s there was increasing criticism of this requirement, particularly on the part of the police who pointed out that one member of the jury if "got at" by the defendant or his supporters could cause a re-trial by simply refusing to agree with the other 11 jurors in a criminal case. After much debate, the Criminal Justice Act 1967 made provision for a majority verdict to be accepted by the judge in a criminal case at her discretion provided that not more than two members of the jury were in the minority (or one member if the jury is reduced to 11 or 10 in number) and provided also that the jury had spent at least two hours seeking to achieve unanimity. If the verdict was "guilty" the fact that it was a majority verdict had to be disclosed in open court.

The majority verdict provisions were extended to civil cases, where a jury had been called, by the Courts Act 1971.

All the provisions concerning majority verdicts have now been consolidated in the Juries Act 1974.

11. HISTORY

The jury as an English legal institution can claim a very long history, in the course of which it has completely changed its role. At present the essential element of the jury system is the fact that the 12 persons called for jury service are completely unknown to the person accused and can thus execute a fair trial free of any bias. Every effort is made to ensure that the jury have no prior knowledge of the case, and will be able to reach their verdict entirely on the evidence presented at the trial. Originally, however, in the earliest days of the English legal system, the jury's role was a combination of local police and prosecutor. Centuries before a paid police force came into being, the responsibility for law and order was a community responsibility. This led to the local "jury" for the hundred having to arrest suspected offenders, and then bring these offenders before the itinerant judge visiting the locality and swear, like prosecution witnesses, to the guilt of the accused. There was nothing unusual in this use of local representatives in the early community. It can be seen also in the local inquiries which led to the creation of the Domesday Book, and the system of inquisitions post mortem—the inquiry held on a death as to the ownership of the lands and goods of the deceased—where again considerable reliance seems to have been placed on local representatives. Throughout the Middle Ages the local community voice was frequently sought in the settlement of litigation disputes concerning the ownership and tenancy of land and the right to an advowson (the right to present to the living of a church).

It was only very gradually and with the passage of centuries that the use of the jury in its modern role, as the uninvolved judges of fact, developed. Even then the original concept continued to exist and this led to the existence of a grand jury and a petty jury. The grand jury numbering 24 members met only at the start of assizes or quarter sessions in order to find a true bill of indictment against the accused. Since the accused had previously undergone the preliminary inquiry by magistrates, who had heard the prosecution case and had decided to commit the accused for trial, the decision of the grand jury became a complete formality. Nonetheless it reveals clearly the original role of the jury as the presenter of the accused for trial. The grand jury was substantially abolished by the Administration of Justice (Miscellaneous Provisions) Act 1933 and finally brought to an end by the Criminal Justice Act 1948. The petty jury of 12 members on the other hand came into being in the thirteenth century to take the place of trial by ordeal, which the ecclesiastical authorities then saw fit to condemn. It became increasingly distinct in its functions from the grand jury, although it long maintained its composition from local witnesses of fact deciding matters from their local knowledge. It was the fifteenth century before the petty jury assumed its modern role in criminal trials as judges of fact.

In civil cases the jury appears to have had its origin in the Assizes of Clarendon in 1166, and the Assizes of Northampton in 1176, establishing the grand and petty assizes. Here again the jury was at first called to decide a case from its local knowledge, and only with the passage of time did it become an impartial judge of the facts. The system allowed for trial to be in two parts—the local jury would hear and deal with the case locally, and then send their findings to the judges at Westminster where the judgment would be given. Jury trial was for centuries as widely used in civil as in criminal cases, and it is only the last 100 years since the Common Law Procedure Act 1854 which has seen the substantial falling off in the use of the jury in civil cases.

12. CONTROVERSIES SURROUNDING THE JURY

There is an ongoing debate between civil libertarians and others about several issues surrounding the jury, all of which are very interconnected:

    (i)   The pros and cons of retaining the jury and jury equity;
   (ii) Randomness; representatives; jury vetting—its desirability and constitutionality; the fairness of prosecution and defence challenges.

(1) Should the jury be retained and does it inject layperson's "equity" into the legal system?

PRO (a) The jury rouses strong emotions and seems to be defended by some historians, civil libertarians, politicians, judges and laypeople as the last bastion of civil liberties. For example, Lord Devlin hailed it as a guardian of democracy:

> "no tyrant could afford to leave a subject's freedom in the hands of his countrymen. So that trial by jury is more than an instrument of justice and one wheel of the constitution: it is the lamp that shows that freedom lives." (*Trial by Jury* (1966))

and Blackstone called the jury "the glory of English law ... the liberties of England cannot but subsist so long as this palladium remains sacred and inviolate". (*Commentaries* (1768))
    It is argued that the jury acts as a check on officialdom, on the judge's

power, and a protector against unjust or oppressive prosecution, injecting jury "equity" by deciding guilt or innocence according to a feeling of justice rather than by applying known law to facts proven beyond reasonable doubt: for example Kalven and Zeisel in "The American Jury" (*New Society* (1966)),

> "It represents also an impressive way of building discretion, equity and flexibility into a legal system. Not least of the advantages is that the jury, relieved of the burdens of creating precedent, can bend the law without breaking it."

(b) Additionally, jury supporters argue that a decision by 12 laypeople is fairer than one by a judge alone, since it is likely that 12 people will cancel out one another's prejudices.

CON (a) The importance of the jury system is overrated, for example, when given the choice, being charged with a criminal offence "triable either way", the vast majority of defendants (about 80 per cent) choose to appear before magistrates (source: *Annual Criminal Statistics*) and, of the remainder, who opt for or are sent to the Crown Court, over 80 per cent plead guilty to one or all charges and thus are not tried by jury but just sentenced by the judge. This point was noted by the Royal Commission on Criminal Justice, 1993, following Home Office research by Hedderman and Moxon. It was one factor influencing the Commission to recommend that the defendant should be deprived of the right to insist on jury trial in triable either way cases. (Recommendation 114.)

(b) The rate of use of civil juries has declined massively since the nineteenth century. By the 1920s only half the civil cases in the K.B.D. were tried by jury, then the Administration of Justice (Miscellaneous Provisions) Act 1933 imposed limits on the use of civil jury trial, which remains a right only in cases of libel, slander, malicious prosecution, false imprisonment and fraud but, under the Supreme Court Act 1981, the court can refuse jury trial if it is of the opinion "that the trial requires prolonged examination of documents or accounts or of any specific or local investigation which cannot conveniently be made with a jury". In other civil cases, the judge has a discretion whether to allow jury trial.

(c) By now, civil juries are rarely used (under 200 trials per year) and examining the reasons why people do not opt for them gives an idea of the drawbacks of jury trial.

The Faulks Committee (1974) recommended that juries should no longer be available as of right in defamation actions because, *inter alia*:

(i) Judges were not as remote from real life as popularly supposed.
(ii) Judges gave reasons, whereas juries did not.
(iii) Juries found complex cases difficult.
(iv) Juries were unpredictable.
(v) Juries were expensive (jury trial is more time consuming, as explanations have to be geared for them, not a judge).

Additional reasons given by the anti-jury lobby for the unpopularity of civil juries are:

(vi) They seldom take notes, are not encouraged to do so, and may not be able to remember all the evidence, thus they are likely to be swayed in the jury room by the more dominant characters' interpretation or recollection of events and to be more vulnerable to persuasive rhetoric than a judge.

Their difficulty in understanding evidence is most acute in fraud trials and was considered by the Roskill Committee on Fraud Trials in 1986. Fraud trials are notoriously long (sometimes over 100 days), expensive and highly complicated. The Committee said:

> "The background against which the frauds are alleged to have been committed—the sophisticated world of high finance and international trading—is probably a mystery to most or all of the jurors, its customs and practices a closed book. Even the language in which the allegedly fraudulent transactions have been conducted will be unfamiliar. A knowledge of accountancy or bookkeeping may be essential to an understanding of the case. If any juror has such knowledge, it is by chance" (para. 8.27).

The Committee recommended the jury be abolished in complex criminal fraud cases and be replaced by a Fraud Trials Tribunal of a judge and two lay members. Their remarks on the anomalous (as they see it) use of the jury epitomise the view that the significance of the jury is overrated (para. 8.21).

"Out of all the citizens (possibly some three million) who, in the course of any year, find themselves in difficulty with the law, only a small portion (32,000 in 1984) will be tried by a jury. The underlying logic of this situation we find puzzling in the extreme. If society believes that trial by jury is the fairest form of trial, is it too costly and troublesome to be universally applied? ... But if jury trial is not inherently more fair, given its extra cost and trouble, what are the merits which justify its retention? Society appears to have an attachment to jury trial which is emotional or sentimental rather than logical."

(d) The notion that the jury applies its own equity has no substance. Baldwin & McConville in *Jury Trials* (1979) found no evidence that juries acquitted people in the face of unjust prosecution. On the contrary, perverse verdicts (*i.e.* verdicts against the weight of the evidence, as assessed by professional observers and assessors) occurred at random. The jury thus had the disadvantage of being unpredictable.

See further pros and cons of the jury in Findlay & Duff, *The Jury Under Attack* (1988) and P. Darbyshire [1991] Crim.L.R., 740.

(2) Arguments about randomness, representatives, jury vetting and the rights of challenge

The legal sources of definitions of the notions of randomness and representativeness are difficult to discover. As mentioned above, they do not appear in the Juries Act 1974, which significantly qualifies randomness but there are statements elsewhere.

The Report of the Departmental Committee on Jury Service (*The Morris Committee*, 1965): "a jury should represent a cross-section drawn at random from the community" and the 1973 *Practice Note* by the Lord Chief Justice "a jury consists of twelve individuals chosen at random from the appropriate panel". (Now superseded by the 1988 direction.) *Note*: this does not imply that the panel should be random. Further, the *obiter* statement of Lord Denning in the *Brownlow* case (1980, above) reviewed the two "rival philosophies" as he called them, of our random jury and the highly selected American jury. He stated:

> "Our philosophy is that the jury should be selected at random from a panel of persons who are nominated at random. We believe that twelve persons selected at random are likely to be a cross-section of the people and thus represent the views of the common man. Some may be moral. Others not. Some may be honest. Others not ... The parties must take them as they come."

Lawton L.J., however, in *Mason* (1980, above) rejected as "misconceived" the argument that, on a true construction of the Juries Act 1974, every person who was not ineligible or disqualified should be permitted, as of right, to sit as a juror.

Challenges, like the statutory exclusory rules, destroy randomness and, for this reason, the Roskill Committee recommend their abolition. It is sometimes argued that civil libertarians are contradictory in supporting randomness, yet complaining that defence rights of challenge have been whittled away (see above).

The focal point of their objection, though, is the imbalance between prosecution and defence rights. As can be seen above, the prosecution have far more drastic rights than defence and there are further objections to the practice of vetting:

(i) That its legal and constitutional foundations are dubious, as argued by McEldowney in "Stand By For The Crown—An Historical Analysis" (1979). The Attorney-General presumably claims prerogative power for vetting yet the Juries Act 1974 sets out jury selection as the Lord Chancellor's responsibility.

(ii) That it is anti-democratic because it was not sanctioned by Parliament in the Juries Act.

(iii) That it is an erosion of jurors' moral rights of privacy, as investigations are carried out in secret, without the jurors' knowing. A lot of irrelevant and prejudicial information is revealed by vetting (for example in the *Mason* case and the 1979 anarchists trial) which the jurors have no opportunity of contradicting.

13. JURY SECRECY

The secrecy of jury deliberations is protected in English law. They deliberate alone in the jury room and disclosure of those deliberations is a contempt under The Contempt of Court Act 1981, s.8. The application of that section is so broad as to preclude bona fide research into jury decision-making, frustrating would-be socio-legal researchers and reform bodies. The Royal Commission on Criminal Justice, 1993, recommended its abolition, as did the Law Commission, in their 1995 annual report.

CHAPTER 5

CIVIL COURTS

In all legal systems a distinction is drawn between civil law and criminal law, and generally a separate system of courts and of court procedure accompanies this division. The English legal system generally follows this pattern; and so this chapter will describe the civil court structure whilst Chapter 6 will examine the criminal court structure and Chapter 7 will outline the procedure followed in the civil and criminal courts.

The fundamental difference between civil law and criminal law is that in criminal law the state is concerned to enforce law and order in the community by ensuring that an accepted code of conduct is everywhere observed. In civil law the state plays little part, other than to provide the forum for the settlement of disputes between individuals. These include breach of contract cases, disputes about liability for alleged civil misconduct—torts, property disagreements, for example as between a landlord and a tenant and family issues, all of which are civil law matters.

As with the rest of the legal system, the work and jurisdiction of the civil courts is currently in a state of massive upheaval. Following the recommendations of the *Civil Justice Review* (1988), the Lord Chancellor was given sweeping powers under the Courts and Legal Services Act 1990 to reorganise the civil business of the High Court and the county courts. The *Review* recommended a significant shift of work for the High Court, as it found that the High Court was clogged up with trivial cases. The Lord Chancellor used his powers to this end, via 1991 statutory instruments, augmented by changes in the court rules and practice directions. He will certainly produce more delegated legislation, shifting yet more work into the county court. Given the thoroughness of the Review and its consequent legislation, it was astonishing to find civil procedure yet again under scrutiny by the legal profession, in the Heilbron Report, 1993 (properly known as *"Civil Justice On Trial—The Case For Change": Report by the Independent*

Working Party set up jointly by the General Council of The Bar and the Law Society) and for the Lord Chancellor's Department by Lord Woolf (1994, about to report in 1996).

The Children Act 1989, which came into force in 1991 and, again, the subordinate legislation made under it, consolidates and significantly changes the substantive law relating to children but it also gives concurrent jurisdiction to the magistrates' courts, county courts and High Court in all matters relating to children.

1. MAGISTRATES' COURTS

It should not be forgotten that magistrates have a substantial civil jurisdiction. Under the 1989 Children Act, implemented in October 1991, their domestic proceedings courts were renamed "family proceedings courts" and the specially trained magistrates who adjudicate are selected from "the family panel". They can make and enforce financial provisions following a family breakdown and can make orders protecting adults and children. They can make a range of orders relating to children, including care and supervision orders and contact and residence orders, replacing, respectively, what used to be known as access and custody orders.

Other civil work of the magistrates' courts includes the enforcement of the Council Tax and VAT.

2. COUNTY COURTS

Since 1846, the county court has provided a nationwide system for the trial of civil cases where a comparatively small amount of money is involved.

County courts do not follow county boundaries. Their name is historical. There are 260 county courts in England and Wales, each with at least one circuit judge and one district judge (formerly registrar; renamed by the CLSA 1990). Among the latter's tasks are dealing with interlocutory matters (matters arising during a trial such as an application for discovery of documents), holding the pre-trial review, considering applications for adjournment, taxing costs, and also disposing of undefended cases or small claims. Following the recommendations of the Civil Justice Review, under the CLSA and delegated legislation, the district judge's general jurisdiction was increased to £5,000 and to £1,000 in small claims (£3,000 since January 1996: see below).

For the hearing of a case the judge sits alone. A jury of eight can be called, but in practice this is rare. An appeal from the district judge's finding goes to the circuit judge, whilst an appeal from the circuit judge goes, subject to certain conditions, to the Court of Appeal (Civil Division). The CLSA, s.7 provides that the Supreme Court Rules can set out leave requirements for appeals.

The Civil Justice Review 1988—problems and proposals on the distribution of civil business

The Civil Justice Review, set up to examine the distribution of work between the county courts and the High Court, reported in 1988 that delay permeated civil litigation, that the High Court was clogged up with too many trivial cases and that the cost of litigation was too high, relative to the amounts claimed, deterring litigants. The Review was unusually successful, as public bodies go, in that most of its recommendations were adopted, in the CLSA 1990 and its 1991 subordinate legislation. They included:

(i) The High Court should be confined to:
    (a) public law cases,
    (b) other specialist cases (for example commercial, admiralty, building contracts),
    (c) general list cases of *importance* (for example involving fraud or test cases) or *complexity* (on the law or facts or number of parties involved) or *substance* (over £25,000 value).

(ii) There should be a flexible financial band of £25,000–£50,000, within which cases could be tried by either court, depending on the availability of judges and the substance of the cases, and no upper limit of county court jurisdiction.

(iii) All personal injury cases should commence in the county court, with discretionary transfer upwards.

(iv) Small claims should be increased to £1,000.

(v) Generally speaking, the same remedies should be available in both courts.

(vi) A plaintiff should be free to commence a case where he chooses.

(vii) The Review Body considered but rejected the proposition that there should be one civil court, replacing High Court and county courts, on grounds of "specialist efficiency". Certain specialist cases need to be handled, from the outset, at High Court level by judges with specialist expertise.

(viii) Registrars' (now district judges') jurisdiction should be increased to £5,000 and the High Court work absorbed by the county courts should be dealt with by circuit judges.

County court jurisdiction

Under the Courts and Legal Services Act 1990, s.3 the county court was given almost all the powers of the High Court. Consequently, it now tries the vast bulk of civil cases, with the High Court reserved for a few special cases, in accordance with the recommendations of the Civil Justice Review. Under the Act, its subordinate legislation and practice directions, the county court should try:

— all personal injury claims under £50,000

— equity and probate cases under £30,000

— and any action worth less than £25,000, unless the court considers, applying the new criteria, that it should be tried in the High Court.

76

Either the county court or the High Court may try actions in the £25,000–£50,000 range, which should be allocated according to the new criteria:

(a) the financial substance of the action;
(b) the importance of the action, especially whether it raises issues relevant to outsiders, or of general public interest;
(c) the complexity of the facts, legal issues, remedies or procedures involved;
(d) whether a transfer is likely to result in a more speedy trial of the action.

There are exceptions to this. In London, all actions under £200,000 commence in the London County Court. Under CLSA, s.4 the court may penalise in costs any party who brings a case in the High Court which it considers should have been brought in the county court.

The 1991 County Court Rules increased the small claims limit to £1,000 and, following Lord Woolf's recommendation, 1995 Rules increased the limit to £3,000 in 1996, except in personal injury cases and possession actions. Under this limit, all claims are subject to a more informal arbitration procedure, conducted by a district judge, unless it is legally or factually complex. The Civil Justice Review said district judges should be encouraged to take on an inquisitorial role in these proceedings, as the parties are not usually represented, and CLSA, s.6 allows rules to be made permitting this. In the 1991 subordinate legislation, the district judge's general powers were increased to £5,000.

Other than small claims and family proceedings, the county court deals with cases involving such issues as probate, property, tort, contract, race relations, bankruptcy, insolvency and admiralty, among other things. Very much of its work is concentrated in debt collection or personal injuries.

Under the Children Act 1989, from October 1991 the county court has had the same jurisdiction in relation to children as the High Court and the magistrates' courts, with cases allocated according to their complexity.

All the divorce county courts have jurisdiction to hear any uncontested private family law matters, with contested matters being dealt with by family hearing centres or care centres. All such cases must start off in the county court and be determined there, unless sent up to the High Court.

3. THE HIGH COURT OF JUSTICE

The High Court of Justice and the Court of Appeal were brought into being as the Supreme Court of Judicature under the Judicature Acts 1873–75. At that time, the High Court consisted of five Divisions—the Queen's Bench, Chancery, Probate, Divorce and Admiralty, Exchequer and Common Pleas. The last two Divisions were merged in the Queen's Bench Division in 1880 and the remaining three Divisions continued unaltered from then until the Administration of Justice Act 1970 redistributed the functions of the Probate, Divorce and Admiralty Division and created the Family Division.

There are 95 High Court judges appointed to the three Divisions according to the pressure of work. When appointed, the judge has to be prepared to serve in any of the Divisions but, in practice, judges tend to continue to serve in the Division to which they have been allocated.

The High Court has its headquarters at the Royal Courts of Justice in the Strand in London but, for the convenience of litigants and their solicitors, there are a number of district registries (for non contentious business) and trial centres in the larger cities in England and Wales. It is thus possible for cases to be dealt with at the county court in certain provincial cities so avoiding the need to take the parties and witnesses to London.

THE QUEEN'S BENCH DIVISION

This, the great common law court, takes its name from the fact that the early royal judges sat on "the bench"—*in banc*—at Westminster. As a result of the reconstruction of the courts in the Judicature Acts 1873–75, and the transfer to the Queen's Bench Division in 1880 of the jurisdiction of the Common Pleas and Exchequer Divisions, this court has absorbed the whole common law jurisdiction. The present jurisdiction of the Division is thus both civil and criminal, original and appellate and the Q.B.D. is much larger than the other two Divisions.

In terms of its civil jurisdiction, with which this chapter is particularly concerned, this can be simply stated as cases in contract and tort. Cases are heard in London or at 26 provincial trial centres. Within the Division is the Commercial Court, where five Queen's Bench Division judges with special commercial experience hear cases of a commercial nature, concerning insurance, banking and the interpretation of mercantile documents like negotiable instruments or bills of lading. The procedure is deliberately kept informal and the strict rules relating to documents and evidence are relaxed.

A Commercial Court judge may be appointed as an arbitrator. As with the Commercial Court, a separate Admiralty Court has been established, to deal with issues relating to ships and aircraft, such as collisions and cargo.

As well as these various responsibilities, Queen's Bench judges are appointed to hear cases in the Restrictive Practices Court, which was created by the Restrictive Trade Practices Act 1956. Under these statutory arrangements, one judge with two specially appointed laypeople form the court to hear a case. A similar arrangement applies to the Employment Appeal Tribunal which hears appeals from Industrial Tribunals. These courts are superior courts of record but not part of the High Court.

The Queen's Bench Division furnishes the judges who try, with a jury, the most serious criminal offences at the Crown Court throughout England and Wales.

The Queen's Bench Divisional Court. In its appellate jurisdiction, the Queen's Bench, like the other two Divisions, has what is rather confusingly called a Divisional Court. This is, in most instances, an appeal court of at least two, but possibly three judges, and in the case of the Queen's Bench Divisional Court it has the following jurisdiction:

(i) Appeals on a point of law by way of case stated from magistrates' courts, tribunals and the Crown Court.

(ii) It exercises the supervisory jurisdiction of the High Court over inferior courts and tribunals and, most importantly, over

governmental and other public bodies. Specialist judges of the Divisional Court regularly hear applications for judicial review from what is called the Crown Office list.
(iii) Applications for *habeas corpus* (challenging the legality of detention).
(iv) Committals for contempt in an inferior court.
(v) Appeals and applications on planning matters.

THE CHANCERY DIVISION

This Division is the direct descendant of the Lord Chancellor's equity jurisdiction, and it is thus substantially concerned with those matters which, before the Judicature Acts 1873–75, belonged to the Court of Chancery. It has also had allocated to it by statute the responsibility for such matters as the winding-up of companies and revenue cases. Its jurisdiction can be summarised as:

disputed intellectual property, copyright or patents;
the execution or declaration of trusts;
the redemption and foreclosure of mortgages;
conveyancing and land law matters;
partnership actions and other business disputes;
the administration of the estates of deceased persons (contested probate);
revenue issues, *i.e.* taxation cases;
bankruptcy and corporate and personal insolvency.

It also contains two specialist courts: the Patents Court and the Companies Court.

The 17 Chancery judges are nominally presided over by the Lord Chancellor but this is for historical reasons and in practice he does not sit. Instead, the Vice-Chancellor heads the Division. Most Chancery cases are heard at the Royal Courts of Justice in London without a jury or at one of eight designated provincial first-tier High Court centres. Because of the specialised nature of Chancery work there is a separate Chancery Bar for the barristers who practice in the Chancery Division and it is from this group of barristers that new Chancery Division judges are appointed. Chancery barristers usually have chambers in Lincoln's Inn. Interlocutory matters are dealt with by Chancery masters.

The Chancery Divisional Court. The Chancery Divisional Court hears certain income tax appeals from the Commissioners of Taxes and it also hears appeals from county courts in bankruptcy and insolvency.

THE FAMILY DIVISION

This Division of the High Court came into being under provisions contained in the Administration of Justice Act 1970. It shares family jurisdiction with the magistrates' court and the county court. The Division is headed by a President and occupies 16 High Court judges.
The main responsibilities of the Family Division are:

(i) the grant of legal title—probate or letters of administration—to authorise named executors or administrators to wind up a decreased person's estate where the matter is uncontested. This work is done at the Principal Registry in London, or at one of 11 district registries in various cities of England and Wales;

(ii) the hearing of defended or complex divorce and matrimonial cases, either in London or at certain designated provincial centres. All matters relevant to the case, such as financial orders relating to maintenance, or children, are also dealt with;

(iii) applications relating to children, under the Children Act 1989: for instance applications for care orders, adoptions, wardship, residence and contact orders. Jurisdiction under the Children Act is concurrent with that of the county court and magistrates' court. Cases will be allocated according to their complexity so the High Court will be dealing with the most complex. Transfers between courts may occur.

The Family Divisional Court. The Family Divisional Court hears appeals from decisions of magistrates in a wide variety of domestic matters; for example, appeals lie from the magistrates' court, under section 94 of the Children Act where magistrates have made an order or refused to make an order under that Act.

An appeal from the decision of a judge sitting in any one of the three Divisions of the High Court will go to the Court of Appeal (Civil Division).

The one exception to this rule, introduced by the Administration of Justice Act 1969, is that it is possible for an appeal to "leapfrog" the Court of Appeal and go direct to the House of Lords provided:

(i)   the trial judge is prepared to grant a certificate;

(ii)   the parties agree to this course;

(iii)   a point of law of general public importance is involved, which relates wholly or mainly to the construction of a statute or statutory instrument; or the judge was bound by a previous decision of the Court of Appeal or the House of Lords; and

(iv)   the House of Lords grants leave.

In view of these stringent conditions not many successful applications are made (about 12 per year).

4. COURT OF APPEAL (CIVIL DIVISION)

The Court of Appeal was created by the Judicature Acts 1873–75 together with the High Court of Justice to form the Supreme Court of Judicature. It was at first intended that the Court of Appeal should be the final appeal court, but a change of plan led to the Appellate Jurisdiction Act 1876, under which the House of Lords in its judicial capacity was retained as the supreme appeal court.

A special group of judges called Lords Justices of Appeal were appointed to form the Court of Appeal in civil cases. The present number is 32, across the two divisions.

The present jurisdiction of the court includes appeals from the three Divisions of the High Court, including divisional courts, from the county courts, from the Employment Appeal Tribunal, from the Lands Tribunal and the Transport Tribunal.

The Master of the Rolls is, in practice, the senior judge of the Court of Appeal (Civil Division). The President of the Family Division and the Vice-Chancellor will sit occasionally. Three Lords Justices usually sit to form a court but in a case of great importance (see *Ward v. James* (1966)) a "full court" of five judges is convened. It will be obvious from the number of judges that the Court of Appeal (Civil Division) will sit in several benches on any one day. This explains the fact that in an average year this court will actually hear around 900 full appeals and 600 interlocutory appeals.

Since the Criminal Appeal Act 1966, the Court of Appeal has had a Criminal Division, replacing the former Court of Criminal Appeal. It is presided over by the Lord Chief Justice to hear about 3,000 criminal appeals per year. Both Divisions sit only at the Royal Courts of Justice in London.

5. HOUSE OF LORDS

The Appellate Committee of the House of Lords is the final court of appeal in matters civil and criminal from all courts in England, Wales and Northern Ireland; and in matters civil from courts in Scotland. It first assumed its present jurisdiction under the Appellate Jurisdiction Act 1876. There is now a maximum of 12 Lords of Appeal in Ordinary—known as the Law Lords—to try these appeals. At least two of the judges will be from Scotland and one from Northern Ireland. In addition to the Lords of Appeal in Ordinary, other judges who can take part in the work of the House are the Lord Chancellor, ex-Lord Chancellors, the Master of the Rolls and peers who have held high judicial office. By constitutional convention, lay peers do not take part in the hearing of appeals.

The court known as the Appellate Committee, for which a quorum is three, normally has five judges sitting to hear the appeal. The case is heard in a committee room of the House of Lords at Westminster. The judges wear lounge suits, although counsel are in wigs and robes, and the atmosphere is comparatively informal. The cases heard always raise a point of law of general public importance, which is the sole ground for obtaining leave to appeal to the House of Lords. In English appeals, leave may be granted by the court below. This may be the Court of Appeal or the Queen's Bench Divisional Court when dealing with a point of law in a case stated from a magistrates' court or with a judicial review. If leave is refused by the court below, it is still possible for a party wishing to appeal to ask the Appeal Committee of the House of Lords itself to give leave to appeal. An additional source of appeal cases, introduced by the Administration of Justice Act 1969, allows a High Court judge, in certain defined and limited circumstances, detailed above, at 3. The High Court of Justice may certify that the House of Lords should consider the case. If the Appeal Committee of the House of Lords agree with the judge the appeal will "leapfrog" the Court of Appeal. Each side, in any appeal to the House of Lords, must submit a "printed case", drawn up by counsel, which must contain a succinct statement of their argument. The oral hearing follows.

Their Lordships, after hearing the appeal, will take time to prepare their "opinions", as their Lordships' judgments are called. It is open to all five judges to give individual opinions and then the majority view prevails. The court finally gives notice of its decision to the House of Lords itself, so that the judgment can be formally recorded. Judgments of the House of Lords are almost always reported, because every one adds some new principle to, or clarifies some existing principle of, law. As the supreme court, the decisions of the House of Lords are binding on all lower courts, and they thus form the most important precedents in domestic law. There are only around 60 such decisions per year.

6. THE EUROPEAN COURT OF JUSTICE

The European Court of Justice consists currently of 15 judges, each of whom must be qualified to hold the highest judicial office in their own country, appointed for a six-year term by the governments of the Member States. The judges are assisted by nine Advocates-General who prepare reasoned conclusions on the cases submitted to the court.

The court is not bound by judicial precedent and has a flexible approach to the interpretation of the Treaties. (See Chapter 12.)

7. THE EUROPEAN COURT OF HUMAN RIGHTS

In 1950 the United Kingdom was an original signatory to the European Convention on Human Rights which was established of the Council of Europe. It deals mainly with political and civil rights. It is possible for individuals, dissatisfied with decisions of United Kingdom courts, to petition the European Commission on Human Rights. If the Commission fails to reach a friendly settlement, disputes will ultimately be heard by the Court of Human Rights, which sits at Strasbourg. Since 1988, the United Kingdom government has been found to be in breach of the Convention in various respects. Changes in English law have sometimes followed but, in 1995, Michael Heseltine reacted angrily to the Court's ruling that the U.K. acted illegally in shooting three alleged members of the I.R.A., in the famous "death on the rock" episode, in Gibraltar. He said the Government would ignore the Court's compensation order, thus illustrating the lack of enforcement powers of international courts.

8. MISCELLANEOUS CIVIL COURTS

JUDICIAL COMMITTEE OF THE PRIVY COUNCIL

This Committee is primarily the ultimate appeal court for appeals from Commonwealth countries and from certain of the independent Commonwealth states which have retained this form of appeal. The Judicial Committee is composed of Privy Councillors who have held or now hold high judicial office. Each case must be heard by not more than five and not less than three members of the Committee. In practice, the court usually consists of three or five Lords of Appeal in Ordinary, often assisted by a senior judge from the country concerned. The Committee also hears appeals from the ecclesiastical courts, and from certain domestic tribunals in England and Wales, such as decisions of the General Medical Council, where doctors have been disciplined by the tribunal. The Privy Council's jurisdiction is derived from statute but its history derives from its medieval role as the body of the monarch's closest advisers.

ECCLESIASTICAL COURTS

These courts at the present time exercise control over clergy of the Church of England. In each diocese there is a consistory court, the judge of which is a barrister appointed by the bishop, and known as the Chancellor. For example, in 1995, a consistory court was convened to hear allegations of sexual impropriety made against the Dean of Lincoln. Appeal lies from the consistory court to, depending on the diocese, the Arches Court of Canterbury or the Chancery Court of York, and from either court a further appeal is possible to the Judicial Committee of the Privy Council.

COURT OF PROTECTION

Under the Mental Health Act 1983, a judge of the Chancery Division can sit as a Court of Protection to administer the estate of a person suffering from mental disability. This "court" is a misnomer as it is, in law, an office of the Supreme Court.

RESTRICTIVE PRACTICES COURT

This court was set up by the Restrictive Trade Practices Act 1956 to examine agreements which restrict prices or the conditions of supply of goods. Sittings of the court consist of one High Court judge and at least two lay members specially appointed. Appeal lies to the Court of Appeal. In 1988, the DTI published a green paper suggesting its abolition and replacement with a system based on EC competition law but this has not been implemented, so far.

THE CORONER'S COURT

The Coroners' Court is used to inquire (by an inquest) into unexplained deaths which have occurred other than through natural causes. For certain inquests the coroner may, and sometimes must, call a jury of from seven to 11 persons to return a verdict as to the cause of death. The coroner must be either legally or medically qualified.

THE EMPLOYMENT APPEAL TRIBUNAL

This court was established by the Employment Protection Act 1975 to hear appeals from decisions of Industrial Tribunals, in particular those relating to unfair dismissal, equal pay and redundancy. The composition of the court for a hearing is one High Court judge sitting with two laypeople who have specialised knowledge of industrial relations. Appeals from the Employment Appeal Tribunal on points of law go direct to the Court of Appeal.

CHAPTER 6

CRIMINAL COURTS

THE CRIMINAL COURT STRUCTURE

There is a basic division of modes of criminal trial in the English legal system into summary trial and trial on indictment. To complicate the matter there are now four categories of offence. These distinctions will be examined and explained later, but the English criminal court structure is based on the simple division into the two types of trial. This chapter will begin by studying the courts which may be involved in or following a summary trial and then proceed to consider the quite different court structure which is provided to deal with trial on indictment.

1. SUMMARY TRIAL

THE MAGISTRATES' COURT

Summary trials are held at magistrates' courts. Until 1949 they were known as police courts and many magistrates' courts are situated close to police stations. This is unfortunate since it conveys the impression that the court sits at the convenience of the police to distribute punishment in accordance with police evidence. Depressingly, it is common to find ever new magistrates' courts and police stations constructed as neighbours or even in the same building. As the police inevitably figure prominently in the magistrates' court, it is not surprising that the public has tended to think of it as the police court. Happily, there are not so many uniformed police officers in today's courts as there were prior to 1985. The Prosecution of Offences Act 1985 replaced police prosecutors with Crown Prosecutors and the 1990s saw private security officers replacing police court security officers. If summary justice is to be seen to be balanced, magistrates should consistently endeavour to make it clear to persons appearing before them that they have no bias in the case. The point is worth emphasising because for most people who must be dealt with by a court, as a defendant, or appear as a witness, the court involved will be the magistrates' court. The impression which they form on that occasion will condition their whole future attitude to the administration of justice. In this sense of the number of ordinary people affected, the importance of fair procedure and unbiased trial before magistrates is of greater importance than the more pompous and spectacular trials on indictment before judge and jury in the Crown Court.

All summary offences are statutorily defined. In general terms they consist of offences which can be treated as of minor importance. They include the vast bulk of traffic offences, the most trivial of which many people wrongly assume not to be normal *criminal* offences. Amongst other common summary offences are minor assaults and drunkenness in a public place. These are only the prime examples of a vast number of summary offences known to the law; to obtain a better idea of the scope of the magistrates' full jurisdiction, reference should be made to an annual publication known as Stone's *Justices' Manual*. This work now runs into several thousand pages. Even a cursory examination of its Table of Contents reveals the enormous range of summary offences which can fall to the magistrates for determination.

The category of offences of medium seriousness is called "triable either way" and includes theft, most offences of assault and criminal damage and some sexual offences. Here, the defendant may opt for trial in the magistrates' court or in the Crown Court, unless the magistrates insist on a Crown Court trial or, in certain instances, where the prosecutor can and does so insist. Most defendants opt for summary trial.

The appointment of magistrates has been considered in Chapter 3 but, so far as the court structure is concerned, the local magistrates' court is the lowest rung of the ladder. Every person who is charged with having committed a summary offence will have their case brought before the magistrates in the magistrates' court for the locality where the offence has been committed. In many instances it is necessary for the accused to be present at the hearing because the court may wish to see him and it does have power to send him to prison. On the other hand, for most Road Traffic Act offences, it is possible for the accused to plead guilty by post and save the need to attend court; so the vast bulk of traffic offences, for instance, speeding, are dealt with in a matter of seconds, in the defendant's absence.

For the hearing, the magistrates' court will usually consist of two or three lay magistrates forming "the bench" and they have powers dependent upon the statute which applies to the case, but at the maximum these allow them to send an offender to prison for up to six months and/or impose a fine of up to £5,000 (fixed by the Criminal Justice Act 1991). If the person concerned is convicted of two or more offences at the same time, the maximum sentence of imprisonment goes up to 12 months. If, after conviction, on hearing the record of the person convicted, the bench feel that their powers of sentence are inadequate, they may commit that person to the Crown Court for the locality so that a higher sentence can be given by that court. A stipendiary magistrate, sitting alone, has the same powers as a bench of magistrates.

At the hearing of a summary case, the bench of magistrates have the assistance of the "clerk of the justices" (justices' clerk) or, more usually, a court clerk. The former is legally qualified, usually as a solicitor. The magistrates' clerk is present to advise the magistrates on the law applicable to the case and to control the administration of the court. The clerk must, however, be careful not to give the impression of being the most important person in the court. The role is an essential one, since the successful combination of the lay magistrates with their legal adviser, the clerk, is fundamental to the success of the English legal system. In total, magistrates deal with over 98 per cent of criminal cases.

Special considerations apply where the accused person is a child or young person, because by statute special arrangements are made for trial by magistrates in youth courts, which were known as juvenile courts, prior to October 1992. The intention is to take cases concerning children and young persons away from the publicity of the ordinary courts and allow them to be dealt with privately by the magistrates.

THE CROWN COURT

If a person who has been convicted by the magistrates of a summary offence wishes to appeal, there are two courses open. An appeal may be made on the facts of the case, or against the sentence, to the Crown Court for the area where the case has been heard, or, if the appeal is concerned with a specific point of law, then the convicted defendant can appeal to the Queen's Bench Divisional Court.

The difference between appealing on fact or law is perhaps best understood from an example. If the prosecution is for the offence of exceeding the authorised speed limit, and there is a conflict between the evidence of the police witnesses and that of the driver and a passenger as to the speed of the vehicle over the given distance, then that is an argument about fact, and an appeal against conviction made by the driver would go to the Crown Court. If, however, the charge is of driving whilst under the influence of drink and the driver argues that the breathalyser equipment used by the police was not of an approved type, then that is a point of law and an appeal "by way of case stated" would go to the Queen's Bench Divisional Court. Where the defendant pleaded not guilty in the magistrates' court he may appeal to the Crown Court against both conviction and sentence: if he pleaded guilty he may only appeal against sentence.

For a summary appeal, the Crown Court is composed of either a circuit judge or a recorder accompanied by not less than two or more than four magistrates. The decision of the court is by a majority and the judge has a second and casting vote if the members are equally divided. Naturally, the magistrates must accept the judge's pronouncements on matters of law. The magistrates will also sit with the judge to deal with persons who have been convicted by a magistrates' court and who have been committed for sentence to the Crown Court.

In its appeal court role, the Crown Court conducts a complete rehearing of the case. This means that a second trial takes place, since the parties and the witnesses will gave their evidence again. The Crown Court then reaches its own independent conclusion. No jury is used in these appeal cases and there is no further appeal possible on fact in a summary case from the Crown Court. If on the appeal a point of law is argued before the court, the court may, having given its decision, agree to state a case for the consideration of the Queen's Bench Divisional

Court. This corresponds to the practice of magistrates stating such cases where the point of law arises in a summary case in the magistrates' court.

QUEEN'S BENCH DIVISIONAL COURT

As has just been seen, an appeal on a point of law from the magistrates' court's decision or the decision of the Crown Court is heard by the Queen's Bench Divisional Court. This court sits only in the Royal Courts of Justice in London and consists of two or three Queen's Bench Division judges. The process by which the appeal is brought is known as a case stated. This means that the convicted person, or legal representative, asks the magistrates to state a case for the consideration of the Queen's Bench Divisional Court. This case is then prepared in writing by the magistrates' clerk setting out the point of law which was raised, the decision of the magistrates and the reason why they decided it as they did. One unusual feature of the appeal provisions is that it is open to the prosecutor to ask the magistrates to state a case for the consideration of the Divisional Court where the magistrates have ruled on the point of law in favour of the person accused. This is only so on a point of law; the prosecutor cannot appeal against the magistrates' finding on the facts.

If the Divisional Court decides that the magistrates were wrong, it has three options open to it: (i) it may reverse or amend the magistrates' decision; (ii) it may remit the case to the magistrates requiring them either to continue hearing the case, or to discharge or convict the accused, as appropriate; (iii) it may make such order as seems just.

The Queen's Bench Divisional Court also exercises the High Court's supervisory jurisdiction over the functioning of magistrates' courts and the Crown Court in their dealings with summary cases. The use of the prerogative orders in the exercise of judicial review is considered below.

HOUSE OF LORDS

Where the case stated raises a point of law of general public importance, provided leave is given by the Queen's Bench Divisional Court or by the Appeal Committee of the House of Lords, an appeal is possible by either the prosecution or the defence to the House of Lords. This is known as a "leapfrog" appeal, described in Chapter 5.

Where an appeal does reach the House of Lords, it is heard and determined by five Lords of Appeal in Ordinary, as in other civil and criminal appeals at this final level. It is not surprising that so few summary cases are heard by the House of Lords, because in the vast majority of such cases the arguments are entirely on fact, and it will only be on rare occasions that a point of law of substance emerges.

2. TRIAL ON INDICTMENT

Indictable offences are recognised at common law, or by statute, and are generally the more serious forms of crime. All forms of homicide, major theft, assaults inflicting bodily harm, rape, and perjury are examples.

As well as indictable offences, "triable either way" offences can also be tried at the Crown Court, at the option of the defendant or magistrates or because of the nature of the prosecution (see above). Additionally, since the Criminal Justice Act 1988, a summary offence may be added to an indictment in the Crown Court.

The word "indictment" means a document which sets out in writing the charges against the accused person. Each separate charge is called "a count" of the indictment.

COMMITTAL PROCEEDINGS

Where a person is accused of an indictable offence the first stage in the court system with which he will normally be concerned is the committal proceedings. What this means is that before there is any question of a trial, the prosecutor must be able to satisfy the "examining magistrates" that there is an adequate case to warrant the magistrates sending the accused person for trial.

At the examining magistrates' proceedings, two or three lay magistrates or one stipendiary sit with a clerk, to hear the prosecution present its case against the accused either in full or, with the consent of the defence and much more commonly, by documentary evidence. A record is taken of the evidence given by the prosecution witnesses and at the end of the hearing the magistrates decide if there is a case to answer or not. The defence, although present, is not required to make any contribution, and it is customary for the legal representative of the accused "to reserve the defence" if the magistrates decide to commit the case for trial. The magistrates' decision is not the result of a trial because they are only concerned with one side of the case. If satisfied that there is sufficient evidence, the magistrates commit the accused for trial. If, on the other hand, they are not satisfied that, were it uncontradicted at trial, a reasonable jury may convict, they discharge the defendant. In the latter event, the prosecution can always return later with fresh evidence and ask the magistrates again to commit for trial. Committal proceedings are described in detail in the next Chapter.

THE CROWN COURT

If the magistrates decide to commit the accused for trial, the case will be put in the list for the Crown Court which sits to hear cases from that locality. There are around 90 Crown Court centres.

The Courts Act 1971 which abolished the courts of quarter sessions and assizes created in their place one unified Crown Court. The Crown Court forms part of the Supreme Court and under the 1971 Courts Act, England and Wales are divided into six circuits based on London, Bristol, Birmingham, Manchester, Cardiff and Leeds. Two presiding judges, who are High Court judges, are appointed to each circuit and they are responsible for the organisational arrangements for the Crown Court. In addition, they will themselves sit to try the most serious indictable cases. Below the two High Court judges in each circuit there are a number of circuit judges and a number of part-time recorders. Within the circuit certain towns are designated as having facilities for the trial of all cases, both civil and criminal. Other towns may be designated for all criminal cases, whilst others again may be limited to criminal cases tried by a circuit judge. The Lord Chancellor's department has responsibility for all the administrative arrangements involved. It should be noted that the Crown Court is a single entity; sittings of it take place as circumstances require.

From what has been said it will be evident that, theoretically, the trial of an indictable case can take place before (i) a High Court judge and jury or (ii) a circuit judge and jury or (iii) a recorder and jury. In law, lay magistrates may also sit with the circuit judge or the recorder as a trial court but this has been abandoned, in practice.

By Practice Direction, the Lord Chief Justice directs that offences should be classified into one of four categories and should be tried accordingly:

Class 1: generally by a High Court judge unless released by the presiding judge to a circuit judge—for example, treason, offences resulting in death and serious breaches of the Official Secrets legislation.

Class 2: generally by a High Court judge unless released by a presiding judge to a circuit judge or a recorder—for example, manslaughter, rape, sexual offences against children; and incitement to these.

Class 3: by a High Court judge or by a circuit judge or by a recorder—all indictable offences other than those falling within classes 1, 2 and 4, for example, affray, aggravated burglary and causing death by dangerous driving.

Class 4: normally by a circuit judge or by a recorder, or an assistant recorder, but can be by a High Court judge. This class includes all "triable either way" offences and certain others, for example conspiracy, robbery, grevious bodily harm.

At the time the Courts Act 1971 was passed, the intention was that an accused person should not have to wait more than eight weeks between committal and trial. Because of the increase in crime it has not been possible to meet this objective but waiting times were cut down progressively in the 1980s to about 13 weeks in 1995 for defendants remanded in custody and 17 weeks for those on bail.

As the court of first instance trying indictable cases, the Crown Court will call for the assistance of a jury of 12 whenever a "not guilty" plea is entered. The High Court judge, circuit judge or recorder, as the case may be, will direct the jury as to the law and will ensure that the case is conducted in accordance with proper procedure. After the jury has returned its verdict of "guilty" or "not guilty", the defendant is sentenced or discharged by the judge.

An appeal from the Crown Court against conviction and/or sentence can be made to the Court of Appeal (Criminal Division). Notice has to be given or the application made within 28 days of the conviction or sentence complained of.

COURT OF APPEAL (CRIMINAL DIVISION)

The Court of Appeal (Criminal Division) was established under the provisions of the Criminal Appeal Act 1966 to replace the former Court of Criminal Appeal. The law which governs the court is now to be found in the Criminal Appeal Act 1968, as amended by the Criminal Appeal Act 1995.

The Court of Appeal (Criminal Division) sits only at the Royal Courts of Justice in London. The court is made up of the Lord Chief Justice, Lords Justices of Appeal and a number of Queen's Bench Division judges specially nominated by the Lord Chief Justice. At least three judges must sit—and the number is not usually more—for the hearing of an appeal. Generally these will be the Lord Chief Justice, or a Lord Justice of Appeal and two or even three Queen's Bench Division judges. In a well publicised speech in 1992, the outgoing Lord Chief Justice attacked the Lord Chancellor for a shortage of Lords Justices of Appeal, resulting in important criminal appeals being heard, in the main, by High Court judges. This is part of the ongoing concern, explained in previous chapters, by the judiciary at the over use of lower level judges to hear serious cases and appeals. To add fuel to the fire of judicial anger, the Criminal Justice and Public Order Act 1994, s.52 permits circuit judges to sit in the Court of Appeal (Criminal Division). The first one sat in 1995.

The jurisdiction of the Court of Appeal (Criminal Division) is:

(i)   to hear appeals against conviction on indictment with the leave of the Court of Appeal or if the trial judge certifies that the case is fit for appeal (Criminal Appeal Act 1995, s.1).

(ii) to hear appeals against sentence pronounced by the Crown Court provided that the sentence is not one fixed by law and provided that the court grants leave. An application for leave may be determined by a single judge, but if leave is refused, the appellant can require a full court, *i.e.* two or more judges to determine the matter.

(iii) to hear appeals referred to it by the new Criminal Cases Review Commission, under the Criminal Appeal Act 1995.

(iv) to hear appeals against a verdict of "not guilty by reason of insanity" or against findings of fitness and unfitness to plead.

(v)   to hear an appeal by the prosecution against an acquittal on a point of law at the trial in the Crown Court. This provision involves an application by the Attorney-General for the opinion of the court on the point of law and is known as an "Attorney-General's Reference". The result cannot affect the acquittal and the defendant is not named in the appeal.

(vi) to hear an appeal by the prosecutor, again as an "Attorney-General's Reference" against a lenient sentence. In this case the court will set out sentencing guidelines for the future but may also increase the actual sentence imposed.

APPEALS TO THE HOUSE OF LORDS

Appeals from the Court of Appeal. Either prosecutor or defendant may appeal, provided the Court of Appeal certifies that a point of law of general public importance is involved and that either court feels that the point should be considered by the House and grants leave. The

House, in disposing of the appeal, may exercise any of the powers of the Court of Appeal, or remit the case to it. (Criminal Appeal Act 1968.)

THE ROYAL PREROGATIVE OF MERCY

The prerogative of mercy, the power to pardon convicted individuals, is part of the residuary royal prerogative exercised by the Crown on the advice of the Home Secretary. Effectively, petitions are sifted and decided upon by the civil servants of the Home Office. The prerogative is exercised in three ways:

(a)   A free pardon: quashing and expunging a conviction.
(b)   A conditional pardon: excusing or varying the conviction, subject to conditions, for example by commuting sentences.
(c)   Remission of a sentence.

Once an individual has been pardoned, they have a right to apply for compensation, under the Criminal Justice Act 1988, s.133. Before this, individuals benefited only from an *ex gratia* payment and the new right to compensation is a result of criticisms of that state of affairs, especially by the House of Commons Select Committee on Home Affairs.

3. COURTS MARTIAL

A special type of criminal court is the Court Martial which is used to enforce the law applicable to the armed forces on service personnel. It is thus a criminal court, in the sense that many of the cases within its jurisdiction concern conduct which would be an offence if committed by non-service personnel. Theft is an obvious example. Offences such as treason, murder, manslaughter or rape must be tried in the ordinary courts if committed in the United Kingdom. A court martial is composed of a small group of serving officers and in important cases the court will be advised by a judge advocate, who is a legally qualified serving officer.

Since 1951 there has been a special Courts Martial Appeal Court to hear, as the name indicates, appeals from a person convicted and/or sentenced by a court martial. The appeal court has the same composition as the Court of Appeal (Criminal Division). From its decision it is possible, with leave, to appeal to the House of Lords but this is very rare. Less than one case a year from this source reaches the House of Lords. Inevitably the case would have to raise a point of law of general public importance. At the time of writing (1996), the courts martial procedure is under review. It has been ruled, unanimously, by the European Commission of Human Rights to be in breach of Article 6(1) of the European Convention on Human Rights, which guarantees a "fair and public hearing before an impartial tribunal". The Armed Forces Act 1996 aims to resolve some of the problems of a lack of natural justice in the procedure.

CHAPTER 7

PROCEDURE

1. ADJECTIVE LAW

Because the relationship between the parties and the aims of the law are so very different between civil and criminal cases, procedure differs accordingly. This chapter examines civil then criminal procedure. It also describes the role of the judge and gives a basic outline of sentencing.

The term used to describe the law of practice and procedure is adjective law; it is contrasted with substantive law which is the law administered by the courts.

2. CIVIL PROCEDURE

THE COUNTY COURT

An ordinary action is begun in the county court by the plaintiff, the person bringing the claim, filing a request for a summons at the county court office on a form which sets out the names, addresses and descriptions of the parties, together with the nature and amount of the claim. The plaint is entered on the court record and a date fixed for pre-trial review. The district judge issues a summons and this and the particulars of claim are served on the defendant at least 21 days before the hearing, with forms on which the defendant may state her defence, admit liability or make a counterclaim. Alternatively she may use a separate document or may not reply at all.

The defendant has several choices open. If she pays the whole amount claimed into court within 14 days, the action is said to be "stayed"; if she pays less than the full amount within the 14 days, the plaintiff has to decide whether to accept or reject that amount in settlement of his claim; another possibility is that the defendant will admit the claim and offer to pay by instalments, and again the plaintiff had to decide whether to accept or not; if the defendant has a defence, or a set-off or counterclaim, it will be for her to take steps to defend accordingly. The vast majority of cases do not come to trial, most claims being settled without a hearing.

On the return day specified the district judge will hold a "pre-trial review". If the defendant does not appear and has filed no admission or defence the district judge may enter judgment for the plaintiff, usually without a hearing. If there is a defence and the case is proceeding to trial the district judge fixes the date for the hearing and gives any necessary directions to assist the parties and the court.

If the case does proceed to a hearing, the trial will be by the circuit judge, unless the claim is for les than £5,000, when the district judge usually deals with the case. In theory it is possible for a jury of eight to be called, in certain tort cases, but in practice the calling of a jury for a county court claim is rare. The actual hearing of the case follows the usual form of the plaintiff presenting his case first, calling witnesses in support of his allegations, with the defendant then answering the claim, calling witnesses to support her defence. A party can be represented by a solicitor, or by counsel if she so chooses. The judge concludes the matter by giving judgment on the claim.

The comparative simplicity of the procedure is the result of the concept of the county court as a local court providing a quick and inexpensive remedy for minor civil claims.

A special procedure is available when the claim is for a debt or other liquidated demand and the plaintiff believes that there is no defence to his claim. This is called a default action and the plaintiff will obtain judgment in default without the need for a trial if the defendant fails to take appropriate steps to defend.

Another possible procedure is a reference to arbitration. This was introduced by the Administration of Justice Act 1973 for small claims, at present those not exceeding £1,000 in personal injury or possession actions, or £3,000 in all other cases. The judge or an outside arbitrator may be appointed to act as the arbitrator and the advantage of the process is that it will be quick, cheap, held in private and lacking in formality. It is intended that no costs will be awarded to either side so that the employment of lawyers to represent parties will be less likely. The aim of the procedure is to provide a method of recovering a small claim without the cost of recovery amounting to more than the claim.

The general jurisdiction of the county courts is to be found expressed in Part 1 of the Courts and Legal Services Act 1990 and a battery of delegated legislation, such as the County Court Rules 1991. These control in detail the procedure which is to be observed in the courts. The practitioner's task is simplified by an annual publication, called *County Court Practice*, and known as "the Green Book".

THE HIGH COURT OF JUSTICE

(a) General

As was seen in the chapter on the structure of the civil courts, the High Court has three Divisions, each derived historically and each having a separate jurisdiction. As a result of this variety in responsibility there are considerable differences in the formal methods used to bring matters to trial before the court. The example which follows is of the most typical kind of action, being a substantial claim in contract or tort to be heard in the Queen's Bench Division. It must not be overlooked that an action brought, for example, in the Chancery Division might take a quite different course, and be the subject of a totally different terminology.

(b) Pleadings

A claim for damages resulting from a breach of contract or the commission of a tort and which falls within the guidelines for commencement in the High Court is normally begun in the Queen's Bench Division of the High Court by the plaintiff, or his legal representative, issuing a writ against the defendant. This writ of summons is obtained from the central office of the Supreme Court or from a District Registry. It is a formal summons from the Lord

Chancellor to the named defendant, notifying her of the commence-ment of the action and requiring her to acknowledge service to the court within 14 days. The writ may be indorsed with a statement of claim but usually the writ is accompanied by a separate statement of claim which sets out in detail the basis of the plaintiff's case. This is a most important document and consequently is usually drawn up by counsel, the presentation of the claim in this form being a highly technical matter.

The writ, having been authenticated by the court, is either served on the defendant in person or served by post, or fax, or DX, or delivered personally to her address. If she fails to acknowledge service as required under the terms of the writ, she is taken to be admitting the claim in full by default, and in such circumstances the plaintiff can apply for judgment in his favour. The actual acknowledgment of service is a formality by which the defendant is expected to signify her intention to defend the action. Assuming that the defendant does acknowledge service, she must take steps to defend the action and, in particular, she must make arrangements to file a defence. This is a formal document which deals step by step with the allegations contained in the statement of claim. It is necessary for the defence to answer the statement of claim paragraph by paragraph, since the court works from the assumption that anything not formally denied in the defence is thereby admitted. The rules state that the statement of claim must be served within 14 days of the service of the writ, and the defence must then be filed with the court within 14 days of service of the statement of claim. In practice the time for filing the defence is extended, because it is almost always necessary for counsel to prepare this document and she is not likely to be able to do so in 14 days. Often the defendant, or the plaintiff, will ask for further and better particulars of the statement of claim, or the defence, before proceeding to answer in documentary form.

It is possible that the defendant, as an integral part of the action, will wish to bring a counterclaim against the plaintiff, or perhaps claim a set-off; this means that she claims to be owed money by the plaintiff, which she proposes to set off against the plaintiff's claim. If this happens and a counterclaim or set-off is filed with the defence, the plaintiff, in turn, will have to proceed to file a defence to counterclaim. In fact the documentary battle can continue through several exchanges with such documents as a reply, a rejoinder and theoretically a surrejoinder, a rebutter and surrebutter as possible, but virtually extinct, candidates.

The object of this documentary "war" is so that "the pleadings", as the documents are collectively known, shall define exactly what are the issues between the parties. In practice, pleadings were criticised in the *Civil Justice Review* for being far too vague and shoddily drafted to be of much use.

When the pleadings are complete, the plaintiff takes out a summons for directions, which is heard by a master, in the presence of representatives of the parties. She deals with any matters outstanding relating to discovery of documents—both sides are required to produce all relevant documents for inspection—or interrogatories— the formal asking of certain questions, the answers to which are recorded as relevant to the issue between the parties—and decide on the place and mode of trial. Thereafter the case can be set down for trial in the court lists.

The *Civil Justice Review* found that, in practice, the summons for directions was not "a major occasion" and recommended that automatic directions should be introduced in both levels of court in general cases. This recommendation is, gradually, being implemented. Discovery, for instance, is now automatic in both the High Court and the county court.

If the plaintiff fails to pursue his claim actively against the defendant, or fails to set the action down for trial, the latter can, as a last resort, ask the court to dismiss the action for want of prosecution. Naturally, the court exercises its discretion sparingly.

In some cases, the lengthy procedure necessary to ensure that a case does actually come to trial may be by-passed by the plaintiff proceeding for summary judgment (under Order 14 of the Rules of the Supreme Court, which regulate all procedural matters in the High Court). Where a statement of claim has been served, and the plaintiff believes the defendant has no real defence, he may apply to a master for summary judgment. If the master is satisfied, after having heard the facts of the plaintiff's case and such defence as the defendant chooses to make out, that there is a proper case he may either order that judgment be entered for the plaintiff forthwith (if there is no real defence) or, if it appears to him that there is an issue which should be tried, give the defendant leave to defend either with or without conditions.

(c) Costs

One of the unsolved problems of civil litigation is the costs of the case. The value of the claim to the plaintiff can be completely overshadowed by the costs of the action. The added consideration is that in the English system whoever loses the case has to pay her own costs and the costs of the other side. Together, these may well total more than the claim. This is even more true if the decision at first instance is challenged on appeal, since the loser then will have four sets of costs to pay, and if the case should reach the House of Lords, six sets of costs will be at stake. No wonder it is said that today the great corporations—local authorities, government departments, statutory undertakings and insurance companies in particular—and individuals who have a legal aid certificate are the only parties who can safely afford to litigate!

It can hardly be satisfactory justice for the individual if a lawyer has to advise a client to settle a case because of the consequence in costs if that client should lose the case. The *Civil Justice Review* found that 90–95 per cent of proceedings were settled pre-trial (General Issues paper, 1987) and they were certainly concerned over the high level of High Court costs. They recommended a single costs regime in the High Court and county courts. The Courts and Legal Services Act 1990, s.4 now provides for rule-making on costs and provides for personal penalties for representatives who waste costs. The Lord Chancellor's introduction, in 1995, of a rule permitting "no win, no fee" agreements between lawyer and client, permitted under the CLSA is an attempt to ameliorate the harshness of the costs regime and reduce the risk involved in litigation, encouraging more people to take their civil disputes to court.

APPEAL PROCEDURE

Appeal lies from the county court to the Court of Appeal (Civil Division) without leave unless the amount at issue falls below £5,000 in tort, contract, etc., or below £15,000 in equity and probate cases, etc. Leave is not necessary where the appeal is the result of an application for an injunction or concerns the upbringing of a child.

From the three Divisions of the High Court of Justice, and from Divisional Courts in civil matters, appeals also go to the Court of Appeal (Civil Division). In 1994, 2,260 such appeals were disposed of. The hearing in the Court of Appeal is not a complete retrial since witnesses are not normally heard again. The appellant, in furnishing notice of appeal, must specify precisely the grounds for appeal and will be limited to arguing these before the court. The parties have six weeks from the judge's judgment to give notice of appeal. The appeal will be heard by three Lords Justices of Appeal in about six months from the time when the appeal was set down for hearing.

A further appeal to the House of Lords is possible, but only if the Court of Appeal gives leave, or the House of Lords, by its Appeal Committee, itself gives leave. Only cases that raise points of law of general public importance reach the House of Lords. Appeals from the Court of Appeal (Civil Division) numbered 42 in 1994. For a hearing, five Lords of Appeal in Ordinary form a court.

Under the Administration of Justice Act 1969, it is possible for an appeal to go direct from the High Court to the House of Lords and so "leapfrog" the Court of Appeal, as described, above, in Chapter 5.

CIVIL JUSTICE UNDER THE MICROSCOPE: DISSECTION SINCE 1985

The problems of English civil procedure have been the subject of constant scrutiny throughout this century and much of the last. Prior to the Lord Chancellor's establishment of the Civil Justice Review in 1985, there had been no fewer than 63 reports, since the turn of the century on the same subject. With tedious and frustrating repetition, they all identify the same core problems so that the opening words of Chapter two of Lord Woolf's interim report, in 1995, give those of us who have been watching the legal system for some years more than a frisson of *dé-jà vu*:

"The process is too expensive, too slow and too complex."

His Lordship quotes a number of famous judicial critics of the civil process who have all drawn attention to the fact that these problems militate against the provision of an accessible system of civil courts which is necessary if people are to be enabled to enforce their rights in civil law. Indeed, the very title of his Lordship's report, *Access to Justice*, seems like an ironic cliché, after years of concern over the lack of it.

The Civil Justice Review body reported in 1988. The review was remarkable for the breadth and depth of its scrutiny of the system, its radical approach and its success rate, in that many of its recommendations were soon translated into law, in the Courts and Legal Services Act 1990 and subsequent delegated legislation. Yet, despite the fact that its reforms were potentially the most radical since the Judicature Acts of 1893–95, they apparently did not solve those fundamental problems. No sooner had the dust settled on the new legislation than the two sides of the legal profession had established the Heilbron Committee, to produce a 1993 report on the continuing problems of civil justice and their proposals for dealing with them. The Lord Chancellor responded by commissioning Lord Woolf, when a Law Lord, to carry out yet another scrutiny of the system and suggest yet another list of proposed reforms. In the meantime, the Master of the Rolls and the President of the Family Division have taken matters of reform into their own hands by issuing new and fairly radical Practice Directions for the conduct of litigation in the High Court. Listed are some of the recommendations and procedural changes consequent upon them:

The Heilbron Report 1993

The report starts with the working premise that:

> "It is axiomatic that in any free and democratic society all citizens should be equal before the law. This means that all litigants, rich and poor, however large or however small is the subject matter of their litigation, should have access to a fair and impartial system of disputes resolution."

They complain that:

— "An air of Dickensian antiquity pervades the civil process."

— "Procedures are unnecessarily technical, inflexible, rule-ridden, formalistic and often incomprehensible to the ordinary litigant for whom they are ultimately designed";

— lawyers and judges are reluctant to change;

— progress of actions lies with the parties and their lawyers rather than the courts; causing avoidable delay.

— fear of costs of litigation deters people from using the courts;

— most people want their dispute resolved rather than their "day in court".

The principles underlying their recommendations were:

— the philosophy of litigation should be to encourage the early settlement of disputes;

— litigants should have imposed upon them sensible procedural time-frames;

— judges should adopt a more interventionist role to ensure that issues are limited, delays are reduced and court time is not wasted;

— there should be an adequate number of High Court judges. (This reflects the ongoing outrage of Bench and Bar with Lord Mackay's over-use of deputies, in the 1990s. See Chapter 2.)

— since time in court is costly, a balance should be struck between the written and oral word and what can be achieved out of court rather than in court;

— justice should, where possible, be brought to the people;

— a widespread introduction of technology is urgently required;

— facilities for the litigant urgently need improving;

— additional resources must be found to improve the system.

Amongst others, here are some of their main recommendations. Some of the procedural reforms in civil trial have already been put into effect by the 1995 practice directions. My comments are bracketed:

— merger of Q.B.D. and Chancery (this is unlikely to be accepted);

— High Court listing should be computerised;

— common procedural rules for the High Court and county court (repeating the *Civil Justice Review*);

— judicial review cases to be heard on circuit and more specialist county court trial centres;

— revival of an ethos of public service amongst court staff and assistance to litigants;

— plain English court documents;

— a more interventionist approach by judges at trial and on appeal;

— limits on discovery, provision of skeleton arguments and bundles and on appeal;

— judicial intervention at trial to avoid time wasting;

— promotion of ADR and training of lawyers therein. (ADR means alternative dispute resolution. It is explained in Chapter 9).

The 1995 Practice Directions

It was, doubtless, the Heilbron Report which prompted the establishment of the Woolf investigation and the issue of the 1995 practice directions. Directions were issued for all three High Court divisions. In them, the Heads of Division emphasised the importance of reducing cost and delay and threatened that "Failure by practitioners to conduct cases economically will be visited by appropriate orders for costs". The court will now limit discovery, oral submissions, examination of witnesses, the issues on which it wishes to be addressed and reading aloud from documents and authorities. Witness statements will generally stand as evidence-in-chief and the parties must, pre-trial, limit the issues. Bundled, photocopied documents and skeleton arguments must be lodged in court pre-trial. Opening speeches must be succinct and, where appropriate, lawyers must verify that they have considered the possibility of ADR with their client. These practice directions have had a significant impact on the shape of the civil trial. The parties and the judge will have read most of the arguments and documentation in advance of trial, thus departing radically from the oral tradition characteristic of the common law, adversarial procedure. The directions also encourage the judge to control the nature and content of the cases presented to him, again signifying a departure from the traditional judge's role as a non-interfering umpire.

The Interim Woolf Report 1995

This repeated many of the recommendations of its predecessors, the *Civil Justice Review* and the Heilbron Report. Amongst Lord Woolf's main recommendations are these:

— the courts must run an effective system of case management, instead of allowing the parties to flout rules and run the cases;

— an expanded small claims jurisdiction of £3,000 (this has been introduced, in 1996) and a fast track for cases up to £10,000. Judicial, tailored case management for cases over £10,000;

111

— encouragement of early settlement, assisted by enabling either party to make an offer to settle, replacing the system of payment into court;

— the creation of a new Head of Civil Justice;

— a single set of High Court/county court rules;

— court appointment of single, neutral expert witnesses;

— promotion of the use of IT for case management by judges and use of video and telephone conferencing.

From 1996 onwards we must continue to watch developments in the civil process closely, as, no doubt, procedural and legislative changes will follow the final Woolf Report, due out in Summer 1996. The Defamation Bill, going through Parliament in 1996 will, if enacted, introduce a "fast track" for defamation cases. The judge will be empowered to dispose of them summarily, awarding damages up to £10,000, where it appears to him that there is no defence which has a reasonable prospect of success. In 1996, Lord Woolf was moved from his position as a Law Lord, to be appointed Master of the Rolls, thus enabling him to oversee his proposed changes in civil justice.

3. CRIMINAL PROCEDURE

SUMMARY OFFENCES

Over the years there has been an increasing tendency to pass the responsibility for trying criminal cases of a less serious nature to magistrates and Parliament has repeatedly downgraded indictable offences to triable either way and triable either way offences to summary offences. Just how vast in scope the magistrates' jurisdiction has become can be seen from a glance at the "bible" of the magistrates' court—the three-volume annual publication of Stone's *Justices' Manual.*

The most obvious work of the magistrates in dealing with summary offences is their adjudication in (i) almost all Road Traffic Act offences; (ii) minor theft cases, such as shoplifting; (iii) drunk and disorderly behaviour; (iv) minor assault; and (v) minor criminal damage cases.

A summary case is usually begun by an information being laid before a justice of the peace requesting that they issue a summons to the person accused. The summons will require that person to appear at a named magistrates' court, at a time stipulated, so that the case against him may be heard. Prosecutions are now a matter for the Crown Prosecution Service but it is possible for one citizen to lay an information related to alleged criminal conduct by another. The Road Traffic Act allows a defendant in the case of certain minor motoring offences to escape having to attend court if he pleads "guilty" by post. This useful provision, it must be stressed, does not extend to other cases, in the majority of which the defendant must either be present in person, or be legally represented. In some instances, particularly where there is a possibility of imprisonment, the defendant must attend.

Duty solicitors are meant to be available to or contactable by defendants who need their help, at each magistrates' court. The solicitors will be from local firms in private practice and will be paid by the state through the Legal Aid Fund.

When the accused appears before the court for the hearing of the charge, the court will state the substance of the information and ask the accused if he pleads guilty or not guilty. If he pleads guilty, he may be convicted and sentenced immediately, unless the magistrates require more information on the defendant, in which case they will adjourn for the preparation of a medical or psychiatric report or a social inquiry report, prepared by a probation officer or social worker. Otherwise, a plea of not guilty will be entered, and the prosecutor responsible for the laying of the information will outline the facts. After outlining the facts relating to the case, the prosecutor calls the prosecution witnesses to substantiate those facts; such witnesses are open to examination by both sides. As in all criminal trials in England and Wales, the onus of proof is on the prosecution to prove the case against the person accused. The quantum of proof required is "proof beyond reasonable doubt". If the magistrates are left with a reasonable doubt they must acquit the defendant, since he is entitled to the benefit of any doubt. It follows that at the conclusion of the prosecution case the defendant, or his legal representative, may claim that there is no case to answer. This submission means, simply, that the evidence produced by the prosecution does not show that the defendant has committed the offence with which he is charged. If the magistrates uphold that submission the case is dismissed forthwith. On the other hand if they do not, then the full case for the defence is then presented to the court. Defence witnesses will be called, and the magistrates will finally be left to decide whether or not the evidence is sufficient for them to convict. If they decide to convict they proceed to sentence the defendant; if they decide not to convict the case is dismissed.

The bench of magistrates can call for the assistance of their court clerk if the case raises issues of law rather than fact. The maximum penalty open to the magistrates, unless a specific statute provides otherwise, is six months' imprisonment, and/or a £5,000 fine. If a defendant is convicted of two or more offences at the same hearing the magistrates have power to send him to prison for 12 months. There is power in the magistrates in many instances to send a convicted defendant for sentence to the next sitting of the Crown Court for that area, if they feel that their own sentencing powers are inadequate.

Appeals

If magistrates discover that they have made a mistake, they may re-open a case to vary a sentence or order where it appears to be in the interests of justice to do so (Magistrates' Courts Act 1980, as amended by the Criminal Appeal Act 1995).

An appeal in a summary case will take one of two forms. The defendant may appeal against conviction to the Crown Court, where there is a complete rehearing of the case, including the calling of all the witnesses heard before the magistrates. The decision of the Crown Court is final on the facts of a summary case and there is no further provision for appeal. If, however, the defence raises a point of law in the magistrates' court, or at the Crown Court, then it is possible for an appeal on the point of law to go, by a process known as appeal by way of case stated, for determination by the Divisional Court of the Queen's Bench Division. From the decision of the Divisional Court on the point of law, a further appeal, subject to leave being obtained, is possible to the House of Lords. Such cases are rare; the sort of matter which has gone on appeal to the House of Lords is when technical points, for example relating to the use of breathalyser equipment by the police, are raised. The procedure followed in an appeal on a point of law is for the magistrates, through their clerk, to have prepared a statement setting out the point of law raised, and explaining why they ruled on it as they did. This is why the process is known as "a case stated". The Divisional Court or the House of Lords then considers the point of law in question and gives its determination; it restricts itself entirely to the point of law raised and to arguments about it.

Post Appeal

The Criminal Appeal Act 1995 gives the new Criminal Cases Review Commission (described below) an unconditional power to refer a conviction or sentence imposed by magistrates to the Crown Court, to be treated as an appeal.

INDICTABLE OFFENCES

When an individual is charged with a more serious crime—an indictable offence—process may be begun, as with summary offences, by laying an information before a magistrate who will then issue either a summons or a warrant for arrest. But after this the procedure is different. If the person concerned has been arrested they may be bailed by the police, conditionally or unconditionally, to return to the police station or appear before magistrates or they must be brought before a magistrate within 24 hours (excluding Sunday) so that they may then either be granted bail or remanded in custody. If the magistrates decide to remand them in custody the maximum limit for a remand is eight days, or, thereafter, 28 days. Statutory provisions are contained in the Bail Act 1976 as amended.

The Police and Criminal Evidence Act 1984 contains detailed statutory provisions governing police conduct in relation to arrest and detention, and the questioning and treatment of persons suspected of having committed crime. Depending on circumstances, suspects may be detained without charge for up to 96 hours, but this is only likely to occur very exceptionally.

The Committal

While the accused person is on bail or remand, the prosecution must be actively preparing their case, because the first stage in the procedure is for the magistrates to hold their examination, or preliminary inquiry in a procedure which is due to be abolished, in 1997. This inquiry, which is also known as committal proceedings, is an impartial investigation of the prosecution case. The examining magistrate or magistrates hear all the prosecution witnesses and then decide whether or not there is a prima facie case to warrant putting the accused person on trial. It is not at this stage a question of whether she is guilty or not guilty, it is a simple test of how substantial is the case against her. Since the onus of proof is on the prosecution, magistrates can save the time of the court of trial by refusing to commit an accused person where the case against her is too flimsy to warrant a trial. Under an "old style committal", all the evidence given at these proceedings is taken down in longhand by the magistrates' clerk. Each witness has then to swear on oath to the truth of her evidence as contained in this statement, which was called a deposition. This procedure is known as "old style committal". "New style committal" allows for written statements to be submitted to the examining magistrates if the parties agree; even to the extent of the defendant, if she is legally represented, agreeing that the magistrates may commit her to trial without considering the evidence. In effect this is committal by consent. The main point is that it rests with the defendant how the committal proceedings are to operate. She can, if she wishes, insist on the old style process of oral evidence and deposition; or she can insist on some witnesses giving oral evidence but accept the written evidence of others. The written statement of evidence must be signed; it must contain a declaration that the person making it believes it to be true and copies must be made available to the defendant. She is thus made fully aware of the case which she will have to meet at the trial. The "new" committal proceedings arrangements make for much greater speed without restricting the defendant's rights in any way. It means, however, that the procedure is dependent on the defendant's being represented. There is a restriction on the media in its publication of committal proceedings. This only permits the publication of the bare details of the names and addresses of the parties, the charges and the decision of the magistrates. An exception is made if the defendant asks for the restrictions on media reporting to be lifted. This change in the law was made on the grounds that as, in committal proceedings, only the prosecution case was published, it could lead to a jury being prejudiced against a defendant. The public can nonetheless attend the committal proceedings.

As might be expected, in the vast majority of cases the examining magistrates are satisfied that the prosecution have a case and so commit the accused person for trial in the Crown Court. The actual court is determined by the locality where the alleged criminal act took place and the accused person receives a written statement of the charge—"an indictment". An indictment may be made up of several "counts", or separate charges.

Transfer for Trial to Replace Committal Proceedings in 1997

At the time of writing and until at least January 1997, committal proceedings will continue to take place, as described above but they have long been criticised, notably by the Royal Commission on Criminal Procedure 1981 and the Royal Commission on Criminal Justice 1993, as ineffective in screening out weak cases. The latter Commission found that only 7 per cent of committals were old style, the rest being a mere formality. They recommended that committals be abolished and replaced by a procedure to permit written submissions of "no case to answer" before trial. Consequently, section 44 of the Criminal Justice and Public Order Act 1994 purported to abolish the functions of a magistrates' court as examining justices and replace committal proceedings with a new system of transfer for trial, to be conducted, usually, in writing. In September 1995, the Home Secretary was about to bring this section into force, when his attention was drawn to various defects in the detail of the proposed transfer proceedings. The 1994 Act has been amended by the Criminal Procedure and Investigations Act 1996. New rules are being drafted and the Home Office hopes that these will be brought into force in early 1997. It is intended that the system of transfer will operate in this way: most transfers to the Crown Court, for trial on indictment, will take place on paper. Where the defence opposes transfer, they may make an application in writing for the dismissal of the charge, which the prosecutor may then oppose, in writing. Oral representations will not be accepted unless, for example, the case is unusually complex, or the defendant is unrepresented, or the prosecutor has substituted new triable either way charges, when the defendant will have to be brought back to court to elect mode of trial. It is envisaged by the Home Office that oral hearings will be needed in only a very small percentage of cases.

The Plea and Directions Hearing

At the Crown Court, the defendant (except in cases of fraud) must appear at a newly devised proceeding called a "plea and directions hearing", designed to prepare for trial and fix the trial date. Requirements for the plea and directions hearing are set out in a Lord Chief Justice's practice direction (1995). In all class one or serious or complex cases, the prosecution provides a summary, identifying issues of law and fact and estimating trial length. The arraignment takes place at the hearing: the defendant enters a plea of guilty or not guilty to each of the charges. Following a not guilty plea, the parties are expected to inform the court of such matters as: witnesses, defence witnesses whose written statements are accepted, admitted facts, any alibi, points of law and special requirements for the trial (for example, live video links for child witnesses). If the plea is "guilty", the judge should, if possible, proceed to sentence the defendant, after hearing his plea in mitigation. This is a plea for leniency, allowing the defendant to argue any partial excuses or explanation for his admitted offences. If the judge or recorder is considering imposing a custodial sentence or non-custodial alternative, she may require a pre-sentence report to be prepared, or, where appropriate, a medical or psychiatric report.

The Criminal Procedure and Investigations Bill 1996

The controversial section of this Bill, which, at the time of writing, seems to be passing through Parliament unopposed by the Labour party, is its provisions for pre-trial disclosure of evidence on the part of the defence. The Government set out its proposals for this legislation in a consultation document, *Disclosure*, in 1995. In brief, they were concerned by the findings of the Royal Commission on Criminal Justice that the defence were gaining an unfair advantage and the prosecution were hampered by disclosure requirements which had become unduly onerous, following recent case law. Defence lawyers could delay trial and put obstacles in the way of a prosecution by requiring the disclosure of more and more evidence yet the accused was still in the position of being able to ambush them with a surprise defence, at trial, thus securing an unwarranted acquittal.

It appears that the Bill will be enacted in this form, in 1996:

— The prosecutor is under a duty to make "primary disclosure" to the accused any evidence which, in his opinion, might undermine the case for the defence. At the same time, he must indicate the nature of any prosecution material relating to the offence, which the prosecutor considers does not fit into the above category and is not "sensitive" (whose disclosure, for instance, would not be in the public interest);

— In cases to be tried on indictment (in the Crown Court), the accused must then give a written defence statement to the prosecutor, setting out his defence in general terms and indicating on what matters and why he takes issue with the prosecutor. If this includes an alibi, he must give details of the alibi witnesses;

— In cases to be tried summarily, the accused may voluntarily give a defence statement;

— At this point, the prosecution must disclose any previously undisclosed material which might reasonably be expected to assist the accused's defence (secondary disclosure). If the accused has reasonable cause to believe there is further material which should have been disclosed, he can apply for disclosure;

— The prosecutor has a continuing duty to keep under review whether further disclosure is necessary;

— Most controversially, the court or jury may make negative inferences against the accused if he has failed to comply with the duty of disclosure.

As can be seen, placing a duty of pre-trial disclosure on the defence creates a massive change in the balancing of the scales of justice, in a system where the accused has, generally, been entitled to see the whole of the prosecution case unfold before disclosing his defence, if he ever chooses to disclose a defence. Like the qualifications to the right to silence, embodied in the Criminal Justice and Public Order Act 1994, this provision has brought forth the wrath of lawyers, notably the Law Society, The Bar, JUSTICE and many academic commentators. For a neat exposition and critique, see *Leng* at [1995] Crim. L.R. 704. He challenges the government's assumption that the concerns of the Royal Commission are well founded. He and other critics feel that draconian measures are being taken to deal with a problem that was confined to exceptional cases. My concern is that, like the modifications to the right of silence, this piecemeal legislation is radically changing the balance of criminal justice in an unprincipled fashion; that such issues of principle would involve amending a written constitution if we had had one and that these layers of pre-trial procedure will be open to abuse, challenge and interpretation. Quite how the unrepresented defendant is meant to cope with and understand the implications of such a duty is beyond me. Doubtless the measure will add significantly to the cost of legal aid. The most shocking aspect of the Bill is that the Opposition "welcomed the Bill as a piece of long overdue legislation." The Bill is scheduled to receive royal assent by July 1996.

Plea Bargaining

At any time prior to or during a criminal trial, it is common for a defendant to change his plea from "not guilty" to "guilty" to one or more counts. Where this change occurs after a case has been listed for trial, it results in what has become known as a "cracked trial". This wastes court time and public resources and, in relation to trial on indictment, was one of the concerns of the Royal Commission on Criminal Justice. This often results from plea negotiations between prosecution or defence, which may be initiated by either side, commonly known as "plea bargaining". One type of deal, more accurately known as "charge bargaining" occurs where the defendant agrees to plead guilty to an alternative less serious charge, in exchange for the prosecution's withdrawing a more serious charge. What is properly called "plea bargaining" is a guilty plea by the defendant, in exchange for some assurance of a lighter sentence than one which would have been passed, had the defendant insisted on his right to trial and subsequently been found guilty by the jury. The Court of Appeal has long sanctioned a system of a 25–30 per cent "sentence discount", rewarding the defendant for pleading guilty but the case of *Turner* (1972) prevented the trial judge becoming involved in a plea bargain to assure the defendant of a specific sentence discount. This prevented the development of a full blown system of legally enforceable plea bargains, conducted in special hearings, before a judge, which exists in most of the United States. The Royal Commission said nothing about such pre-trial negotiations involving the judge but, in order to try and obviate the occurrence of cracked trials, recommended a "sentencing canvass", offering the defendant a graduated system of sentencing discounts: the earlier the plea, the greater the discount. Whilst acknowledging the danger that this might induce innocent people to plead guilty, the Commission concluded that this risk would not be increased by "clearer articulation of the long accepted principle" of sentencing discounts.

Section 48 of the Criminal Justice and Public Order Act 1994 gives statutory recognition to this centuries old system of informal sentencing discounts and, indeed, makes it mandatory, by requiring the sentencing judge to take into account the timing of a guilty plea and stating so in open court. Neither the Act nor the plea and directions hearing practice direction, outlined above, says anything of the sentence canvass which the Royal Commission recommended should be offered to the defendant pre-trial, by the judge in chambers.

Trial on Indictment

If the plea is "not guilty" the court proceeds to swear in 12 jurors, who will be responsible at the end of the trial for deciding whether the accused is guilty or not guilty. Once the jury is sworn in, the prosecution will open the case by outlining the facts and then calling the prosecution witnesses to give evidence to prove those facts. The defence can cross-examine all such witnesses. At the close of the prosecution case the defence counsel presents the defence case and calls witnesses for the defence, possibly including the defendant. These witnesses too can be cross-examined on their evidence. It will be noticed that the accused person is not required to give evidence. This rule is called the right to silence and is discussed below. The court has to decide whether the prosecution's accusation is proved beyond reasonable doubt. It does not hold an inquiry into the case. If it did do so, it would be forced to have the accused answer questions which were relevant to the circumstances of the alleged crime.

When the final speeches by the prosecution and defence counsel have been made, the judge "sums up" for the benefit of the jury. This summing-up is the last speech which the jury hear before they retire to consider their verdict. In it the judge has to balance the arguments of the prosecution and the defence, but leave the jury to decide on the issue of guilt, beyond reasonable doubt, of the accused.

As a result of the abolition of the requirement for a unanimous verdict by the Criminal Justice Act 1967, it is possible for the judge to accept a majority verdict of the jury, provided that there are not more than two in the minority. If there are three or more in the minority this is known as a "hung jury" and the trial is abandoned. The judge will then usually order a retrial, if the prosecution so desires, before a different judge and jury. If the jury has dropped to 11 or 10 in number there can be a majority verdict if there is not more than one dissenter. Every effort is made, however, to obtain a unanimous verdict and the jury must have been out for at least two hours before the judge is able to accept a majority verdict. If the verdict is "not guilty" the accused is immediately discharged; if the verdict is "guilty", after a plea in mitigation by his counsel, he will be sentenced by the judge.

The Right to Silence

Until the Criminal Justice and Public Order Act 1994, the defendant had a virtually unqualified right to silence, both in the police station and at trial. In court, this extended to the right not to be asked questions and the judge could comment on a defendant's exercise of the right but not adversely. The right was considered by the Criminal Law Revision Committee, in 1972, the Royal Commission on Criminal Procedure, 1981, and the Royal Commission on Criminal Justice, 1993, and it has long been a subject of controversy. Proponents hail it as a major safeguard of the English legal system that the defendant cannot convict himself out of his own mouth. It leaves the burden of proof entirely on the prosecution. Opponents criticise it as a rule protecting the guilty. They believe it encourages the police to intimidate suspects into confessing and some have said that it is sentimental to argue that the accused should not be allowed to convict himself.

In 1987, the Home Secretary set up a working party to examine the effects of abolishing the right to silence but this was quietly disbanded at the peak of public concern over wrongful convictions. The 1993 Royal Commission considered the value and operation of the right to silence. The majority recommended that adverse inferences should not be drawn from silence at the police station and recommended retaining the existing caution (that is, the warning given by police before questioning by them). Only when the prosecution's case had been fully disclosed should the defendant be required to offer an answer to the charges made against him at the risk of adverse comment at trial on any new defence he then discloses or any departure from a previously disclosed defence (in other words, in the event of an "ambush defence").

The Criminal Justice and Public Order Act 1994 goes much further than this and, critics would say, effectively vitiates both stages of the right to silence. Sections 34–39 allow the court to draw "such inferences as appear proper" from the accused's failure to mention, under police questioning, any fact which he could have been expected to mention, or failure, under questioning, to account for any objects, marks or substances, or failure, under questioning, to account for his presence at a particular place, or failure to give evidence or answer questions at trial.

The new provisions on silence in the 1994 Act are one of the most heavily criticised and discussed areas of a provocative statute. Already, the operation of the sections in practice has been the subject of critical comment. It is said that the sections offer no protection to the mentally disordered suspect and that the newly re-drafted police caution is so lengthy and complex that it is only fully understood by a minority of suspects. The Court of Appeal has already ruled, in October 1995, in three appeals against conviction on the grounds that trial judges had wrongly directed the jury on the effects of these sections. The Court of Appeal held (*R. v. Cowan*) that the trial judge was required to remind the jury of certain rules still protecting the defendant, for instance, that the burden of proof lay on the prosecution, that the defendant was entitled to remain silent, that an inference drawn from silence could not on its own prove guilt, that the jury had to be satisfied that the prosecution had established a case to answer before drawing any inferences from the defendant's silence and, finally, that if they concluded that his silence could only sensibly be attributed to the defendant's having no answer or none that would stand up to cross-examination, they could then draw an adverse inference.

Those who criticised these sections as being a breach of Article 6 of the European Convention on Human Rights were disappointed by the case of *Murray v. United Kingdom* (1996), in which the European Court of Human Rights ruled, in respect of a similar provision in Northern Ireland, that there was no such thing as an absolute right of silence and it was only a matter of common sense to permit the drawing of adverse inferences where a defendant said nothing in the face of overwhelming evidence.

124

Appeal

A convicted person may appeal from the Crown Court to the Court of Appeal (Criminal Division), with leave of the Court of Appeal or if the trial judge grants a certificate that the case is fit for appeal (Criminal Appeal Act 1968, s.1 as simplified by the Criminal Appeal Act 1995, s.1). He may appeal against sentence, with leave of the Court of Appeal (1968 Act, ss.9–11). Applications for leave to the Court of Appeal are normally considered on paper, by a High Court judge. If he refuses leave, the application may be re-heard by the Court of Appeal in open court.

POWERS OF THE COURT OF APPEAL

Section 2(1) of the Criminal Appeal Act 1995 sets out new and simplified grounds upon which the Court of Appeal may allow a criminal appeal. The Court of Appeal:

"(a) shall allow an appeal against conviction if they think that the conviction is unsafe; and
(b) shall dismiss such an appeal in any other case."

The Court of Appeal *may* "receive any evidence which was not adduced in the proceedings from which the appeal lies". (Criminal Appeal Act 1968, as amended by the 1995 Act, s.4.) The Court *must*, in considering whether to receive any evidence, have regard in particular to:

(a) whether the evidence appears to the Court to be capable of belief;
(b) whether it appears to the Court that the evidence may afford any ground for allowing the appeal;
(c) whether the evidence would have been admissible at the trial;
(d) whether there is a reasonable explanation for the failure to adduce the evidence at trial.

125

(Criminal Appeal Act 1968, s.23(2), as amended by s.4 of the 1995 Act, paraphrased, my emphasis).

Section 5 of the 1995 Act gives the Court of Appeal a new power to direct the newly created Criminal Cases Review Commission to investigate and report on any specified matter relevant to the determination of an appeal against conviction, where such an investigation is likely to result in the Court being able to resolve the appeal and where the matter cannot be resolved by the Court without such a reference.

The 1995 amendments to the Court of Appeal's powers all result from the recommendations of the Royal Commission on Criminal Justice. These were a culmination of years of criticism from JUSTICE (1989, etc.), the House of Commons Select Committee on Home Affairs (1981), academics, M.P.s and many others. It was repeatedly said that the grounds of appeal in the 1968 Act were narrow and ambiguous, that the Court of Appeal interpreted their powers too narrowly, that they were too ready to uphold a conviction, even where they accepted there had been an irregularity at trial, and that they were too reluctant to admit fresh evidence.

It is important to understand that the Court of Appeal does not provide a rehearing in criminal cases, unlike an appeal from a magistrates' court to the Crown Court. The limited powers of the Court of Appeal were spelt out in the successful appeal of the Birmingham Six in 1991, *R. v. McIlkenny and ors.*, in a judgment read out by the judges in turn:

> "Nothing in section 2 of the Act, or anywhere else obliges or entitles us to say whether we think that the appellant is innocent. This is a point of great constitutional importance. The task of deciding whether a man is innocent or guilty falls on the jury. We are concerned solely with the question whether the verdict of the jury can stand.
> Rightly or wrongly (we think rightly) trial by jury is the foundation of our criminal justice system. ... The primacy of the jury in the criminal justice system is well illustrated by the difference between the Criminal and Civil Divisions of the Court of Appeal. ... A civil appeal is by way of rehearing of the whole case. So the court is concerned with fact as well as law. ... It follows that in a civil case the Court of Appeal may take a different view of the

126

facts from the court below. In a criminal case this is not possible . . . the Criminal Division is perhaps more accurately described as a court of review."

Further, the Court of Appeal may substitute a conviction for an alternative offence, or order a retrial, where it feels this is required by the interests of justice.

The defendant may appeal against the sentence imposed by the Crown Court to the Court of Appeal who may substitute any other sentence or order within the powers of the Crown Court, provided it is not more severe than originally. The Criminal Justice Act 1988, s.36 gives the Attorney-General a new prosecutorial power to refer any "unduly lenient" Crown Court sentence to the Court of Appeal, who then have the power to quash it and substitute any sentence within the Crown Court's powers. The Attorney may then refer any such decision of the Court of Appeal up to the House of Lords.

The Attorney-General may, under the Criminal Justice Act 1972, also refer a point of law to the Court of Appeal, on behalf of the prosecution, following an acquittal. The Court of Appeal simply clarifies the law for the future, leaving the acquittal verdict untouched. The point may then be referred to the House of Lords.

A further appeal to the House of Lords is possible by the prosecution or the defence but only if the Court of Appeal certifies that the case reveals a point of law of general public importance and either that court or the House of Lords grants leave on the principle that the point is one which ought to be considered by the House of Lords. There are very few criminal appeals heard by the House of Lords each year.

POST APPEAL: RESOLVING MISCARRIAGES OF JUSTICE

Until 1996, the Home Secretary had power to refer cases to the Court of Appeal but would not normally do this unless all avenues of appeal had been exhausted and there was fresh evidence upon which the Court of Appeal might decide that the conviction was unsafe and unsatisfactory (1968 Act, s.17). For example, this power was used in

1987 to refer the convictions of the Birmingham Six to the Court of Appeal and again in 1991.

The Royal Commission on Criminal Justice, paying heed to the multitude of critics who complained that the Home Secretary was too reluctant to use his power to refer, recommended that it should be replaced by that of a criminal cases review authority, whose job it would be to investigate miscarriages of justice, in cases referred to them by the Court of Appeal, or drawn to their attention in other ways. Following this recommendation, section 17 was duly repealed in the 1995 Act, which created a Criminal Cases Review Commission (ss.8–25). The Commission is a body corporate, independent of Government, whose 11 members are appointed by the Crown on the advice of the Prime Minister. One third of them must be lawyers and two thirds must be experienced in the criminal justice system.

Under section 9, they have a very broad power to refer any conviction or sentence *at any time* after an unsuccessful appeal or a refusal of leave, to the Court of Appeal (my emphasis). The condition for their making a reference is that they "consider there is a real possibility that the conviction, verdict, finding or sentence would not be upheld" because of an argument or evidence not raised in the convicting court or an argument, point of law or information not raised prior to sentence. Section 13(2) provides an even wider power to refer any case which does not satisfy those conditions, in exceptional circumstances. When deciding whether to refer, the Commission has a duty to take account of representations made to them and they have wide investigatory powers. They may seek the Court of Appeal's opinion, direct an investigation by the police or any other relevant public body, require the production of documents, reports or opinions or undertake any inquiry they consider appropriate.

The 1995 Act preserves the prerogative power to pardon a convicted individual. This is a residual monarchical prerogative, exercised traditionally by the Home Secretary and s.16 gives him the power to refer any case under his consideration to the Commission for their opinion.

For critiques of the 1995 Act, see articles by Smith and Malleson at [1995] Crim. L.R. 920 and 929. Concern is expressed over how liberally or restrictively the Court of Appeal will interpret the wording of the new grounds of appeal and over the fact that the new Commission will be using the police to investigate miscarriages of justice, some of which will have been caused by police malpractice. One omission from the Act is that the power to order retrials under the 1968 Act, s.7 is left untouched, despite considerable debate, in the Royal Commission and elsewhere, over the circumstances in which it is appropriate to order a retrial.

OFFENCES TRIABLE EITHER WAY—MODE OF TRIAL

The Criminal Law Act 1977 divided offences into three categories. First, offences triable only on indictment in the Crown Court. Secondly, offences triable only summarily in the magistrates' court. Thirdly, offences triable either way. The Criminal Justice Act 1988 added a fourth category, summary offences triable on indictment.

The Magistrates' Courts Act 1980 lays down that for an offence triable either way, the magistrates' court shall hear representations from the prosecutor and the defendant as to the appropriate mode of trial. (The court has no discretion if the Attorney-General or the Director of Public Prosecutions seeks indictable trial.) Having heard the representations and considered all the circumstances, the magistrates may decide that the defendant should be tried on indictment. If so, that decision is final. If they consider that summary trial is appropriate the magistrates tell the defendant so, but offer him the option of trial by jury. Experience has shown that the vast majority of defendants who have an option choose to have the case tried by magistrates.

Drawing conclusions from Home Office and other research on mode of trial decisions by magistrates and defendants, the Royal Commission on Criminal Justice concluded that the system was not being used as intended. They found that, while defendants often opt for Crown Court trial in the belief that their chances of acquittal are greater, they nevertheless change their plea to guilty at the Crown Court; that defendants often opt for Crown Court trial in the mistaken belief that, if convicted, the Crown Court judge will impose a lighter sentence than magistrates and that magistrates send a number of cases to the Crown Court where the defendant ultimately receives a sentence within the magistrates' own sentencing powers. They recommended that the defendant should no longer have the right to insist on jury trial. Where prosecution and defence could not agree on mode of trial, the decision should be referred to the magistrates. The Royal Commission was subject to academic criticism, alleging that it had misinterpreted the Home Office research. Nevertheless, the Home Office published a consultation document, *Mode of Trial*, in 1995. In it, they outline various options designed to shift more cases from the Crown Court to the magistrates' courts. They point out that national mode of trial guidelines issued by the Director of Public Prosecutions have already gone some way towards achieving this. They sought opinions on three other options: the reclassification of more offences as triable only summarily, the withdrawal of the defendant's option to insist on jury trial in the Crown Court and a requirement that the defendant enter the plea before the trial/hearing venue is chosen.

The Government chose to enact the third and least draconian of these options. Given the sentimental attachment of the English to jury trial in criminal cases, it would be politically inexpedient to remove the defendant's right to opt for jury trial in all triable either way cases. Instead, clause 34 of the Criminal Procedure and Investigations Bill 1995 (which is due to be given royal assent in July 1996) requires the magistrates, before determining mode of trial, to ascertain the accused's plea. Where he indicates a not guilty plea, they must proceed to deal with the case summarily. Where the accused pleads not guilty, they may choose to send the case up to the Crown Court or, where they decline to do so, they must still give the defendant the option of summary trial or trial on indictment at the Crown Court. In other words, if the defendant expresses an intention to plead guilty, he loses the right to opt for the Crown Court. The magistrates must hear the case but retain the right to send it up to the Crown Court for sentence, where they feel their own sentencing powers are too low. There will of course, be nothing to prevent the accused from indicating a not guilty plea at this stage, then changing his plea to guilty at the Crown Court. In such cases, the clause will fail to achieve its desired objective.

4. THE JUDICIAL FUNCTION IN CRIMINAL AND CIVIL TRIALS

Judges receive very little training in preparation for their change of role and this has been the subject of comment. A brilliant advocate may after all make an unsatisfactory judge.

The function of the judge in the common law, adversarial model is to preside in court, to conduct the hearing according to the accepted rules of procedure and evidence, to give rulings on points of law and, where appropriate, to sum up the factual evidence in order to assist the jury. It is no part of the judge's role to initiate the adduction of new evidence or to take an inquisitorial role. If there is no jury, the judge hears and determines the case and, where appropriate, gives a reasoned explanation of the legal principles which she has decided to apply.

In giving judgment, the judge is inevitably creating new law—judge-made law. The decision must be consistent with existing legal principles and, as such, must be linked to a consideration of previous case decisions by earlier judges. This system is known as the doctrine of judicial precedent and will be considered at length in Chapter 11. Even where the judge's task is to interpret a word or phrase appearing in a statute, she will still need to be guided by other previous judicial interpretations relevant to the one with which she is concerned. There are two ways of looking at the role of the judge in giving judgment—one is to see her function as "*jus dicere*", simply saying what the law is, and always has been, on the facts of the particular case; the other is to regard it as "*jus dare*", meaning to give or create the law applicable to the facts revealed. On either view the discretion of the judge is very limited in view of the application of the doctrine of judicial precedent.

THE CONCEPT OF JUDGE AS ARBITER

The essence of the role of the English judge, or magistrate, is that she acts as an unbiased umpire whose job it is to listen to evidence presented by both sides, without interfering in the trial process. This is often contrasted with the role of the *juge d'instruction*, the French first instance judge who performs an inquisitorial role in some trials, directing criminal investigations, cross-examining the defendant and compiling a *dossier* of evidence for the trial court. Of course, there is no comparable English equivalent. The point is simply that the court takes a much greater role in compiling the evidence and is involved at an earlier stage in the process. Similarly, the role of the German judge is to take an active part in the assembling of evidence and the questioning of witnesses, before and at trial. It is said that these European judges, from civil law countries, take part in an inquisitorial system, whereas ours is adversarial or accusatorial. This is a rather crude comparison, as we shall see. It is sometimes said that the judge's role, especially in the civil trial as a non-interfering umpire, is a reflection of the English sense of fair play: each side has an equal opportunity to win the litigation "game" by convincing the judge of the merits of their argument, collecting good evidence and citing favourable case authorities. During 1991–93, The Royal Commission on Criminal Justice considered whether the court should have an investigative role before and during the criminal trial and the Heilbron committee (1993) and Lord Woolf (whose final report is due in 1996) have recommended an interventionist role for the civil trial judge, especially in terms of case management.

THE PRACTICAL MEANING OF JUDGE AS ARBITER

1. Summoning witnesses

The judge and court do not select witnesses. It is left to the parties to call the witnesses they see fit to boost their case. The civil judge has no power to call witnesses unless both parties consent. (He can, however, appoint an independent expert witness, on the application of any party. In a 1995 case, where the defendants wanted to call 29 experts, the judge ordered the appointment of one court expert, instead.) In criminal cases the judge does have such a power but it is used very rarely. This can have two undesirable results.

(a) There may be conflict between expert witnesses, where each side has an opposing expert witness and the judge has no power to call an independent adviser for herself. It may be that such conflicts are reduced slightly in civil trials by the compulsory exchange of expert evidence, pre-trial, and by a rule operating since 1986, in cases other than those on personal injuries, in the High Court, whereby the court can direct a meeting between experts to see whether they can agree a report. Nevertheless, a judge (and jury) will still frequently find themselves having to decide between two experts in a criminal case (for example on psychiatric or forensic evidence).

(b) It may lead to a vital witness not being called who would have given penetrating evidence against both sides (for example where, in a civil case resulting from a road accident, one witness may be able to give evidence that both parties were driving far too fast).

2. The conduct of the trial

The judge does not interfere in the presentation of evidence by examining and cross-examining witnesses. This is left to the parties or their advocates. The role of the judge was set down clearly by Lord Denning M.R. in *Jones v. National Coal Board* (C.A. 1957) and can be summarised thus: he should:

(a) listen to all the evidence, only interfering to clarify neglected or obscure points;

(b) see that advocates behave and stick to the rules;

(c) exclude irrelevancies and discourage repetition;

(d) make sure he understands the advocates' points;

(e) at the end, make up his mind where the truth lies.

3. The judge's expertise on law and fact

Generally speaking, the judge relies on the advocates to present legal and factual arguments. Of course, the specialist judges of, say, the Admiralty Court, are appointed because they need a certain level of understanding to appreciate specialist argument but they do not choose which precedents to examine. A judge can, if a vital precedent has been ignored, invite counsel's arguments upon it. In tribunals, of course, panel members are appointed because of their factual expertise, the antithesis of a county court or Q.B.D. general list judge, who is meant to be a Jack-of-all-trades.

The rule of non-intervention, set out above, does not apply to *legal* argument addressed to the judge. Students watching this in court will see that very often a dialogue goes on between counsel and the judge, especially in civil cases and the appellate courts.

English law is emphatic that judge or magistrates must not interfere in a case. To do so invokes accusation of a breach of natural justice. Justice must be seen to be done. Bias need not be proven for proceedings to be quashed: *R. v. Sussex Justices, ex p. McCarthy* (H.L. 1924).

Th rule of non-interference is subject to certain exceptions:

(a) Small claims in the county court. Research by Appleby (1978) showed some registrars employed an inquisitorial technique. Many of those who appear are unrepresented and, therefore, the progress of the case depends on the district judge being somewhat interventionist. The *Civil Justice Review* recommended that registrars (now district judges, since the CLSA) adopt a more standardised inquisitorial role in small claims and the CLSA, s.6 provides for the County Court Rules to prescribe the manner of taking and questioning evidence, thus permitting official sanction for a more inquisitorial role.

(b) The unrepresented. The plight of the unrepresented has been well documented in socio-legal research (Dell, (1971); Carlen, (1976); Darbyshire, (1984)). Where a defendant is unrepresented, mostly in the magistrates' courts, as virtually all Crown Court defendants are represented, he is wholly dependent on the goodwill and expertise of the bench or, more realistically, the clerk, to help him put his case and examine witnesses and explain what is being asked of him, for example, choice of venue in a triable-either-way offence. Some clerks are much more prepared and skilled to help than others.

Unrepresented parties in civil proceedings, known as litigants in person, have become a cause of concern in the 1990s. Their numbers are increasing, most probably because of the lack of availability of legal aid. High Court and Court of Appeal judges have become so concerned about their prevalence that they convened a working party, which reported in 1995. Their report points to the disadvantages suffered by litigants in person. They encourage the development of *pro bono* services offered by solicitors and barristers and they urge the Lord Chancellor to enhance the funding of the Citizen's Advice Bureau in the Royal Courts of Justice and to give serious consideration to the needs of such litigants. The Supreme Court has since taken further measures to assist them. For instance, in late 1995, a new Chancery Guide was issued, which includes a section specifically designed to help them and point them in the direction of further assistance.

(c) Matrimonial proceedings. Under the Magistrates' Courts Act 1980, the court is under a duty to help the unrepresented party, in family proceedings, to present their evidence.

Coincidentally, in relation to both the civil and the criminal process, there have been recommendations in the 1990s to move towards a more interventionist role for judges. The interim Woolf Report (1995), described above, envisages a positive role for judges in civil trial management, to speed a case along both through its pre-trial and trial stages, as do the practice directions on civil trial, issued by the heads of division in 1995, outlined above. Similarly, the Royal Commission on Criminal Justice (1993) recommended:

> "Wherever practicable in complex cases judges should take on responsibility for managing the progress of a case, securing its passage through the various stages of pre-trial discussion to preparatory hearing and trial and making sure that the parties have fulfilled their obligations both to each other and to the court." (Recommendation 254),

and the 1995 practice direction on Plea and Directions Hearings in the Crown Court, described above, goes some way towards this aim.

5. ROYAL COMMISSION ON CRIMINAL PROCEDURE

A Royal Commission on Criminal Procedure reported in 1981 and many of its recommendations have been enacted. The Prosecution of

Offences Act 1985, instituted a Crown Prosecution Service in place of prosecution by the police and the Police and Criminal Evidence Act 1984, introduced a comprehensive code of police powers and practices in the investigation of crime and amended the rules of evidence in criminal proceedings in certain respects.

6. ROYAL COMMISSION ON CRIMINAL JUSTICE

In 1991, in response to public anxiety over a well-publicised series of miscarriages of justice, overturned by the Court of Appeal, including the cases of "The Guildford Four", "The Birmingham Six", the Maguires and others, which reflected very badly on the fairness of the English system of pre-trial procedure, trial and appeal, the Home Secretary and Lord Chancellor appointed a Royal Commission on Criminal Justice (RCCJ), which reported in 1993. Its terms of reference were to examine the effectiveness of the criminal justice system in securing the conviction of the guilty and the acquittal of the innocent and to examine in particular:

(i)   the supervision by senior officers of police investigations;
(ii) the role of the prosecutor in supervising the gathering of evidence and arrangements for its disclosure to the defence;
(iii) the role of experts and the forensic science services;
(iv) access to experts and legal services by the defence;
(v)   the accused's opportunities to state his case;
(vi) the powers of the courts in directing proceedings, including the possibility of their having an investigative role during and pre-trial; uncorroborated confession evidence;
(vii) the role of the Court of Appeal;
(viii) arrangements for investigating miscarriages of justice when appeal rights have been exhausted.

The sixth term of reference was very far reaching. It involved considering importing inquisitorial procedures used in civil law systems and would mean a significant departure from the English adversarial model. This has sparked off a renewed interest in inquisitorial systems, such as those of Scotland and other European countries.

The Commission, in the event, decided against importing inquisitorial elements from foreign systems. They commissioned a great deal of research into the workings of the English and foreign criminal processes and examined many aspects of our system, from the point of police investigations, to the post appeal process. They made 352 recommendations, too many to summarise here, although most of the recommendations relevant to this book are discussed in this edition and their outcomes reported. Some of their proposals are very far reaching and it is said that if they are all effected, they will tip the scales of justice in favour of the prosecution. Many recommendations have already provoked new government legislation, although not always in line with the Commission's wishes. Examples of this are certain sections of the Criminal Justice and Public Order Act 1994, the Criminal Appeal Act 1995 and the Criminal Procedure and Investigations Act 1996. Changes in practice have also followed, such as those required by the 1995 practice direction on plea and directions hearings. At the time of writing, 1996, it is assumed that there will be further legislative outcomes of the 1993 report.

CHAPTER 8

EVIDENCE

1. MEANING

The task of the court is to unravel and identify the relevant facts in the case, and then determine the dispute for the parties by applying the appropriate legal principles to those facts. The law of evidence assists the court to this objective by establishing rules about the means by which the facts of a case are to be presented to the court. The facts which are at the basis of the dispute between the parties, whether in a civil or a criminal case, are called "the facts in issue"; and in every case it will be the substantive law and procedure which will decide which facts are the facts in issue. Evidence comes into its own in that it is the branch of the law which provides the means by which those facts in issue can be proven.

Some of the confusion associated with the law of evidence arises because there are at least three senses in which the word can be used.

(i)   In the formal legal sense, as described above, the word is used to mean the way in which the facts in issue can be proved.

(ii) By a natural abbreviation the word is sometimes used to describe those facts which may be proved, instead of the means by which those facts may be proved.

(iii) The word is frequently used alone in the sense of "admissible evidence", where the consideration is whether the facts in question are, under the principles of the law of evidence, such as the court will permit to be given in the manner proposed. In such instances the evidence is said to be "admissible", or "inadmissible", as the rules allow.

It will be gathered that the law of evidence is not an easy subject, and it has been vigorously criticised by C.P. Harvey, Q.C., in his book, *The Advocate's Devil*, where he writes: "Founded apparently on the propositions that all jurymen are deaf to reason, that all witnesses are presumptively liars, and that all documents are presumptively forgeries, it has been added to, subtracted from and tinkered with, until it has become less of a structure than a pile of builder's debris." Nevertheless, the pages which follow will endeavour to select some of the more important aspects of the subject for consideration. What is certain is that it is impossible to understand the method of trial in a civil or criminal case without an appreciation of the relevant rules of procedure and evidence.

2. THE BURDEN OF PROOF

The essential mechanism for calibrating the scales of justice is the burden of proof.

In a civil case the courts take the view that the responsibility for proving the facts alleged to substantiate the claim made, or the defence submitted, falls on the party propounding those facts. It can thus be said that the general burden of proof is fixed at the beginning of the trial on the plaintiff, or the defendant, asserting the affirmative of an issue. Once that evidence has been given, however, the particular burden of proof may shift throughout the trial as each party gives in turn their version of the facts in dispute.

In a criminal case, because the English system follows the accusatorial principle whereby the prosecution accuses the defendant of committing a specified criminal offence, the onus of proving that the defendant is guilty of the offence charged is on the prosecution. The prosecution cannot look to the defendant for any assistance in the case, in that he cannot be required to answer questions or afford explanations of his conduct. If he wishes, the defendant can remain silent throughout the proceedings but, as we have seen in Chapter 7, the jury may be invited to draw adverse inferences from the accused's failure to account for specific items of prosecution evidence (Criminal Justice and Public Order Act 1994, ss.34–39.) Critics of the statute argue that these sections have relieved the prosecution of some of their burden of proof.

The *standard* of proof, which must be distinguished from the *burden*, requires that the prosecution, in bringing a case, must have sufficient evidence available to satisfy the court, "beyond reasonable doubt", that the accused person is guilty of the offence charged.

The direct result of this approach is the long-running claim that in English criminal law the defendant is entitled to be presumed innocent until the prosecution have satisfied the court of guilt beyond reasonable doubt. Again, critics of the Criminal Justice and Public Order Act 1994 claim that it has derogated from this so-called presumption of innocence.

There are a number of situations in which the defendant in a criminal case may have the burden of proving particular facts. For example, if the defence sets up a plea of insanity or diminished responsibility, it is for the defence to satisfy the court that this plea is justified. Again under section 25 of the Theft Act 1968, where a person is found in possession of any article for use in the course of, or in connection with, any burglary, theft or cheat, it may well fall to the defendant to justify possession of the article. Ashworth and Blake, at [1996] Crim. L.R. 306 argue that a legal burden of proof is now placed on the defendant in a growing number of offences.

Finally, having disposed of "the burden", the further question arises, what is "proof"? the *Oxford English Dictionary* defines "proof" as the process which convinces the mind of something and in the evidential sense this occurs when the court accepts that a particular circumstance has been shown to its satisfaction to have been established as a relevant fact in issue. Proof means showing that a fact *is in issue*, rather than established *to be true*.

One essential difference between civil and criminal cases in the *standard* of proof is that, whereas in a civil case proof is required "on the balance of probabilities", in a criminal case, because the freedom of the individual may be involved, a higher standard is applied and the proof is required to be beyond reasonable doubt or such that the court is "sure" of guilt.

3. TYPES OF EVIDENCE

(i) Oral evidence

The word "evidence" comes from the Latin word "videre", meaning "to see", so that oral evidence is the testimony of a witness given by word of mouth relating to a matter which she has actually seen or of which she has some direct personal knowledge. In giving this testimony on oath in public as a witness, the person called before the court is subjected to an examination in three stages. She is first asked to answer certain questions by the party who is calling her. This is known as examination-in-chief. Then when this is concluded the legal representative of the other party will proceed to ask the witness questions, designed to show that her testimony is not reliable, or to get her to admit to facts which correspond to the other party's side of the case. This stage is known as cross-examination. Finally the side which orginally called the witness is allowed to clarify, by further questions, the answers given by the witness in cross-examination. No new material can be introduced. This stage is known as re-examination.

(ii) Documentary evidence

In many civil cases much of the evidence before the court will consist of relevant documents as, for example, the correspondence which has passed between the parties, or the various contract documents relating to the claim. Similarly, in certain criminal cases, such as fraud or forgery, a document or documents can be relevant evidence. Documentary evidence is usually hearsay evidence, which is admissible only in exceptional circumstances, particularly in criminal cases.

The court may require to see and inspect the original document, and in civil procedure there is provision for what is called Discovery of Documents, so that the parties and the court have access to all relevant documents in advance of the hearing. One recent reform of civil procedure, to speed and ease the process, has been to make discovery automatic in most cases. In civil cases, since 1995, both sides prepare "bundles" of photocopied documents presented to the opposition and the court which are referred to by all parties and judges throughout the trial. This was prescribed in 1995 Practice Directions described in Chapter 7.

(iii) Real evidence

Real evidence usually takes the form of the inspection of a material object by the court. The poker alleged to have been the murder weapon, or the second-hand car the subject of the contract, may be examined by the court as a means of proof of a relevant fact in issue. Such objects are usually called "exhibits".

If it is not convenient to bring an object into court, or if the court wishes to inspect a building, or make a site visit, then this "view" is taken to be real evidence. The same term is used of the impression which a witness makes on the court resulting from her demeanour in the witness-box.

4. CLASSIFICATION OF EVIDENCE

(i) Direct evidence and circumstantial evidence

Direct evidence relates to the facts in issue themselves. For example, the witness who actually saw the incident which gives rise to the criminal charge, or which is a vital aspect of a civil case, can given direct evidence. Similarly, an original document, such as a will, or a material object which is, in itself, a fact in issue is direct evidence.

Circumstantial evidence is evidence of certain facts from which the facts in issue can be inferred. The presentation to the court of a number of related circumstances—or facts not in issue—can lead to the inference in a criminal case that the accused is guilty of the crime charged. A murder case where the body of the victim has not been found is a clear instance of a situation where circumstantial evidence is likely to be the only evidence available to prove the charge. Inevitably with circumstantial evidence, the arguments will be about the proper inferences to be drawn from the evidence. Notice that the conviction of Rosemary West, in 1995, for 10 counts of murder, making her the most prolific female serial killer in British legal history, was based entirely on circumstantial evidence. There was no direct evidence against her: no evidence that she had even met some of her victims. There was overwhelming circumstantial evidence against her, notably the bodies under the cellar in her home.

(ii) Primary and secondary evidence

Primary evidence is the most effective evidence to prove a particular fact in issue. The witness who saw the incident is to be preferred to a person who heard a version some time later; the actual letter containing an alleged offer in a contract case is to be preferred to the recollection of one of the parties as to the terms of the letter.

Secondary evidence is the term used to describe evidence which is introduced to take the place of certain primary evidence which is not available to the court. In the case of a document this may be a copy of the original or other evidence relating to its contents.

At one time the courts had a rule that only the "best evidence" of the facts in issue would be allowed. This rule has been relaxed, so that now the courts will permit the facts to be proved by any admissible means. Obviously, however, the courts will expect the parties to call primary rather than secondary evidence, unless good reason for the failure can be shown.

(iii) Original and hearsay evidence

The difference between these two kinds of evidence is, in general terms, the difference between first-hand evidence and second-hand evidence.

Original evidence may be oral, documentary or real as, for example, that of the witness who was present at the incident in question and can testify of their own knowledge as to what took place.

Hearsay evidence, in contrast, is evidence of what some other person, who is not before the court, has said or written. Naturally the attitude of the courts is to insist, in so far as this is possible, that that other person should be brought before the court, so that the court can itself assess the demeanour of the witness, and the opposing party can proceed to cross-examine her on what she had said or written. For this reason the courts have been unwilling to accept hearsay evidence where it is presented as proof of the truth of what was said or written. Confusion can arise because what appears to be hearsay may in another sense be properly treated as original evidence; for example, if it is presented to the court to prove that a statement was made or a letter was written, rather than that its contents are true.

In criminal cases the general principle is that hearsay evidence is inadmissible. This rule was relaxed to allow certain declarations of deceased persons to be put in as evidence, as also voluntary confesions by the accused and certain statements contained in public documents. The rule was further relaxed by statute, the most recent example being sections 23–32 of the Criminal Justice Act 1988, which provides a fairly comprehensive code for the admission of documentary hearsay, including computer-generated documents, in the Crown Court and magistrates' courts. The 1995 trial of Rosemary West saw an un-precedented use of this section to admit, as electronic documentary hearsay, the murder confessions of Fred West, her dead husband. The 1988 Act also permits, for instance, the admission of video recordings of a child's testimony. This is hearsay, since the Act (as amended) provides that the child shall not be examined-in-chief on any matter dealt with adequately in the video.

In civil cases the rule against hearsay has been substantially relaxed by statute and recently abolished, in the Civil Evidence Act 1995, following a 1993 report by the Law Commission. They also reported, in 1995, on criminal hearsay, prompted by the 1993 Royal Commission but recommended the rule be reformed but not abolished: for full discussion see [1996] Crim. L.R. 4–33.

A provision of the Civil Evidence Act 1968 lays down that the findings of a court in a criminal case are to be available as evidence in any subsequent civil case. This provision will, *inter alia*, prevent the virtual reopening of the criminal case in the hope of getting a change of verdict by the commencement of civil proceedings, for example for defamation, based on the same facts.

It remains the position that hearsay evidence which has no relevance to the facts in issue, whether in civil or criminal cases, is, like other forms of evidence which are irrelevant, inadmissible.

5. DIFFERENCES IN THE LAW OF EVIDENCE IN CIVIL AND CRIMINAL CASES

GENERAL

Although the principles of the law of evidence are common to both civil and criminal cases, certain special rules apply in criminal cases. One such difference was observed in the treatment of the hearsay rule where the criminal case approach is much more stringent. Other examples are:

(i) Waiver

Evidence can, at the discretion of the parties, be waived in civil but not in criminal cases. This distinction follows the fundamental rule that a civil action can be "settled out of court" by the parties before trial and can be settled with the approval of the court during the trial, whereas criminal proceedings, once begun, cannot be withdrawn unless the court gives consent.

(ii) Character

The rules relating to the giving of evidence of character differ as between civil and criminal cases.

In a civil case the plaintiff may not give evidence of her own good character nor call a witness to give such evidence. On the other hand a witness can be cross-examined as to her character so as to test her credibility as to the evidence she has given. In the occasional case, as, for example, where justification is pleaded as a defence in defamation, the character of the plaintiff may be a relevant factor in which case evidence of her character may be given.

146

In a criminal case the prosecution must not buttress its case by deducing evidence of the accused's bad character to support its allegations against him. If, however, the accused himself puts his character in evidence, or if he attacks the character of the prosecution witness, then in either case the prosecution can cross-examine him as to his character and bring any previous convictions of the accused to light except where these are to be treated as "spent", in accordance with the Rehabilitation of Offenders Act 1974. Reference to such convictions is at the judge's discretion.

(iii) Admissions

In a civil case, as was seen in the chapter on procedure, the documents which make up the pleadings must expressly answer every allegation contained in the opponent's claim. Any such allegation which is not expressly denied, or traversed, is taken to be admitted.

By way of contrast, in a criminal case the prosecution has to prove every factor relevant to the guilt of the accused. The only qualification to this rule is that it is permissible for the defence to make formal admissions to the court in order to obviate the need for those particular facts to be specifically proven.

(iv) Confessions

Whereas confessions are inapplicable in civil proceedings, they are often crucial in a criminal case.

The Police and Criminal Evidence Act 1984 contains provisions designed to exclude confessions obtained by oppression or in any circumstances which might render the confession unreliable. There are also provisions under which evidence obtained unfairly can be excluded by the court.

(v) Previous convictions

A rule protecting the defendant in a criminal trial is that the court must not be told of any previous convictions.

Save in the exceptional circumstances specified, the Rehabilitation of Offenders Act 1974 provides that after certain periods of time a conviction is to be regarded as "spent". The length of time in question varies with the sentence imposed. Sentences of more than 30 months' imprisonment are excluded from rehabilitation. Once a conviction is "spent" it should, in practice, no longer be referred to. Subject to this legislation, the court is formally informed of the previous convictions of the defendant only after he has been found "guilty" and is about to be sentenced. One important exception to this rule is the admissibility of "similar fact" evidence. In a criminal case, the judge may permit the prosecutor to adduce evidence that the accused has been convicted of or accused of an offence which bears a similarity to the offence charged, or that he is disposed to a particular type of activity. Such evidence should only be admitted if it has a really material bearing on the issues to be decided. The judge must weigh its probative value against its prejudicial effect against the accused and only admit it if it would not be unfair to the accused. A high degree of similarity is required between the previous behaviour and that presently alleged. A memorable example of the admission of similar fact evidence was in the 1995 trial of Rosemary West. Her defence was that she knew nothing of the murders of the girls whose bodies were found, bound and gagged, buried at her house and her previous home. She claimed that her late husband, Fred, had acted alone. In order to rebut this and to prove that they acted together, the prosecution was allowed to call Caroline Owens, who told the court how she had been picked up by both of the Wests, then bound, gagged and raped by the two, acting together. The Wests' convictions for this offence were allowed in evidence. Evidence of Rosemary West's sexual proclivities, even of her prostitution, was also allowed, under this rule, as was the evidence of her stepdaughter, that she had suffered repeated sexual abuse from the Wests, from the age of eight.

(vi) Identification evidence

The problem of visual identification evidence constantly gives cause for concern as it has been shown by experience to be rather unreliable.

In *R. v. Turnbull* (1976) the Lord Chief Justice gave detailed advice to judges presiding in cases where visual identification evidence is all-important. They must warn the jury of the dangers of relying on identification evidence and draw the jury's attention to the circumstances in which such evidence was obtained.

(vii) Alibi as a defence

An important statutory provision requires the defence in a criminal case to give the prosecution notice of its intention to rely on an alibi at the pending trial.

(viii) Opinions

The general principle is that the opinions of witnesses are not relevant, because the court in every case is concerned with the proof of facts. The one exception made is that the opinion of an expert witness, for example a doctor, may be accepted where the opinion is based directly on expert knowledge, which must first be established.

(ix) Estoppel

This rule of evidence prevents a party, usually in a civil action, from asserting or denying a particular fact. For example, once a decision in a matter has been arrived at by a court, that matter is said to be "*res judicata*", and that issue cannot be raised again. Where it applies, estoppel results in a party being "stopped" from introducing evidence which would otherwise be admissible. Estoppel may arise by agreement, by representation, by conduct or by deed.

(x) Judicial notice

One qualification to the rule that all relevant facts must be proved is that in civil and criminal cases the judge will take notice of such matters as the contents of Acts of Parliament or the law and custom of Parliament. Facts of which judicial notice is taken do not, therefore, require to be proven.

(xi) Compelling attendance

A court has long reserved the power to compel a witness to attend and give evidence before it. In civil proceedings the court may issue a document, called a *subpoena*, which will require the attendance of a witness; in criminal proceedings the Criminal Procedure (Attendance of Witnesses) Act 1965 allows for the making of a witness order, or witness summons, to compel attendance. A failure to attend then becomes a contempt of court.

There are a few exceptions where a person will not be made to be a witness, for example a wife, of husband, is not normally compelled to give evidence in criminal proceedings against the other spouse.

Another example of a very different kind is that, in civil and criminal proceedings, persons enjoying diplomatic immunity cannot be compelled to give evidence.

(xii) Public policy

In a criminal case it is a matter of public policy whether or not a prosecution is proceeded with, and the Attorney-General by a writ of *nolle prosequi* can always intervene to terminate proceedings in progress.

In a civil case the courts have long accepted that, as a matter of public policy, the Crown has the right to decline to allow apparently relevant evidence to be given. This was known as crown privilege or privilege in the public interest. Obviously the claim is not to be lightly accepted by the courts, and in *Conway v. Rimmer* (1968) the House of Lords laid down that, in every such instance, the court will require the central government Minister concerned to justify the claim that it is not in the public interest for the evidence to be given.

Since that leading case, the concept has become known as public interest immunity, an area of evidence far too complex for examination here. Debates on whether a Minister has a duty to sign a public interest immunity (PII) certificate, have been prolific in newspapers and law journals in 1996. This arose as a result of *The Scott Report*, in 1996. This report, by Lord Justice Scott, on the "Arms To Iraq" scandal, involved the issue of whether Ministers had a duty to sign "PII" certificates to prevent the admission of evidence that they secretly condoned the sale of parts of a "Supergun" to Iraq, prior to the Gulf War, contrary to publicly stated government policy. The evidence would have been overwhelming defence evidence in the criminal trial of the Directors of Matrix-Churchill, who were charged with illegal arms sales.

CHAPTER 9

TRIBUNALS, INQUIRIES, ARBITRATION AND A.D.R.

1. TRIBUNALS

FUNCTION

In addition to the civil and criminal courts, which have been examined in Chapters 5 and 6, there also exists in the English legal system a vast number of tribunals set up by Acts of Parliament to hear and decide disputes on a court-like basis. These tribunals are frequently referred to as "administrative tribunals", because many of the issues which arise and need to be determined do so under a statutory scheme of administration. Examples are the Social Security Appeal Tribunals whose predecessors were set up under the National Insurance Act 1946 and now hear appeals concerning income support, family credit, national insurance, etc. It was plainly foreseeable that, when the national insurance system was brought into operation by the 1946 Act, there would be disputed decisions and so provision was made for the establishment of tribunals. Thus, in some instances the conflict is between the citizen on the one side and a state agency on the other but this is not always the case; there have been examples of Parliament setting up tribunals where the dispute is between private parties. Perhaps the best example in this field is the creation of rent tribunals charged with resolving disputes between landlord and tenant over rent and security of tenure in certain dwellings.

There is complete diversity of function amongst tribunals and no classification is completely satisfactory. There are tribunals concerned with the various state benefits and tribunals reviewing the detention of mental patients and hearing complaints about the professional conduct of doctors in the National Health Service. There are tribunals concerned with matters affecting agricultural land, public transport, the valuation of land, income tax assessments and a wide range of more specialised matters extending from copyright in plant varieties to betting levy assessments and immigration appeals. All that can be said is that in every instance Parliament has brought the tribunal into being and given it limited jurisdiction over the matters specified in the Act.

There is no reason why the dispute in question should not have been given to a court to decide, and in this sense the use of tribunals is best seen as an alternative to the court system. It is not a worthwhile exercise to try to distinguish a court from a tribunal, since their function is one and the same. Both are bodies responsible for determining disputes and some tribunals are much more like courts than others.

ADVANTAGES AND DISADVANTAGES

The reasons which are advanced for the use of tribunals rather than the ordinary court are several. A major consideration is that the costs of a tribunal hearing are negligible, particularly as compared with a High Court action. There are no court fees to the parties and as legal representation is not essential the costs of this can be avoided. Tribunals can give a fixed date for the hearing in contrast to court proceedings where the case is entered in the list and all parties and witnesses have to be present to await the case being called, which inevitably increases the cost of an action brought in the courts.

In order to put the parties at their ease and to obviate the need for legal representation the procedure followed at a tribunal hearing is as informal as possible. There is nothing like the formal rules of court or the documentary method of proceeding—the pleadings—used in the High Court. The members of the tribunal can take part in the proceedings and may assist either or both parties in the presentation of the case. Hearings are held to suit the convenience of the parties and as far as possible tribunals are accessible in that they sit locally and as business demands. At the conclusion of the hearing the tribunal arrives at its decision, which may be announced forthwith or notified to the parties reasonably quickly after the hearing.

Another important factor in favour of tribunals is that the members of a tribunal, because of their limited jurisdiction, soon become specialists in the particular field of law with which they are concerned. The members of a Rent Assessment Committee inevitably become expert on the level of rents within their locality; and similar expertise is a characteristic of all tribunal work. Whereas a judge has a wide jurisdiction, a tribunal member rapidly becomes a specialist; this leads to a consistency of treatment of cases locally which cannot be matched by the courts. The system also has the advantage of bringing lay people into the legal system, as with magistrates and jurors, so ensuring that the lawyers are not the totally dominant force in all disputes. In fact the composition of a tribunal, as will be seen, is almost always a combination of lawyer and lay people.

Perhaps the most important argument in favour of the system is that if all the tribunals were abolished the courts would simply be unable to cope with the work which would have to be transferred to them. It has been estimated that tribunals deal in total with approximately one-quarter of a million cases every year. The Royal Commission on Legal Services highlighted this matter (para. 15.1) by pointing out that "the total number of cases heard by tribunals in 1978 was six times the number of contested civil cases that were disposed of at trial before the High Court and county courts. The number of hearing days in tribunals has in recent years exceeded the total number of hearing days before judges in the High Court and county court, including days in chambers."

Those persons who can see disadvantages in the tribunal system point to the dangers of having a cheap, informal hearing with an immediate decision; they point out that the rules of court, the pleadings, and the formal procedure and rules of evidence of the courts are there because experience has shown that these lead in the long run to the most satisfactory result—the establishment of legal principles in accordance with the ideals of justice. They regard this by-passing of the court system as a dangerous lowering of standards, and foresee the introduction of tribunals by the executive as a matter of administrative expediency whenever new legislation calls for the resolving of disputes.

Judging from the continuing use made of tribunals by successive governments and their willingness to establish new tribunals, especially in recent years, the critics are not making much headway.

CHARACTERISTICS

Creation. All tribunals are of statutory origin and share one common feature, the task of adjudication.

Composition. The composition of the tribunal varies from one to another. Whereas a Lands Tribunal hearing consists of one member to decide the dispute, an Industrial Tribunal hearing will require three members to be present. In general terms, the majority of tribunals will be made up of three members, with a lawyer chairman and two lay representatives. For Industrial Tribunals the lay representatives will be selected from nominations made by employers and union organis-ations and for Agricultural Land Tribunals the two lay representatives are in the same way chosen from nominations of the Country Landowners' Association and the National Farmers' Union. Where the tribunal is concerned with specialist matters, as in the case of the Medical Appeal Tribunal, which assesses the degree of medical disability from which a claimant of, for example, a mobility allowance is suffering, inevitably the tribunal is made up of experts, in this instance medical specialists of consultant status.

The appointment of members to serve on tribunals usually falls, under the statute creating the tribunal, to the minister of the central government department whose ministry is responsible for the service to which the tribunal's jurisdiction relates. Accordingly, the Secretary of State for the Environment appoints members of Rent Assessment Tribunals and the Secretary of State for Social Services appoints members of the Social Security Appeal Tribunals. The minister is usually guided by the nominations of interested organisations, but retains a discretion in the matter. In appointing a lawyer chairman, however, most are appointed directly by the Lord Chancellor or selected by the relevant department or tribunal president from a panel appointed by him.

Procedure. Although there are procedural rules affecting certain tribunals (for example, the Mental Health Review Tribunal Rules 1983, made as a statutory instrument under the authority of the Mental Health Act 1983), other tribunals have no formal rules of procedure. Nonetheless, all tribunals tend to follow a similar pattern, since they are all determining disputes and consequently all have a court-like appearance. However, at the hearing, as has been seen, informality predominates. Where there are rules, they deal with such matters as the composition of the tribunal, the time and place of the hearing, the right of audience and representation, the hearing and the procedure to be adopted, inspection (if applicable) and the notification of the tribunal's decision to the parties.

Cases. Case loads of different tribunal systems vary enormously. Whereas Social Security Appeals Tribunals may decide over 80,000 annually, some, for instance, the Copyright Tribunal, may hear only three or four.

Organisation of tribunals. The organisation of tribunals depends entirely on the statute which creates the tribunals.

The tribunals concerned with tax, state benefits and health problems are, as might be expected, organised on a national basis.

The General Commissioners of Income Tax have over 350 divisions in England and Wales, whereas there are 14 Mental Health Review Tribunals. Many tribunals are so rarely used that there is only one of them, for instance, the Copyright Tribunal and some tribunals have never been constituted. For instance, no Mines and Quarries Tribunal has ever been convened, since provision was made for it in 1954.

Appeal. Because, generally, tribunals are intended to decide issues involving fact, there is no appeal from most tribunals on the facts. One exception is the Social Security Commissioners, lawyers of 10 years' standing, who hear appeals from the determinations of the Social Security Appeal Tribunals; others are the Lands Tribunal which hears appeals from Valuation Tribunals and The Employment Appeal Tribunal, hearing appeals from industrial tribunals.

Appeal on a point of law is possible to the High Court or Court of Appeal from the decisions of some tribunals under various statutes. For instance, appeal on a point of law lies from the Immigration Appeal Tribunal under The Asylum and Immigration Appeals Act 1993, to the Court of Appeal. If a tribunal misconducts itself, or makes a mistake of law, an interested party can apply for judicial review or appeal by way of case stated on a point of law to the Queen's Bench Divisional Court. This court has powers to control all inferior courts and tribunals if they make a mistake of law. The full picture on appeals from tribunals is too complex to be sketched here. The Law Commission suggested rationalising and simplifying appeals in a 1993 report.

THE TERM "TRIBUNAL"

As well as the administrative tribunal, the word is also familiar in the term, "domestic tribunal". Such a tribunal is one concerned with the discipline of members of a particular profession or organisation. Solicitors, for example, are subject to the disciplinary code enforced by the Solicitors' Disciplinary Tribunal; the same sort of disciplinary institution is used by doctors, architects and surveyors, and has become common under trade unions' rules. There is the possibility of appeal to the courts against the findings of certain domestic tribunals, for example, to the Privy Council from the General Medical Council.

Another tribunal, which in practice takes the form of an inquiry, is a statutory tribunal of inquiry, established ad hoc, to investigate a matter of "urgent public importance". A Royal Commission on Tribunals of Inquiry recommended that Parliament should use this power sparingly. With all the publicity that such a tribunal of inquiry attracts, there is a danger that individuals involved will get less protection than they would have had in an action in a court of law.

THE DEVELOPMENT OF THE ADMINISTRATIVE TRIBUNAL SYSTEM

Tribunals, as an important feature of the legal system, are of comparatively recent origin, having achieved particular prominence in the last 50 years. This is not to say that there were no tribunals in earlier years, but the use of tribunals developed rapidly with the advent of the Labour government in 1945, committed, as it was, to the introduction of "the welfare state". As each statute became law so it was necesary to have a tribunal to deal with the disputes which would arise. What were known as the National Insurance and Industrial Injuries Tribunals, the

National Assistance Appeals Tribunal, the National Health Service Tribunal and the Medical Appeal Tribunal were all established at this time.

The success of the tribunal is evidenced by the willingness of the government, through Parliament, to create new tribunals. Conveyancing Appeal Tribunals, for example, were set up under the Courts and Legal Services Act 1990.

Naturally the increasing use of tribunals has been called in question from time to time. The Committee on Ministers' Powers, which reported in 1932 (the Donoughmore Committee Report, Cmd. 4060 (1932)), was more concerned with delegated legislation, but it considered the place of tribunals in administrative jurisdiction generally. Then the Franks Committee on Administrative Tribunals and Enquiries, which reported in 1957 (the Franks Report, Cmnd. 218 (1957)), carried out a thorough examination into the whole system of tribunals and inquiries. Its report led to the 1958 Tribunals and Inquiries Act, consolidated in the 1971 Act and then the 1992 Act, now the key statute on tribunals.

The Committee's Report was reassuring about the need for tribunals and inquiries in modern government and about the standards achieved. The Committee, basing its recommendations on the need for "openness, fairness and impartiality", decided tribunals were clearly part of judicial machinery, not part of the executive.

The 1958 Act, as well as setting up the Council on Tribunals, has ensured that tribunals must give reasons for their decisions, that on points of law there should be an appeal to the High Court, that chairmen of most tribunals should be drawn from a panel of lawyers, that the dismissal of members of tribunals should need the consent of the Lord Chancellor and that, wherever possible, rules of procedure should be prepared, approved and published for tribunals and inquiries.

THE COUNCIL ON TRIBUNALS

The most important recommendation of the Franks Committee was that there should be a standing body responsible for the supervision of tribunals and inquiries. This was given effect immediately by legislation which established the Council on Tribunals. The Council consists of from 10 to 15 part-time lay members and has to report annually to Parliament on the operation of tribunals and inquiries. If the Council wishes it can submit a special report to Parliament at any time. It investigates complaints from members of the public, instigates its own examination of the way in which the system is working and assists the central government departments which are responsible for the membership of tribunals and for the procedural rules under which tribunals and inquiries are held.

2. INQUIRIES

Although inquiries have in name come to be associated with tribunals, they are designed to serve a quite different purpose. Whereas tribunals, like courts, are intended to reach a decision, inquiries are set up to obtain facts and opinions from all the parties concerned on the matter in issue so that the person who has to make the decision following on the inquiry can do so from a fully informed standpoint. Generally, an administrative inquiry is held to provide a minister with the fullest possible information before coming to a policy decision. For instance, inquiries will be held into the siting or rerouting of roads and the development of airports and power stations, as well as those into objections to much smaller developments. Such an inquiry has a secondary value in that it enables interested parties to feel that their views have been fully aired and made known to the person making the decision. How far such a process is to be regarded as "letting off steam", and exactly what effect it has on the policy-makers, have always been politically charged questions.

An administrative inquiry is also known as a "local" and "public" inquiry, thus emphasising two of its characteristics. It is held in the vicinity of the matter in dispute and it is almost always open to the public, both to attend and, with reservations, to give evidence. As Parliament has come to find this procedure valuable, so it has increasingly made provision in statute for an inquiry to be held before the minister takes a particular policy decision.

3. ARBITRATION

As an alternative to trial in the courts, the commercial world has come to favour a process which is known as arbitration. This is the reference of a dispute for determination to a third party, who may not be a judge or an officer of a court. The person appointed is known as an arbitrator. The arbitrator must conduct the hearing in a judicial manner, usually according to the provisions of the Arbitration Act 1996.

When an arbitration agreement is entered into it either specifies the arbitrator by name or, more commonly, it makes provision for the arbitrator to be appointed by the president for the time being of some appropriate professional body. This latter provision simply means that if an arbitration is found to be necessary, the parties then ask the office-holder named to exercise this power of appointment. It is possible for a judge of the Commercial Court to be appointed an arbitrator and, in the county court, small claims are dealt with by the district judge acting as an arbitrator.

The advantages which are claimed for arbitration, as a process compared with court proceedings, are several in number. Generally, arbitration is less expensive because, although the arbitrator has to be paid a fee, there is no court fee and no need to pay for the services of a solicitor and counsel in the preparation of the pleadings and in the presentation of the case in court. Because the arbitration takes place in private and there is no formal court procedure, there is often no need for legal representation at all. The arbitration can be fixed at a time and place convenient for all the parties and there is no delay, no waiting for the case in the court list to be reached, with parties, witnesses and lawyers standing in the corridors of the court, and costs mounting hour by hour. Another advantage is that the arbitrator chosen can be an expert in the particular field in which the dispute arises. The hearing can thus make rapid progress as compared with a similar hearing before a judge, where witnesses will have to be called to provide the judge with basic information before she can hope to get to the stage of understanding, let alone resolving, the dispute. The decision is immediate and, like the hearing, is private, and if necessary, as a last resort, the court can be called upon to enforce the arbitrator's award. With all these advantages it is not surprising that arbitration agreements are widely entered into and are generally found to be satisfactory.

There are, as might be expected, disadvantages which can be set up to temper the widespread enthusiasm for arbitration. It does not, for instance, follow that the process will necessarily be cheaper than litigation, because a professional person will charge a professional fee, and, furthermore, if the award should then be challenged in the courts, the costs of the arbitration will have been substantially wasted. To those who take the view that one gets what one pays for, the supposed advantages of speed, cheapness, informality and lay representation are all in themselves likely to prove weaknesses. The arbitrator has long had a discretion to refer a legal problem arising in the course of the arbitration to a judge for determination, in the meantime adjourning the hearing. The arbitrator must conduct the arbitration in accordance with the rules of natural justice and in a judicial manner; and must give reasons for the award. Any misconduct on the part of the arbitrator can result in the Queen's Bench Divisional Court being asked to intervene to quash the award and require a rehearing.

Following a growing number of ill-founded applications for judicial review, leading to long delays in settling awards, Parliament passed the Arbitration Act 1979 (now consolidated in the 1996 Act). This Act, which is comparatively complex, allows parties to exclude judicial review in certain defined instances and alternatively allows a right of appeal subject to stated conditions on any question of law arising out of an arbitrator's award. The court is given discretion in deciding whether to grant leave for an appeal on the point of law in question.

4. ALTERNATIVE DISPUTE RESOLUTION (A.D.R.)

This has been the fashionable development of the 1990s. Many British lawyers, most notably the Lord Chancellor, have taken an active interest in this American import, as a means of avoiding the public and private expense and the private pain of litigation. There are three main categories of scheme: *Mediation, Conciliation* and *Arbitration* (below). Schemes may be private or court-linked.

Mediation is the least formal. The parties voluntarily refer their dispute to an independent third party who will discuss the issues with both sides, normally in separate rooms and, by acting as a "go-between", the mediator will assist them to discuss and negotiate areas of conflict and identify and settle certain issues. The best known of such schemes in 1996 are those which will be offered to family disputants under the Lord Chancellor's controversial Family Law Bill 1996. Critics of this part of the Bill say that parties to a family dispute may be forced, unwillingly, into mediation if it is made a condition of their being granted legal aid.

Conciliation lies midway between informal mediation and formal arbitration. The process is very similar to mediation but the third party may offer a non-binding opinion which *may* lead to a settlement. Many county courts have in-court conciliation schemes.

Arbitration is the most formal (and established) type of A.D.R. (see above). It may be the last resort where conciliation fails. In certain schemes, a conciliator may transform into an arbitrator, where necessary, and pronounce a binding decision.

Be aware also of the *mini-trial*, a mock trial, used to air and rehearse the issues prior to negotiation.

Lord Chancellor Mackay became increasingly keen to emphasise the benefits of A.D.R., throughout the 1990s and its merits were recognised in both the Heilbron Report and Woolf Report on civil justice. The 1995 Practice Note on case management in the Q.B.D. and the Chancery Division requires the parties' solicitors to certify whether they have considered resolving the dispute by A.D.R. and discussed this with their client.

CHAPTER 10

LEGAL AID AND ALTERNATIVE LEGAL SERVICES

If the Rule of Law states that everyone should be equal before the law then, arguably, this implies that everyone should have equal access to the law and to justice. This means, broadly: being able to make full use of legal rights, through adequate legal services, *i.e.* advice, assistance and representation, regardless of means; also, the ability to make full use of the court structure and rights of appeal.

Those issues are dealt with in this chapter and above, in relation to the adversarial process (for example, *Civil Justice Review*).

1. LEGAL AID

This phrase has two meanings. *Generally*: state funded legal representation, advice and assistance, carried out by a barrister or solicitor. *More specifically*: representation and ancillary work (for example, preparation). *Legal advice and assistance* falls under "legal aid" but refers to all help falling short of representation: advice, letter writing, telephone calls, etc., and assistance by way of representation (ABWOR).

Here, I describe the legal aid system in the context of a critical analysis of the Legal Aid Act 1988 and developments since 1988. *Access to justice issues are:* Does the legal aid scheme leave gaps in the population served or type of service provided? Why do people not make enough use of existing services? Are practitioners geared to providing the services needed?

BACKGROUND TO THE 1988 ACT

Civil and criminal legal aid schemes were developed post war, the former administered by the Law Society and the latter by the courts.

Legal advice and assistance, under the "green form scheme" was added by the Legal Advice and Assistance Act 1972. The Legal Aid Act 1974 consolidated and later statutes expanded provision. The 1988 Act is a major shift away from the post-war model but, in some aspects, makes no change.

THE LEGAL AID ACT 1988

The *purpose* of the statute is outlined in section 1, to establish a new "framework" for publicly funded advice, assistance and representation "with a view to helping persons who might otherwise be unable to obtain (it) on account of their means". The Act was hailed as "a Trojan horse" by the Law Society because it provided only a framework, giving the Lord Chancellor broad rule-making powers.

The Legal Aid Board (s.3)

The Legal Aid Board (L.A.B.) administers legal aid, replacing the function of the Law Society, as the government's *Efficiency Scrutiny Report* (1986) thought it undesirable that the profession, remunerated by legal aid funds, should hold the purse-strings. Within weeks of its appointment, the Board reorganised the 15 legal aid area committees into five groups and massively cut administrative staff.

The Board's powers (s.4)

The Board may consider and advise the Lord Chancellor on legal services policy. To this end, it both responds to his requests for advice and initiates its own investigations. In the first category, it has produced consultation papers on "franchises" for "green form" legal advice and on multi-party actions, and, in 1995 it published its response to the Lord Chancellor's green paper on legal aid. In the second category, it has published one on the duty solicitor scheme and one on criminal legal aid.

Its franchising proposals have proved highly controversial. The Board was given wide powers to "*contract out*" the provision of certain legal services to "persons or bodies" (other than lawyers in private practice). For example, the function of giving advice on housing or welfare benefits might be "contracted out" to a Citizens Advice Bureau or law centre. The government's white paper, which proposed the Act, *Legal Aid in England and Wales: A New Framework* (1987), said that, once this was done, such topics would be removed from the "green form" scheme. This was opposed by the Marre Committee (1988). A parallel suggestion was that delivery of certain legal services be opened up to "competitive tendering" between solicitors and others. The Law Society predicted it could cause confusion, as clients, approaching a solicitor for advice on two topics, would be told they could be advised on only one. They also feared a reduction in consumer choice with long queues to see few advisers.

Aware of hostility from solicitors which has continued throughout the 1990s, the Board adopted the notion of "franchising" as less provocative than these alternatives. The Board offers fixed term, renewable contracts to franchisees to deliver legal services under certain categories, for example, family, housing, employment, welfare, immigration, personal injury. Franchisees are empowered to deter-mine all green form and ABWOR applications but must satisfy certain requirements, such as independence, an effective management infra-structure, non-discrimination, expertise in welfare benefits, an adequate library and efficiency in keeping clients informed. The Board was proposing that applications would only be granted to firms or agencies with a minimum gross turnover of £40,000 in legal aid fees but this requirement was dropped, as their own and Law Society research indicated that, in some localities, no one could satisfy this criterion. The Board has granted about 1,300 franchises, by 1996. It is currently experimenting (1996) in granting franchises to non-solicitor agencies (*e.g.* Citizens Advice Bureaux). In 1995, to encourage franchising, the Lord Chancellor rewarded franchised legal aid providers with a higher increase in fees than other providers. He repeated this differential fee increase in 1996 and has been condemned as bribing solicitors to become franchised. The Law Society originally threatened to boycott any scheme of franchising but are now prepared to countenance it, providing it is on satisfactory terms. They were not satisfied with the terms offered until 1994.

The Board has power to *make grants and loans*, which has enabled it to take over the funding of eight law centres, although the Law Society failed to amend the Bill to provide for specific funding for them.

The Board may propose to the Lord Chancellor that its *functions be extended*. In debate, he said this "will provide an opportunity for some rigorous and adventurous thinking".

The Board's duties (s.5)

They must *report annually* to the Lord Chancellor. The Law Society proposed a (failed) amendment that this should contain statistics of the percentage of households currently eligible for legal aid. This reflects an anxiety that the Government, in economising, is reducing this percentage. The Law Society continues to complain that eligibility is declining and they and the Legal Action Group commissioned statistical research which showed that, by 1990, only 47 per cent of adults were eligible for legal aid in general cases and 52 per cent in personal injury cases, even after the Lord Chancellor's relaxation of the means test for aid in personal injury actions and rules permitting child personal injury litigants to be independently means-tested.

Advice and assistance (Part III)

This part gives the Lord Chancellor wide powers but, for the time being, he will preserve the *green form scheme*, under which advice and assistance, up to a certain limit (two hours' worth, or three hours' worth in matrimonial cases) is mostly given by solicitors in private practice, after they have conducted a means test on the client. Contributions are payable above a certain level of disposable income and capital, according to a sliding scale, which makes allowance for dependants. The means tests for civil and criminal legal aid (described below) follow the same pattern but with different monetary limits. As these are updated annually, they are not published here. Readers should consult the *Law Society's Gazette* or the Legal Action Group (L.A.G). *Bulletin* for details of current rates.

The Lord Chancellor may provide for free green form advice. This power is currently used to provide advice under the duty solicitor scheme, for example. He may also exclude certain topics from the green form scheme and he has used this power to exclude wills and conveyancing, with certain exceptions, from green form advice.

Research by Baldwin and Hill, for the Lord Chancellor's Department (1988) N.L.J. 631, 644), concluded that the green form scheme was a "crucial element in publicly funded legal services". Their report is repeatedly cited by solicitors in defence of the scheme and against franchising.

The Act preserves the notorious *statutory charge* on advice and assistance (s.11) and civil legal aid (s.16), under which the cost of legal aid can be recovered from an assisted person, over and above her contribution, from any property or costs recovered. This may destroy the benefit of litigation and critics have long sought its abolition.

The Act also preserves another heavily criticised power, which can *penalise unassisted parties* who litigate successfully against a legally aided opponent. Costs may only be awarded against the legally aided party if she instituted proceedings *and* the court is satisfied the unassisted party would otherwise suffer severe financial hardship *and* if it is just and equitable that she should recover costs from public funds (ss.13 and 18). Lord Denning M.R. called this rule "the ugly, unacceptable face of British justice", in *Thew v. Reeves* (C.A. 1981).

ABWOR (assistance by way of representation) appeared in the Legal Aid Act 1979. The Lord Chancellor introduced it for domestic cases, in magistrates' courts and extended it, in 1982, to Mental Health Review Tribunals.

Civil legal aid (Part IV)

The Lord Chancellor has power (s.14) to extend or restrict the categories of court or tribunal for which legal aid is available and

Schedule 2 lists them and lists exclusions: for example, relator actions and defamation proceedings. The R.C.L.S. thought the latter could cause injustice.

Legal aid is currently provided for *only five tribunal systems*, the Employment Appeal Tribunal, Lands Tribunal, Commons Commissioners, Mental Health Review Tribunals and Restrictive Practices Court. Critics have long argued that legal aid should be available before all tribunals and research suggests that representation enhances the litigant's chances of success. The policy behind exclusion was, originally, an attempt to keep tribunals informal, by discouraging lawyers. Lawyers nevertheless do appear, for those who can afford them, and some tribunals have become very legalistic.

The Law Society, the R.C.L.S. (1979) and the Marre Committee all recommended an extension of legal aid in tribunals. Nevertheless, in the white paper, the government expressed a present intention not to do this. Instead, procedure should be simplified and research completed on the efficacy of representation. (This was published in 1989.) The 1995 green paper (see below) announced, to the delight of the legal profession, that the government intended to conduct a pilot study to see whether legal aid should be available for tribunal representation.

Another gap in the provision of civil legal aid is that it is not automatically available for *appeals to the House of Lords*, as it is in criminal appeals (where the prosecutor appeals, s.21). Arguably, the state should pay for House of Lords appeals as their opinions are as crucial in developing the law as the work of Parliament.

Under section 14, the Lord Chancellor can extend provision of legal aid, in terms of the applicant's capacity. The Law Society has urged that this power be used to permit *legal aid for class actions* or groups. The Lord Chancellor is still concerned with the issue of how to fund group actions, for example, on medical negligence and disasters, and he required the Legal Aid Board to produce its consultation paper on "multi-party actions" (1989). The 1995 green paper suggests several different alternatives for dealing with multi-party actions, and other very high cost cases, which would come out of a special budget.

The Lord Chancellor retains power to stipulate means and merits tests (s.15). On *merits*, statute requires that the applicant satisfies the Board that he has reasonable grounds for taking or defending proceedings not more appropriately dealt with by ABWOR. In practice, the granting committees scrutinise the "cost efficiency" of the action and decide whether they would advise an unassisted client to risk his own money.

On the *means test* the *Efficiency Scrutiny Report* recommended a flexible upper income limit. The classic criticism of the means test is that the upper income limit, above which a person is disentitled to legal aid, is unfair, depriving even well-off people of access to justice in very expensive cases.

The Act introduced a heavily criticised power to recoup *contributions* throughout the period of representation, rather than for the previous 12 months limit (s.16). Critics said this would encourage the assisted party's opponent to prolong litigation, to induce a settlement.

Criminal legal aid

This is subject to a different *means* test. Contributions, on a sliding scale, are mandatory. *Justices' clerks* could grant legal aid, prior to 1989. In practice, this meant a court clerk. The white paper promised new regulations permitting them to refuse it and these were passed in 1989.

The availability of criminal legal aid in the Crown Court causes little concern, since about 97 per cent of defendants there are aided. Problems arise in magistrates' courts where diverse policies are exercised by clerks and their Benches. The Legal Action Group in its *Bulletin* regularly publishes legal aid "league tables" showing differences in the rate of grant from court to court (for example in 1990, Kingston granted only 72 per cent of applications while Harrogate granted over 99 per cent).

The reason for these discrepancies is that the *merits test* for criminal legal aid, retained by section 21, is open to subjectively different interpretations: "Representation may be granted where it appears ... desirable to do so in the interests of justice." This test has been applied in accordance with "the Widgery criteria", guidelines devised in 1966. These criteria, despite criticism (for example by the R.C.L.S.), are incorporated, in slightly modified form, in statute (s.22), requiring the court to take account of the following factors:

(a) likelihood of a sentence depriving the accused of liberty or livelihood, or serious damage to reputation;
(b) substantial question of law;
(c) inability of understanding;
(d) the nature of the defence involves tracing and interviewing witnesses or expert cross-examination;
(e) a third-party interest in the accused's being represented.

The criteria are open to highly subjective and differing interpretations, from one justices' clerk to another. (It is essentially the clerks who develop legal aid distribution policy as this "grass roots" level.) In 1983, the Lord Chancellor's Department said it was studying ways of securing consistency between courts. The Legal Aid Board has published national guidelines. The 1995 green paper (see below) was heavily critical of the way magistrates' courts administer the tests for granting legal aid.

Lawyers' remuneration

The Lord Chancellor retains the power to fix fees by regulation (s.34).

The Act abandons the principle of "fair and reasonable remuneration" for work done, in favour of standard fees, as proposed by the white paper. The Lord Chancellor must consult the profession before fixing fees. He argues that standard fees will speed payments and improve solicitors' cash-flow.

The profession distrust the Lord Chancellor to fix fair rates. Both sides complained of poor pay for criminal work throughout the 1980s. The Law Society argued, in 1988, that firms are giving up legally aided work. Lord Mackay claimed the opposite and asked the Law Society to provide evidence and both sides have repeated their claims ever since. Lawyers point out that legal aid fee levels have not been kept up with inflation and that, in performing certain legally aided services, they are actually making a significant loss.

The profession criticised the white paper plans and Act as a

government cost-cutting exercise. Indeed, the Explanatory and Financial Memorandum in the Bill claimed it would save £10 million a year.

THE RISING COST OF LEGAL AID: ANOTHER LORD CHANCELLOR'S REVIEW

In the autumn of 1990, the Lord Chancellor made several speeches
signalling his concern over the rising cost of legal aid. He pointed to the
gross cost of legal aid, £715 million, which had doubled in five years,
and warned that the legal aid fund was not to be regarded as a "blank
cheque". Critics soon responded that the net cost was £560 million
because of the fund's receipts from contributions and the statutory
charge, not to mention VAT, but they acknowledged that even the net
cost had doubled in five years. Lawyers were swift to point out that
they were not profiting unduly from this increase, especially as their
fees had not been kept up with inflation. For instance, both the Legal
Action Group and the Law Society attributed the spiralling cost to
government policy and social trends. PACE 1984 introduced the free
24-hour duty solicitor scheme. Recorded crime has increased and more
people are brought to court.

To annoy legal aid practitioners further, the Legal Aid Board, in its
1991 report, complained of the rising unit cost of the average criminal
legally aided case in the magistrates' court, blaming the increase on
declining productivity of lawyers and the courts. The Board's research
indicated that there were longer waiting times and that cases took
longer and received more attention from solicitors, on average.

In the meantime, the Lord Chancellor established a three-year
review of eligibility for civil legal aid, which published a consultation
paper in June 1991. It set out five major alternatives to the current
system: the litigant's own resources, bank loans, contingency fees (the
subject of another consultation paper), compulsory legal expenses
insurance, and the option most discussed by the Lord Chancellor: the
"safety net". Under this last alternative, the litigant pays for the cost of
his case up to £2–3,000, before legal aid takes over. The obvious
problem here is the unpredictable costs of the other side, should the
litigant prove unsuccessful, and the fact that the system is likely to put
off impecunious litigants, even with meritorious cases.

In his 1990–96 speeches, the Lord Chancellor demonstrated that he is also keen to question the very need for litigation and traditional forms of dispute resolution. He had a working group on ADR, for instance and his 1996 Family Law Bill promotes mediation in family breakdowns.

CURRENT CRITICISMS

Apart from the ongoing concern about eligibility levels, remuneration, franchising, the distribution of criminal legal aid and the lack of aid in tribunals, the Lord Chancellor invoked further wrath from the legal profession when, in 1991, he withdrew green form legal aid from refugees seeking asylum. The charities who were expected to provide advice, instead of solicitors, boycotted this work.

2. ALTERNATIVE LEGAL SERVICES

The traditional pattern for the provision of legal services, through the medium of the solicitor and/or barrister in private practice, paid for by the client, or by the statutory legal aid scheme, is only part of the picture. Because of gaps left by the traditional pattern, "unmet legal need" is generated and alternative services have been developed to try to meet it.

UNMET NEED FOR LEGAL SERVICES

This means individuals or groups have problems which are amenable to a legal solution but which do not receive one. The Marre Report identified the biggest area of unmet need as for advice on social welfare law, including housing, immigration and debt, particularly in rural areas, parts of London and Northern and Midland conurbations.

Causes

These have been identified by many pieces of research:

1. The creation of new categories of legal rights, without the funding to enforce them.
2. People may not realise they have a legal problem. For instance, they may be in dispute with a landlord or local authority and not know that a lawyer could help. Sometimes, professional advisers, such as social workers, may not recommend legal help because they to have failed to identify the problem as legal or because of traditional antipathy between the two professions.
3. Poverty: fear of high lawyers' fees; ignorance of the legal aid scheme.
4. Fear of authority: suspicion and fear of the Establishment, including lawyers; intimidation by legal jargon.
5. Inaccessibility of lawyers: solicitors open up offices in commercial centres of towns, rather than the outskirts or the country and they predominate in rich areas, for example the Royal Commission on Legal Services, 1979 found one solicitor's office per 2,000 people in Bournemouth but only one per 66,000 in Huyton.
6. Lawyers' training has traditionally concentrated on lucrative business, for example revenue, company, commercial, conveyancing, property, not welfare law, and this is reflected in the subjects law students choose to study.

LAW CENTRES

These are staffed by salaried solicitors, articled clerks and non-legally qualified experts, sometimes called "para-legals". They are financed by local or central government or charity and receipts from legally aided work, or a mixture (see below). They are established in poor areas (now about 57) and develop a "shop front" image to attract clients and combat feat of lawyers. They are run by management committes and represented by the Law Centres Federation which provides a co-ordinating and political function and training.

History. The Rushclife Committee recommended a nationwide network of state salaried lawyers providing advice for a low, fixed fee. This was provided for in the Legal Aid Act 1949 but never implemented.

Reformers in the 1970s, especially Labour lawyers, sought to copy the neighbourhood law centres that were developing in the United States, with state salaried lawyers dispensing advice on poverty law.

The first law centre was established in North Kensington, amidst great opposition from the Law Society. They established a barrier to solicitors practising in law centres. To gain a practising certificate, they need a "waiver" of professional restrictive rules. To this, the Society attaches a condition forbidding them from working on a list of legal topics, usually comprising: conveyancing, company, commercial, probate, divorce, personal injury and adult crime.

Since 1970, the Society has reversed its stance on law centres and now fully supports them. It has learned through experience that local firms benefit from the existence of a law centre in the vicinity by referrals of clients it cannot or will not deal with.

Work. Apart from individual casework, such as tribunal representation, some centres prefer working for groups, not individuals, since an individual problem may be symptomatic of a more widespread one, for example local authority tenants against their landlord, women's groups and ethnic minority groups.

As well as providing legal services, law centres see their role as educative and campaigning (for example, against individual targets and for law reform). They visit schools and community groups to educate on legal rights.

Problems. Apart from a high turnover of staff and generally a larger clientele than they can deal with, law centres have always suffered vulnerable funding. Both central and local government funding is subject to political change and several law centres have closed when funds have dried up, sometimes reopening. Often, they run on short-term grants from central or local government and/or charity plus legal aid earnings and there are always some who do not know where their next year's budget is coming from. All this is exacerbated by the fact that the law centre may find itself campaigning against the hand that feeds it, *i.e.* central or local government.

The R.C.L.S. recommended a nationwide network of centres, funded by government and administered by a quango but the government stated, in 1985, that they viewed demands for funding for law centres as a local matter and this had recently been reiterated. The Lord Chancellor has permitted the Legal Aid Board to take over grant aid to eight law centres receiving government funds but has made it clear that this must not be extended. He has commissioned the L.A.B. to examine law centre funding and they are currently suggesting that their experiment in funding non-solicitor agencies by franchising (due to be completed in 1996) should be extended to the franchising of law centres.

OTHER ALTERNATIVE LEGAL SERVICES

Legal Advice Centres

Legal Advice Centres, of which the Efficiencey Scrutiny identified about 600, are sometimes attached to Citizen's Advice Bureaux, universities or polytechnics. Lawyers give free advice, often in the evenings. If the client needs more, he may be referred to a solicitor.

Citizens Advice Bureaux

Citizens Advice Bureaux (C.A.B.) are much favoured by the R.C.L.S. and the present government. The R.C.L.S. found that half their client problems had a legal content and their workers are well trained in identifying legal problems. Some Bureau workers represent people in tribunals and small claims.

Trade Unions

The R.C.L.S. found about half responding unions had legal departments to advise members.

Community groups, campaigning interest groups and advice centres

For example, housing advice centres, MIND, the Child Poverty Action Group, the Automobile Association, all provide legal advice and sometimes fund legal representation for their members/clients.

The five-pound fixed-fee interview

Under this scheme, volunteering solicitors provide half-an-hour's diagnostic advice for five pounds. Very few people have heard of it, however. Baldwin and Hill, in research funded by the L.C.D., found "scarcely any" of the solicitors they interviewed regarded the scheme "as of any real importance at all", [1988] N.L.J. 344.

ALAS! In 1987, the Law Society introduced this scheme, under which volunteer solicitors offer free initial interviews to accident victims. Baldwin and Hill favoured extending it to other legal problems.

OTHER IMPROVEMENTS IN ACCESS TO JUSTICE

Duty solicitor schemes. By 1982, there were schemes in 130 magistrates' courts, organised by local solicitors. Following R.C.L.S. recommendations, the Legal Aid Act 1982 provided for a national scheme.

The Police and Criminal Evidence Act 1984 provided for national scheme in police stations, activated in late 1986. Under both, advice is given free and funding, supervision and policy development are by the Legal Aid Board.

Following a heavily criticial research report in 1990 by Bridges and Sanders, which disclosed a reluctance on the part of duty solicitors to attend police stations, the Board tightened up the scheme's obligations on solicitors. Generally speaking, they must now offer initial telephone advice and attend in specified circumstances. Since 1996, para-legals giving advice under the duty solicitor scheme must be adequately trained and certified competent. Given the poor rates of legal aid remuneration and the unsocial hours involved, some solicitors say it is not surprising that research shows that detained suspects receive inadequate legal advice.

MARRE RECOMMENDATIONS

1. To counteract low public awareness, lawyers should promote public education, public relations and informative advertising.
2. To overcome the public's fear of lawyers, they should develop an approachable, "shop-front" image, use interpreters and encourage ethnic minority practitioners.
3. Client dissatisfaction should be countered by reducing delay, using management training and keeping clients better informed.
4. Lawyers' services should be made more available by expanding the green form scheme to telephone and postal advice in rural areas, etc.

CIVIL JUSTICE REVIEW RECOMMENDATIONS

The outcomes are contained in brackets.

1. Judicial interventionism where parties are unrepresented. (CLSA, s.6 provides rule-making power: see above.)

2. A statutory right to lay representatives in minor county court cases. (CLSA, s.11.)
3. Redesigning of explanatory leaflets. (New leaflets have been given the "crystal award" for clarity, by the Plain English Campaign.)
4. More assistance from court staff.
5. Closer links between courts and advice agencies.
6. Experiments with evening and written adjudications.
7. Reconsideration of contingency fees (the system whereby the lawyer acts for a share of the damages recovered, prohibited as unethical, as it encourages "ambulance-chasing", for example approaches to victims of well-known disasters like the Zeebrugge Ferry and Bhopal disasters). (The Lord Chancellor issued a consultation paper in 1991 (see above) and has since used his powers under the CLSA 1990, s.58 to permit conditional fees, allowing an "uplift" of up to 100 per cent on the fee, where lawyers win the case. Solicitors are now entitled, since 1995, to act on a "no win, no fee" basis but few have, so far, taken advantage of this opportunity, although it is permissible in human rights, insolvency and medical negligence cases.)

3. THE LEGAL SERVICES REFORMS OF 1995–96

The 1980s and 1990s have seen a phenomenal increase in the cost of legal aid: annual growth in expenditure of 17.5 per cent during the period 1985–95. This has not, however, been accompanied by better access to legal services: during the same period, eligibility rates fell from 70 per cent of households to about 50 per cent. The Lord Chancellor became increasingly concerned over this and published a green paper, in 1995, *Legal Aid—Targeting Need*, which invited a complete rethink of the funding and delivery of legal services, challenging the traditional model of delivery via lawyers in private practice. Below, I summarise the Government's concerns over the old scheme and their main proposals for change:

Concerns

1. The old scheme "encourages a system of lawyer led services, and delivers what lawyers are best able to supply .... The solicitor has more information about the cases he or she is pursuing, and is therefore able to run the case in the way most suiting his or her aims. This is often not the way that either the client or the Legal Aid Board would choose to run the case if they had the choice."

2. The existing scheme does not encourage value for money or control expenditure.

3. The scheme is fragmented inefficiently into five types of legal aid.

Proposals

4. Suppliers of legal services would work under a system of block contracts. A predetermined budget would replace the open-ended expenditure which has allowed the cost of legal aid to spiral.

5. Government proposed priorities for legal aid would require parliamentary approval.

6. Contracts could be granted, by the Legal Aid Board, for advice and assistance and representation or a combination. Contracts would be for certain types of work, such as criminal, or family, or social welfare, depending on the need for legal services in any particular area. The Legal Aid Board would check that suppliers were fulfilling the terms of the contract and cases being handled cost effectively and in the way best suited to the needs of the client.

7. Only suppliers meeting quality standards would be allowed to offer legally aided services, as opposed to the former system, wherein any solicitor could work, unchecked, under the legal aid scheme.

8. Non-solicitor agencies, such as Citizens' Advice Bureaux and Law Centres, could receive block contracts for the provision of

advice on social welfare law (housing, immigration, employment, debt and welfare benefits).

9. Since the Government is promoting mediation in divorce, contracts would be granted to mediation suppliers.

10. The Legal Aid Board would keep a central budget for exceptionally high cost cases.

The Legal Aid Board published a response to the green paper, in November 1995. It agreed with many of the proposals, such as block grants and quality control, which it saw as extending the franchising system. It warned, however, that criminal legal aid could not be restricted to a pre-determined budget, since, if funds ran out and defendants in criminal cases were refused legal aid, the Government could fall foul of the European Convention on Human Rights.

The Government will finalise its plans for reform and publish them as a white paper, with a draft Bill attached, sometime during the course of 1996.

CHAPTER 11

SOURCES OF ENGLISH LAW

1. ORIGINS

In everyday conversation it is quite common to hear someone say "You can't do that, it's against the law." One example is where a car driver slows down on entering a village because of the 30 miles per hour speed limit signs. If asked why she has slowed down she would doubtless point to the speed limit signs and explain that she does not want to be fined for breaking the law indicated by those signs. This is, of course, quite correct, but this approach is that of the layperson; the lawyer pursues the matter a stage further by seeking to know the origin of the law. She would require to know the authority for the making of that law and then would go on to examine the conditions which have to be fulfilled before the law comes into force. For example, the lawyer would want to know exactly the form and colour which the signs must take, so as to be sure that the particular ones in question are effective, because unless they comply with the regulations, then it is not a breach of law not to comply with them. Similarly she would examine the procedure which had been followed involving the making of the order by the Highway Authority, and its submission to, and approval by, the Minister of Transport, to see that all the formalities had been complied with. This is because any failure in the procedural formalities would invalidate the order, and thus exceeding the limits specified would not be an offence. It can be seen that the lawyer's approach is a technical approach; in seeking to be satisfied of the authenticity of a law she is inevitably concerning herself with the sources, or origins of the law, which is the subject-matter of this chapter.

By the word "sources", in this context, is meant the various ways in which law in the English legal system can come into being, and will be recognised and given effect in the English courts. It is not always a simple matter to know whether some particular conduct is a breach of the law or not.

At the present time the main sources of law reflect the complexity of modern society. Most new law is produced by delegated legislation, its source being either E.C. law or an Act of Parliament, but an equally important source of the law is the decisions of the judges in cases forming precedents in the higher courts, because the judge in each case is stating what the law is in the circumstances of the particular case and so, in effect, making new law. The practical effectiveness of legislation depends on its being published. Equally, the importance of case decisions by judges can only be of practical value if there is a full system of law reporting, with the law reports being published immediately following the decision and being made easily accessible to lawyers and other interested parties.

The major problem with these two sources today is not accessibility so much as the tremendous bulk of law being produced; more and more the maxim that "everyone is presumed to know the law" is demonstrably false. It is increasingly the case that the lawyer has to specialise in a particular branch or branches of the law in order to keep pace with developments. Indeed, a 1990 Law Society Survey showed that most solicitors now consider themselves to be specialists. Outside a special field of knowledge the lawyer is likely to flounder nearly as badly as the lay person. The only difference will be that the lawyer by training will know where to look for the law, if it proves necessary to pursue a legal point outside that field, whereas the lay person will not.

The other accepted sources of law in the English legal system are custom and books of authority; neither of which is fractionally as important today as legislation and case law. Custom was significant in the development of substantive law. This is because law, as it is first established, is derived from custom. Books of authority fall into a different category, mainly serving to elucidate legal points of difficulty in cases, either by reference to textbooks stating the law as it was, or from more recent academic treatises or articles.

Each of these sources of law will now be considered in detail.

2. LEGISLATION

GENERAL

Much new law is made in documentary form by way of an Act of Parliament. In the British constitution, a fundamental doctrine is that of Parliamentary sovereignty which recognises that supreme power is vested in Parliament and that there is no limit in law to the lawmaking capacity of that institution. This is now massively tempered by membership of the E.C. Nevertheless, unless it conflicts with E.C. law, what Parliament passes in the form of an Act will be put into effect by the courts.

This acceptance by the courts of Parliamentary supremacy is entirely a matter of history derived directly from the seventeenth century conflict between the Stuart Kings and Parliament. In that conflict, the courts took the side of Parliament and one result of their joint success was that, thereafter, the courts have been prepared to acknowledge the supremacy of Parliament within its own sphere, whilst Parliament has readily allowed the independence of the judiciary to become an acknowledged factor in the constitution. The contrast with the American system and other systems with a written constitution is, however, very marked in that in America the Supreme Court does have the power to overrule legislation as being "unconstitutional". No such power exists in the English legal system. So far as the English courts are concerned, an Act of Parliament, which has been given Royal Assent and placed on the Parliamentary roll, is the law and, provided it does not contravene E.C. law, must be given effect. In *British Railways Board v. Pickin* (1974) an attempt was made to persuade the court to intervene, on the grounds that the Board had obtained powers in a private Act of Parliament by misleading Parliament. The Court of Appeal (Civil Division) was sympathetic to the complainant but on appeal the House of Lords refused to contemplate intervention, holding that the complaint was entirely a matter for Parliament. The only role of the courts in relation to legislation which manifests no conflict with European Community law, is to "interpret" the statutory provisions to the circumstances of any

185

given case. Just how this task of interpretation is approached is examined below.

THE QUEEN IN PARLIAMENT

First, however, it is essential that some brief explanation of the institution "Parliament" should be attempted; once this has been done, the documentary form of an Act of Parliament will be examined and thereafter the work of the judges in interpretation will be considered.

An examination of E.C. sources of law and its assimilation into United Kingdom law properly belongs here but, as it is a large topic, it deserves a separate chapter.

Parliament is made up of three constitutent elements: the monarch, the House of Lords and the House of Commons. An Act of Parliament will thus in normal circumstances have the approval of all three elements but it is possible, although it happens very rarely, that an Act of Parliament can be passed without the approval of the House of Lords, under the Parliament Acts. This occurred in 1991 with the War Crimes Act. The monarch's place in Parliament has long become a formality. Despite the splendour of the throne in the House of Lords and the Queen's Robing Room and the Royal Gallery, the only occasion on which the monarch plays any part in the proceedings of Parliament is when she attends the opening of a new session of Parliament. At this ceremony the Queen, after making a formal entrance, reads the speech from the throne, which is the Government's statement of its legislative proposals for the coming session of Parliament. The speech is drawn up by the Prime Minister and her or his colleagues and does not in any way reflect the personal views of the monarch. The other activity of Parliament with which the Queen is concerned is the requirement that all legislation must receive the Royal Assent before it becomes law. The Royal Assent has not been refused since the reign of Queen Anne in 1707 and it is safe to say that it will never be refused, such is the strength of the constitutional convention that the monarchy does not interfere in politics.

The House of Lords is composed mainly of hereditary peers and the far more politically active life peers (as well as bishops, Law Lords, etc.). Originally the senior house, made up of persons who advised the monarch, it has in this century suffered a major diminution in its powers. By the Parliament Acts 1911 and 1949, the previous veto of the House of Lords over all legislation has been replaced by a one-year delaying power over public Bills, other than financial measures where there is no delaying power at all. Allowing for this lack of power, the House of Lords continues to play a useful role in the consideration of Bills, by ensuring that the form of a Bill stands up to detailed scrutiny. It also serves as a debating chamber of national significance, and legislation of a technical and comparatively non-controversial kind can be introduced there. This has occurred with increasing frequency in recent years.

From being in its origin the least important part of Parliament, the House of Commons, now made up of 650 democratically elected members, has become the most important element. The Prime Minister is always now drawn from the Commons, and the vast majority of government Ministers have seats there. Since the House of Lords has little more than a delaying power over legislation and in practice this is used very rarely, and as the monarch's role is a formal one, it can be seen that the majority party in the House of Commons can make law almost as it wishes. This power is, of course, controlled by the pressure of public opinion expressed through the press, radio and television and also by the views of members, both inside and outside Parliament, of the majority party itself. Nevertheless, the lack of a written constitution has, it is said, allowed for the concentration of power into the hands of the Cabinet and, in particular, the Prime Minister. Effectively, most legislation emanates from Cabinet proposals. Some have called this an "elective dictatorship".

PROCEDURE

In order for a legislative measure to become an Act of Parliament and to be recognised as such by the judges, it has to undergo one of several procedures. This process involves the measure being drafted in the appropriate legal terminology, usually by Parliamentary counsel to the Treasury employed full-time as civil servants, and then presented in the House of Commons, or possibly the House of Lords, as a Bill. In the case of a government Bill, the various clauses of the Bill will have been agreed by the department which has instructed Parliamentary counsel to draft the Bill.

Before the Bill becomes an Act of Parliament, and the clauses become sections, it must undergo five stages in each House. These are—First Reading; Second Reading; Committee Stage; Report Stage; Third Reading. The first reading is a formality: the second reading takes the form of a debate on the general principles of the measure; the committee stage sees the Bill examined in detail, clause by clause; the report stage brings the House up to date with the changes which have taken place in the Bill at the committee stage; and the third reading allows for verbal changes only. These five stages can be taken very quickly, although in the normal way they will be spread over a period of weeks or even months. Much depends on the nature and length of the Bill, and how politically controversial it is.

Once the Bill with any amendments has been approved both by the House of Commons and the House of Lords, it needs only the Royal Assent to become an Act of Parliament. Usually a number of Bills receive the Royal Assent individually through Lords Commissioners authorised expressly by the Queen. The result is that every Act of Parliament begins: "Be it enacted by the Queen's most Excellent Majesty, by and with the device and consent of the Lords Spiritual and Temporal, and Commons, and this present Parliament assembled, and by the authority of the same, as follows:—" If, as rarely happens, an Act is passed without the consent of the Lords, the phrase referring to the consent of the Lords Spiritual and Temporal is omitted.

The Act of Parliament comes into effect when the Royal Assent is given, unless the Act contains its own starting date, or it has a provision which allows different parts of the Act to be brought into force at different times, by a Minister making a statutory instrument to that effect. For instance, parts of the Criminal Justice and Public Order Act 1994 are being brought into force during 1995, 1996 and 1997.

THE FORM OF AN ACT OF PARLIAMENT

Language

Because an Act of Parliament creates new law, the language in which it is expressed must be precise in the extreme; in addition, the provisions of every Act must be related to any existing legislation on the same subject. These factors combine to cause legislation to be most complicated and notoriously difficulty for the lay person to understand.

Although the earliest statutes were produced in Latin and French, the change to English took place in the reign of Henry VII and, whereas in earlier centuries statutes had long titles and often a lengthy preamble, since the Short Titles Act 1896, Acts of Parliament have been given a short title and preambles have become the exception.

Citation

The method of citing an Act of Parliament is now governed by the Acts of Parliament Numbering and Citation Act 1962. This Act stipulates that from 1963 every Act is to be given a chapter number for the year in which it receives the Royal Assent. This abolishes the centuries-old system by which Acts were given a chapter number for the session of the parliament in question designated by the regal year of the monarch. This system could produce difficulties as in 1937 which under the former system would be cited as "1 Edw. 8 and 1 Geo. 6." The present system is to refer to an Act by its short title and chapter number for the year in question: for example—The Criminal Appeal Act 1995 (c. 35).

The publication of an Act of Parliament is, under present circumstances, a matter for the Queen's Printer in the form of the Controller of Her Majesty's Stationery Office. From August 1996, it is planned that H.M.S.O.'s status will change and its replacement, under private ownership, will be renamed. At the time of writing, June 1996, it is planned that Acts will be printed and published by this privatised organisation in the same way as by H.M.S.O. but all other details are yet to be finalised. When the Royal Assent has been given, the Queen's Printer has two vellum prints prepared and authenticated by the proper officers of each House, and one is deposited at the House of Lords and the other in the Public Records Office. In practice, H.M.S.O. makes new legislation available for sale to the public as soon as it has been given the Royal Assent. It also publishes annually a collection of the statutes for the year.

Public Bills and Private Bills

A Public Bill is legislation which affects the public at large, and applies throughout England and Wales.

A Private Bill is legislation which affects a limited section of the population, either by reference to locality or by reference to a particular family or group of individuals. These are known respectively as Local and Personal Bills.

A Private Member's Bill is a Public Bill introduced by a back-bench Member of Parliament, as opposed to Public Bills which are usually government sponsored and introduced by the responsible minister.

Consolidation, Codification and Statute Law Revision

Consolidation is the process by which provisions in a number of Acts of Parliament are brought together and re-enacted in one Act. It is not a method for changing the law but it does make the law easier to find. In order to ease the passage of such measures Parliament passed the Consolidation of Enactments (Procedure) Act 1949 and this enables the Lord Chancellor to submit to a joint committee of Parliament a memorandum showing how the new Act proposes to incorporate the existing statutory provisions. If the joint committee is satisfied and recommends acceptance, the new Act should pass the necessary stages in both Houses without undue delay and without a long debate. The procedure is now much used and every year several such Acts find their way on to the Statute Book. In 1996, for example, the legislation concerning arbitration was consolidated in the Arbitration Act 1996.

Codification is the term used for an Act of Parliament which brings together all the existing legislation and case law and forms a complete restatement of the law. It can involve changes in the law and is thus one method of law reform. For this reason there is no simplified parliamentary procedure. The Arbitration Act also falls into this category, since it codifies principles derived from the case law on arbitration.

The Law Commission, which was set up under the Law Commissions Act 1965, has, as one of its responsibilities, to keep under review all the law with a view to its systematic development and reform including, in particular, the codification of the law. It is consequently working at the present time on possible legislation which will, at some future time, codify particular branches of the law.

Statute law revision is the procedure under which obsolete provisions in statutes are repealed and legislation is kept up to date. This is now a matter for the Law Commission which has overall responsibility for advising the repeal of obsolete and unnecessary enactments. Since 1993/94, a Special Public Bill Committee "fast-track" procedure has been used for legislation proposed by the Law Commission and other non-contentious Bills. This "Jellicoe procedure" employs a committee of specialists (*e.g.* judges and lawyers on The Arbitration Bill 1996) instead of a committee of the whole House. The Lord Chancellor's ill-fated Domestic Violence Bill 1995 was supposed to be one such Bill. Unfortunately, it proved to be very controversial and was lost.

DELEGATED LEGISLATION

This is the name given to law made in documentary form by subordinate authorities acting under law-making powers delegated by Parliament or the sovereign, acting under her prerogative. Such legislation can take the following forms:

Orders in Council

Parliament sometimes permits the government through Her Majesty in Council to make law by way of an Order in Council. This is particularly true where an emergency is imminent; for example, under the Emergency Powers Act 1920 the Crown can, in the stated circumstances, by Proclamation declare a state of emergency. The Crown can then by Order in Council issue regulations for securing the essentials of life to the community. Orders in Council are sometimes issued under a prerogative power, as was the Order in Council concerned in the case of *C.C.S.U. v. Minister for the Civil Service* (1984), otherwise known as "the G.C.H.Q. case", which Margaret Thatcher used to issue a ban on trade unions in G.C.H.Q. An Order in Council requires the formality of a meeting of the Privy Council in the presence of the Queen. Practically, the decision to use prerogative power in this way is made by the Cabinet, or a small section thereof.

Statutory instruments

A more common form of delegated legislation is the power frequently given to Ministers of the Crown to make law for a specified purpose. The document containing this law is called a statutory instrument and thousands are issued every year. As each one is published it is given a number for the year, for example, the Justices of The Peace (Size and Chairmanship of Bench) Rules 1995 is S.I. 1995 No. 971. Statutory instruments have become of major importance as a source of law. Some central government departments are responsible for large numbers of statutory instruments.

Bye-laws

Parliament has long been willing to delegate to local authorities and certain other public bodies the power to make local laws limited to their particular functions. Thus local authorities can make town laws, or bye-laws, for their areas. For instance, there are often many rules governing behaviour in parks or leisure centres. Even so the authority has to obtain confirmation of the bye-laws from the named central government minister before the bye-laws take effect. The power to make bye-laws also belongs to public bodies such as the British Airports Authority.

STATUTORY INTERPRETATION

Rules for statutory interpretation

Inevitably, disputes arise as to the meaning or application of legislation and the task of the judges in this context is, therefore, described as that of statutory interpretation. To guide the judges, Parliament has provided them with the general assistance of the Interpretation Act 1978, and often the additional assistance of an interpretation section in the statute itself. The Interpretation Act 1978 in one of its better-known sections provides that "unless the contrary intention appears (a) words importing the masculine gender include the feminine (and vice-versa) (b) words in the singular include the plural, and words in the plural include the singular". Even with the help of the Interpretation Act and such definitions as are offered by the particular statute which is being considered by the court, the judges are constantly faced with cases which turn on the interpretation of a word or phrase in a statute for which no adequate definition is provided by the legislature. The vast majority of Court of Appeal and House of Lords cases concern statutory interpretation. As a result of the many decisions of the courts in such cases there are a number of rules, known as the rules of statutory interpretation, which appear to be the guidelines used by the judges.

It is important to understand that judges do not articulate the application of these "rules". The names of these "rules" are now simply a construct for academic analysis. Recent commentators argue that judges now take a "contextual approach". (See Cross, *Statutory Interpretation*.)

The first principle is that the judge should apply the words according to their "ordinary, plain and natural meaning". This is known as the literal rule, the application of *"litera legis"*.

In *Cresswell v. B.O.C. Ltd* (1980) the applicant sought rating exemption on the grounds that his fish farm fell within the statutory provisions governing agricultural buildings and land. The linguistic consideration in the last resort was whether "fish" were "livestock". Applying the literal rule, the Court of Appeal was unanimous in saying they were not. As a direct consequence of this decision, fish farms were expressly given rating exemption in the Local Government, Planning and Land Act 1980.

A second principle which is derived from the literal rule, and which has become known as the golden rule, is that the literal application need not be applied, if to do so would lead to absurdity or to inconsistency within the statute itself. An outstanding example of the golden rule occurred in *Re Sigsworth* (1935), where a man was found to have murdered his mother. In the statute dealing with the distribution of the mother's estate it was laid down that the estate was to be distributed amongst "the issue". The son was her only child. The judge held that the common law rule that a murderer cannot take any benefit from the estate of a person he had murdered prevailed over the apparently clear words of the statute. The same principle seems to have been applied in the death of the playwright Joe Orton where a substantial legacy had been left to the person responsible for his death and Orton was treated as intestate so far as the legacy was concerned.

A third principle is that if the literal or golden rules fail to assist, the judge is entitled to consider the "mischief" rule. This rule, which was first settled in *Heydon's Case* in 1584, allows the judge to consider (1) what was the common law, (2) what was the defect or mischief in the common law, (3) what remedy Parliament in the legislation has provided for the defect. Here a judge is entitled to examine existing leglislation and case law before coming to a decision, with the intention that the ruling will "suppress the mischief and advance the remedy." In *Kruhlak v. Kruhlak* (1958) the court held, in connection with affiliation proceedings, that a married woman living apart from her husband, even in the same house, is "a single woman" for the purposes of that legislation. The mischief at which the statute in that case was aimed was the situation of an illegitimate child with no means of support. You can imagine the impact of such a broad interpretation. It opened up a new class of claimants who would have been deprived of a remedy had the phrase been interpreted literally. This rule is sometimes referred to as interpretation *"ratio legis"* as distinct from interpretation *"litera legis"*.

The court is not easily persuaded to reject the plain words of the statute. Lord Scarman in *Stock v. Frank Jones (Tipton) Ltd* (1978) explained that "if the words used by Parliament are plain there is no room for the anomalies test, unless the consequences are so absurd that without going outside the statute, one can see that Parliament must have made a drafting mistake ... but mere manifest absurdity is not enough; it must be an error (of commission or omission) which in its context defeats the intention of the Act".

Other rules and presumptions

As well as these major rules associated with statutory interpretation, there are a number of other rules and presumptions, which the judges have introduced to help them in their task of interpretation.

One such minor rule is that where, in a statute, specific words are followed by general words, the general words must be given effect in the light of the foregoing specific words. This is called the *"ejusdem generis"* rule. An example is *Hobbs v. C.G. Robertson Ltd* (1970) where the Court of Appeal had to construe the following phrase concerning the provision of goggles in the Construction (General Provision) Regulations 1961:—"breaking, cutting, dressing or carving of stone, concrete, slag or similar materials"—to circumstances where a workman injured an eye, through the splintering of brickwork from a chimney breast which he was required to move. The court applied the *ejusdem generis* rule in holding that brick was not "a similar material" to stone, concrete or slag; the provision of goggles was, therefore, not compulsory and the workman's claim failed. A connected rule is that where, in a statute, there is a list of specified matters, which is not followed by general words, then only the matters actually mentioned are caught by this provision of the Act. The Latin phrase for this is *"expressio unius est exclusio alterius"*. In *R. v. Inhabitants of Sedgley* (1831) a statutory provision for rating occupiers of "lands, houses, tithes and coal mines" was held not to apply to any other kind of mine. The rule *"noscitur a sociis"* means that where two or more words follow each other in a statute, they must be taken as related for the purpose of interpretation. For example, in *Inland Revenue Commissioners v. Frere* (1965) the House of Lords held that in the relevant statute the phrase "interest, annuities or other annual payments" the word interest meant annual interest.

It is accepted practice that a statute must be taken as a whole. Consequently it follows that a judge must relate a word or phrase in a statute to its place in the context of the whole measure.

Other presumptions are that:

(i) no change in the existing law is presumed beyond that expressly stated in the legislation;

(ii) the Crown is not bound unless the Act specifically makes it so;

(iii) legislation is not intended to apply retrospectively unless this is expressly stated to be the case;

(iv) any change in the law affecting the liberties of the subject must be expressly and specifically stated;

(v) any liability for a criminal offence must be on the basis of fault, unless the words of the statute clearly intend otherwise;

(vi) the legislation applies throughout the United Kingdom unless an exemption for Scotland or Northern Ireland is stated. Because Scotland, in particular, has its own legal and local government system, it is common for Parliament to legislate for Scotland separately;

(vii) if the provisions of two Acts appear to be in conflict the court will endeavour to reconcile them, since there is no presumption of implied repeal. If reconciliation is not possible, logic demands that the later provision be given effect;

(viii) legislation must be construed so as not to conflict with E.C. law.

Extrinsic aids

It became a firm rule that a judge was confined to the Act of Parliament in question. The judge could not, in the task of interpretation, seek assistance from other sources, known as extrinsic aids, such as the *Hansard* reports of what took place in Parliament in the course of the enactment of the legislation in question. The reason for this rule is that people should be entitled to know the law by taking an Act at face value. Furthermore the intentions of, say, the Lord Chancellor, in introducing the Courts and Legal Services Bill may have differed from the "intention of Parliament", in passing the Act, after it had been debated and amended. Because of this rule the judge was unable, theoretically, to make use of Parliamentary debates, reports of committees or commissions or what the government Ministers involved had said about the measure as evidence of Parliamentary intent. This rule, that no extrinsic aids would be used, ensured that Parliament had a complete obligation to express itself precisely when making new law.

Serious inroads into this rule, significantly altering the judicial role in statutory interpretation, were made by the House of Lords in *Pepper v. Hart* (1993). In this case, the question arose whether, under the Finance Act 1976, Parliament had intended schoolteachers at private schools to be taxed on the full value of the benefit in kind of the private education offered to their own children. The House of Lords ruled, erroneously, that this had been Parliament's intention. Their Lordships' attention was later drawn to the statement of the sponsoring minister. From this, it became clear that the true intention was that the teachers should only be taxed on the cost to their employers, which was minimal so an Appellate Committee of seven Law Lords was reconvened and the case reargued, with reference to *Hansard*.

Their Lordships held that Parliamentary materials should only be referred to where:

"(a)   legislation is ambiguous or obscure or leads to an absurdity;
(b)   the material relied on consists of one or more statements by a minister or other promoter of the Bill together if necessary with such other Parliamentary material as is necessary to understand such statements and their effect;
(c)   the statements relied on are clear."

(per Lord Browne-Wilkinson)

Despite their Lordship's warnings that this new activity was to be the exception, judges and counsel in cases since 1993 have made frequent use of the *Pepper v. Hart* principle, even where there is little ambiguity in a statute and case law has extended the rule to allow reference to preparatory material, such as green papers and white papers, and reports of the Law Commission and Royal Commissions.

Drawing attention to the dangers of all this, the editors of the 1995 edition of *Cross on Statutory Interpretation* say it creates more work for lawyers, in advising clients and preparing litigation. Resorting to all these extrinsic aids, they comment, is no substitute for the clearest possible drafting of the text of the statute.

Intrinsic Aids

The judge is, however, entitled to find assistance from the intrinsic aids contained in the statute itself; these include the long title, marginal notes, headings, which may be prefixed to a part of the Act, and Schedules, which are part of the Act although they do not affect words used in the body of the Act unless these are ambiguous. Preambles may also be used in statutory interpretation, although they are rarely used in modern statutes. E.C. legislation makes regular use of preambles. The famous "Eurobananas" Regulation of 1994, regulating standards of bananas, contains a preamble longer than the text. The E.C.J. examines these preambles as a matter of course, in interpreting E.C. legislation. Punctuation is referred to in interpreting the meaning of a sentence in the same way as we use it as an essential guide to the sense of normal everyday English.

Different considerations apply in the case of a statute which incorporates an international convention. Here, exceptionally, the court must have regard to the full background and reference may be made to relevant material which explains the provisions in the convention. For a discussion by the House of Lords of this matter, see *Fothergill v. Monarch Airlines Ltd* (1980) where the amount involved was £16.50 and the linguistic problem was whether "damage" included "loss".

It can be gathered from the strictness of the judicial approach that if the words of a statute fail to deal with a particular situation, there is no power in a court to fill the gap, despite the fact that Lord Denning M.R. often claimed "We fill in the gaps." This absence of provision is known as "*casus omissus*", and in general the principle requires Parliament to pass a new statute to make good the deficiency. Lord Simonds in *Magor and St. Mellors R.D.C. v. Newport Corporation* (1952) said on this point "the power and duty of the court to travel outside them (the words of a statute) on a voyage of discovery are strictly limited. ... If a gap is disclosed, the remedy lies in an amending Act".

This view is unrealistic. Generally Parliament, save in taxation cases, is very slow to amend faulty legislation. In recent years, however, the House of Lords seems to have grasped the nettle and become much more willing to give a purposive construction to legislation. In the *Fothergill Case* (above) Lord Diplock is explicitly critical of Lord Simonds' approach and lays the blame for unsatisfactory rules of statutory interpretation on the judges' "narrowly semantic approach to statutory construction, until the last decade or so".

Criticism

Not unnaturally, considerable criticism has been expressed from time to time at the inflexible attitude of some judges in the task of statutory interpretation. In view of the difficulty of using language with an exactness which covers every conceivable situation, including the future, critics claim that the task of construction would be better done if judges took off their blinkers and considered all the circumstances which are relevant to the interpretation of the legislation in the particular case. Judging from the wide application given to *Pepper v. Hart*, many modern judges agree with this criticism. Taking a broad, purposive approach, they apparently relish the opportunity to consult extrinsic aids.

Another, in some ways more serious, criticism is that there is a lack of consistency in the application of the rules. It is suggested that judges may use whichever rule leads to the result which they wish to achieve; on one occasion they will rely on the literal rule, whereas on another they will reject the literal rule and apply the mischief rule.

The Law Commission in a report in 1969 called "The Interpretation of Statutes" criticised the narrow approach of the judges and recommended (i) that when Parliament produces an Act it should also provide what the Commission calls explanatory material; and (ii) that Parliament should enact a statute to specify what aids of interpretation the court might look at. It suggests the inclusion of reports and command papers on which the legislation is based, punctuation and marginal notes within the Act and relevant treaties and documents; it does not, however, propose that reports of proceedings in Parliament should be included. No action has been taken on this report. In a 1992 critique, *Making The Law*, the Hansard Commission recommended that for every Act of Parliament, the relevant government department and Parliamentary Counsel should prepare "notes on sections", an updated version of the "notes on clauses" prepared for a Minister during the passage of a Bill. These should be published with the Act and used by the courts in interpreting it.

Another consideration is that the judicial approach to statutory interpretation in the English legal system is completely at odds with the methods used in the European Court of Justice where the approach to construction is very flexible.

3. CASE LAW

GENERAL

Remembering that the English legal system is a common law system, indeed the mother of all common law systems, the significance of case law, *i.e.* common law in creating and, presently, refining our laws cannot be underestimated. The law produced by the courts can be just as important as the law produced by Parliament. For instance, in 1991, the House of Lords abolished the rule protecting a husband from criminal responsibility for raping his wife.

By case law is meant the decisions of judges laying down legal principles derived from the circumstances of the particular disputes coming before them. From earliest times in the history of the legal system, continuing attention has been paid to the reasoned judgments expounded by judges to justify their case decisions. When Chaucer in the Prologue to the *Canterbury Tales*, written about 1380, was describing the Serjeant-at-Law, he expressly states that this barrister was an exceptional lawyer, because he knew all the important case law decisions since the Norman Conquest. From his description it can be seen that even in medieval England the decisions of the judges were of great importance.

THE DOCTRINE OF JUDICIAL PRECEDENT—MEANING

The reason why such importance is attached to case decisions is explained by this doctrine of judicial precedent, which is also known as "*stare decisis*" (to stand upon decisions). This doctrine, in its simplest form, means that when a judge comes to try a case, she must always look back to see how previous judges have dealt with previous cases (precedents) which have involved similar facts in that branch of the law. In looking back in this way the judge will expect to discover those principles of law which are relevant to the case under consideration. The decision which she makes will thus seek to be consistent with the existing principles in that branch of the law, and may, in its turn, develop those principles a stage further.

Because the branches of English law have been gradually built up over the centuries, there are now hundreds of thousands of reported case decisions available with many more on databases such as *Lexis*, so that the task of discovering relevant precedents and achieving consistency is by no means simple. An added factor, and one of the greatest importance, is that the standing of a precedent is governed by the status of the court which decided the case. Decisions of the House of Lords are obviously to be treated with the greatest respect, whereas a decision of a county court judge has normally limited effect. This quite common sense approach has developed into a rigid system under which precedents of the superior courts, if found to be relevant to the facts of a particular case, are treated as "binding" on the lower courts, so that the judge in the lower court must follow the reasoning and apply it to the case in hand. The judge is thus obliged to decide the case in accordance with binding judicial precedent.

THE DOCTRINE OF JUDICIAL PRECEDENT—OPERATION

In order to understand the way in which this doctrine works in practice, it is necessary to consider the application of it through the hierarchy of the courts.

The House of Lords

As the supreme appeal court in matters civil and criminal, decisions of the House of Lords are binding on all the courts lower in the hierarchy. This is so not only where the facts of the later case are identical, which will be very rare, but also where the facts of the case call for the application of the same legal principle as in the House of Lords case. Until 1966, by reason of the binding nature of judicial precedent, a decision of the House of Lords, once made, remained binding on itself, as well as on all the courts lower in the structure. In 1966, by a formal Practice Statement, the House of Lords judges announced that in future they would not regard themselves as necessarily bound by their own previous decisions. The Practice Statement is worth quoting at length, as it gives us a neat summary of the arguments for and against a rigid system of binding precedent.

"Their Lordships regard the use of precedent as an indispensable foundation upon which to decide what is the law and its application to individual cases. It provides at least some degree of certainty upon which individuals can rely in the conduct of their affairs, as well as a basis for orderly development of legal rules. Their Lordships nevertheless recognise that too rigid adherence to precedent may lead to injustice in a particular case and also unduly restrict the proper development of the law. They propose, therefore, to modify their present practice and, while treating former decisions of this House as normally binding, to depart from a previous decision when it appears right to do so. In this connection they will bear in mind the danger of disturbing

202

retrospectively the basis on which contracts, settlements of property and fiscal arrangements have been entered into and also the especial need for certainty as to the criminal law. This announcement is not intended to affect the use of precedent elsewhere than in this House."

There have not been many instances since the 1966 Practice Statement of the House of Lords departing from a previous decision. In *Herrington v. British Railways Board* (1972) the court revised a long-standing legal principle concerned with the duty of care owed to a child trespasser; and in *Miliangos v. George Frank (Textiles) Ltd* (1976) it reversed a rule that a judgment could only be given in sterling. In *R. v. Shivpuri* (1986) the House of Lords departed from a decision given only one year earlier when reconsidering the law relating to criminal attempts.

The Court of Appeal

The Civil Division of the Court of Appeal by its decisions binds all the courts in the structure except the House of Lords. Its decisions in civil cases are of very great importance in the system. The Court of Appeal does bind itself for the future, according to the decision in *Young v. Bristol Aeroplane Co.* (1944); although it may escape if (i) a later decision of the House of Lords applies; (ii) there are previous conflicting decisions of the Court of Appeal; or (iii) where the previous decision was made "*per incuriam*", *i.e.* in error, because some relevant precedent or statutory provision was not considered by the court.

This statement of theory has produced considerable conflict in its application on a number of occasions in recent years. This is not surprising in that Lord Denning M.R., when the senior judge of the court, was not convinced of the wisdom of so rigid a system and his colleagues tended to put differing emphasis on the application of the rules depending on the circumstances of the case. An interesting example of an expedient approach to the problem is *Tiverton Estates Ltd v. Wearwell* (1975) where one division of the Court of Appeal

(Civil Division) was able to convince itself that it need not follow *Law v. Jones* (1974) which had been decided by another division of the court only six months earlier. The case dealt with a property law point of great practical importance.

The Criminal Division of the Court of Appeal does not consider itself always bound by its own decisions. Where the liberty of the subject is concerned the court feels itself free to overrule a previous decision if it appears that in that decision the law was misunderstood or misapplied "and if a departure from authority is necessary in the interests of justice to an appellant": *R. v. Spencer* (1985). An example of this occurred in *R. v. Shoult* (C.A., 1996). A court led by Lord Taylor, L.C.J., declined to follow *R. v. Cook* (C.A., 1995), in considering an appeal against a prison sentence for a drink-driving conviction.

The High Court

Decisions of a single judge in the three divisions of the High Court are binding on the lower courts but not on other High Court judges. If a High Court judge is presented with a precedent from a previous High Court case he will treat the precedent as "persuasive", and not as "binding". This means that he will consider the reasoning of the judge in the earlier case and will probably follow it; but is not obliged to do so. Decisions by a Divisional Court are binding on judges of the same Division sitting alone but not necessarily on future Divisional Courts: see *R. v. Greater Manchester Coroner, ex p. Tal* (1985).

The county court, the Crown Court and magistrates' courts

The decisions of these courts are seldom reported and not binding.

TERMINOLOGY

Binding and persuasive

It has already been explained that depending on the status of the court a precedent may be binding or it may be persuasive. Precedents which come from the Judicial Committee of the Privy Council or from countries within the common law jurisdiction, like Canada and Australia, are also said to be persuasive and the adoption of concepts from those foreign jurisdictions has led to developments in English common law, for instance, in criminal law and the tort of negligence.

Other terms

Where a judge finds that a precedent to which he is referred is not strictly relevant to the facts of the case concerned, he is said to "distinguish" that case. As such, the case is not binding upon him.

If, on the other hand, the judge holds that a precedent is relevant, and applies it, he is said to "follow" the reasoning of the judge in the earlier case.

When an appeal court is considering a precedent, it may "approve" the principle of law established in the case, or it may "disapprove" the precedent. It can "overrule" the principle of law established in a precedent if the case was decided by a court junior in status to it.

A decision is said to be "reversed" when a higher court, on appeal, comes to the opposite conclusion to the court whose order is the subject of the appeal.

RATIO DECIDENDI AND *OBITER DICTA*

The most important and binding element of a judgment is the legal reasoning which leads the judge to decide the particular issue in favour of the plaintiff or the defendant, the reason for the decision or "*ratio decidendi*" as it is known; and then the remainder of the judgment, which deals by way of explanation with cases cited and legal principles argued before the court, is called "*obiter dicta*" or things said by the way. The whole of a dissenting judgment is "*obiter*".

It is the "*ratio*" of a decision, which constitutes the binding precedent; or "*rationes*" if there is more than one reason. So that when in a case a judge is referred to a precedent, the first task of the court is to decide what was the "*ratio*" of that case, and to what extent it is relevant to the principle to be applied in the present case. Whilst an "*obiter dictum*" is not binding, it can, if it comes from a highly respected judge, be very helpful in establishing the legal principles in the case under consideration.

So important is it that a judgment should be accurately recorded that, before publication in the "official" law reports, judges are asked to check for accuracy the court reporter's version of the judgment.

ADVANTAGES AND DISADVANTAGES OF THE DOCTRINE OF JUDICIAL PRECEDENT

The main advantages of the doctrine are that it leads to consistency in the application and development of the principles in each branch of the law, and by virtue of this characteristic it enables lawyers to forecast with reasonable certainty what the attitude of the courts is likely to be to a given set of facts. The system is flexible in that it can find an answer to any legal problem, and it is essentially practical in that the courts are perpetually dealing with actual circumstances. It must also be said that one result of the recording of cases over the centuries is that the tremendous wealth of detail leads to considerable precision in the principles established in each field of law.

To balance these advantages, critics of judicial precedent will argue that the way in which the discretion of the judge is restricted is undesirable, and can lead to a judge, who wishes to escape from a precedent, drawing illogical distinctions. Added to this is the difficulty, which can occur in some appeal court decisions, of discovering exactly what principle led to the particular decision. This has been known to be the case when the House of Lords decides an appeal by a majority vote of three to two, and the three judges in the majority appear to arrive at their decision for different reasons. An example of this difficulty is *Harper v. National Coal Board* (1974) where the Court of Appeal was, for this reason, unable to discover the *ratio decidendi* of the House of Lords' decision in *Dodd's Case* (1973).

A final factor, which is a practical problem, is that there are so many cases being dealt with each year that inevitably there is increasing complexity in each branch of the law. The sheer bulk of cases on commercial or criminal law is almost overwhelming and causes textbooks to become increasingly specialised and substantial. Even so, it can well happen that a case of importance is not reported, other than on *Lexis*, and so may go unnoticed for some considerable time. Such a case remains a precedent.

LAW REPORTS

A direct result of the application of the doctrine of judicial precedent is that cases must be properly reported and that the published reports must be readily accessible. One consequence is that in the English legal system there is a vast collection of law reports, of varying degrees of accuracy, stretching back over the centuries.

The earliest case summaries were collected in manuscript form in what became known as the *Year Books*. These seem to have been privately prepared and circulated among the judges and leading barristers. It is impossible now to know exactly how the system then operated, but it is obvious from Chaucer's Serjeant-at-Law that considerable attention was paid to previous case decisions.

With the invention of printing, the production of law reports for sale to the legal profession, between the sixteenth and nineteenth centuries, became common practice. These reporters varied widely in their accuracy and reliability, but their law reports remain available, and have now been republished in a series called *The English Reports*.

Since 1865, law reporting has been placed on a different basis, although it remains a matter for private enterprise. A Council was set up in that year and in 1870 was incorporated as the Incorporated Council of Law Reporting. It consists of representatives of the Law Society and the Inns of Court and publishes what have come to be treated as the official *Law Reports*. These are in four series: Appeal cases (A.C.), Queen's Bench (Q.B.), Chancery (Ch.) and Family (Fam.). The reports are published some considerable time after the judgment has been given, but are regarded as authentic. The Council also publishes the *Weekly Law Reports* (W.L.R.), which are available sooner and there is another series called the *All England Law Reports* (All E.R.), which is also published weekly, by a firm of law publishers. All decisions of the Crown Court, High Court and above, whether or not reported elsewhere, are stored on *Lexis*, the best known law database. Various series of law reports are now available on CD-Rom. As well as these full reports, a number of law magazines carry summaries of recent case decisions, as do *The Times* and *The Independent*. Certain professional publications, like the *Estates Gazette*, the *Justice of the Peace*, and *Knight's Local Government Reports*, publish case reports of interest to their particular readers.

It has long been the practice for the work of law reporting to be done by barristers who attend the court throughout the hearing of the case. The preparation of a law report, and in particular the head-note summarising the relevant facts and the legal principles arising, is a specialised task.

CONCLUSION

It will now be apparent that case law is, and has always been, a major source of English law. Some branches of the law have been painstakingly built up over the years by the gradual application of case decisions; contract and tort in particular are substantially derived from the principles established by hundreds of judgments in actual cases. Even those branches of the law which are based on statute are nonetheless affected by case decisions, since these decisions construe the statutory provisions in question.

4. CUSTOM

In the development of the English legal system the common law was derived from the different laws of the existing Anglo-Saxon tribal groups in, for example, Kent and Wessex. The term "common law" emphasises the point. As England became one nation, with one king and one government, so the laws of the Anglo-Saxon regions had to be adapted into a national law common to the whole country. Since the difference between the regions stemmed from their different customary laws it is no exaggeration to say that custom was the principal original source of the common law and in this historical sense, custom, as the basis of common law, continued to play a part over the medieval period.

Customs thus were absorbed into the legal system, sometimes in the form of legislation and sometimes, particularly in the earliest period, by the judges giving decisions which were based on custom. The gradual result was that custom virtually disappeared as a creative source of law. An exception exists at the present day on a limited scale for cases where the courts can be convinced that a particular local custom applies. Usually in such cases, custom is pleaded as a defence as permitting the conduct in question. It is unusual, nowadays, for an argument to be based on custom and the rules for its acceptance are strict.

5. BOOKS OF AUTHORITY

GENERAL

The fundamental division, which is drawn in connection with legal books as a source of law, is into those of considerable antiquity and those of recent origin. Both categories are of importance and have a part to play in the system, but only the books of antiquity can strictly be regarded as a source of law.

BOOKS OF AUTHORITY

In this category fall certain ancient textbooks, any one of which by long standing judicial tradition, can be accepted as an original source of law. Not all old textbooks are so treated, only a limited number in each major branch of the law being universally accepted by the judges and the legal profession as having achieved the necessary standing. These books are then accepted by the courts as authoritative statements of the law at the time when they were written. Whether a particular book is accepted as authoritative depends on its professional reputation; there is no way of knowing other than by a study of professional practice.

The following works, most of which were written by judges, are accepted as books of authority—

Glanvill, *De Legibus et Consuetudinibus Angliae*, (c. 1189): authoritative on the land law and the criminal law of the twelfth century.

Bracton, *De Legibus et Consuetudinibus Angliae*, (c. 1250): mainly commentaries on the forms of action with case illustrations. A major study of the common law.

Littleton, of *Tenures*, (c. 1480): a comprehensive study of land law.

Fitzherbert, *Nature Brevium*, (c. 1534): a commentary on the register of writs.

Coke, *Institutes of the Laws of England*, (1628): an attempted exposition in four parts of the whole of English law.

Hale, *History of the Pleas of the Crown*, (1736) (60 years after Hale's death): the first history of the criminal law.

Hawkins, *Pleas of the Crown*, (1716): a survey of the criminal law and criminal procedure.

Foster, *Crown Cases*, (1762): authoritative within its scope, which is concerned with the criminal law.

Blackstone, *Commentaries on the Laws of England*, (1765): a survey of the principles of English law in the mid-eighteenth century intended for students.

From the time of Blackstone on, writers of legal textbooks have fallen into the second category, that is those of recent origin.

MODERN TEXTBOOKS

Modern textbooks are not treated as works of authority although they are frequently referred to in the courts. Counsel are permitted to adopt a textbook writer's view as part of their argument in a case. Judges will often quote from a modern textbook in the course of giving judgment; for example, in *Re Ellenborough Park* (1956) the Court of Appeal adopted the definition of an easement as defined in Cheshire's *Modern Real Property*. Sometimes the judge will decide that a statement in a textbook on a particular point is incorrect; for example, in *Watson v. T.S. Whitney & Co. Ltd* (1966) the Court of Appeal decided that on a particular point both Halsbury's *Laws of England* and the High Court's *Annual Practice* were wrong.

In *R. v. Moloney* (1985) the House of Lords held that the definition of "intent" in Archbold's "Pleading evidence and practice in criminal cases" 40th and 41st editions, the virtual bible of criminal court practice, was "unsatisfactory and potentially misleading".

The reason why no textbooks, since Blackstone's *Commentaries* were published in 1765, have been accepted as works of authority seems to be that (i) case reports have become fuller and much more easily accessible and (ii) by that time the principles of the common law were fully established, so that there was no question of a later textbook being itself a source of law.

One old rule which seems to have died out is the rule that a living person could not be an authority in his own lifetime. Under the present arrangements a living textbook writer can be quoted in court, and occasionally the court may refer with advantage to articles in learned law periodicals. For instance, in *R. v. Shivpuri* (1986) the House of Lords paid tribute to an article in the Cambridge Law Journal by Professor Glanville Williams. This article had a considerable influence on the court in persuading it to reverse its previous ruling.

CHAPTER 12

E.C. LAW: ITS IMPACT ON ENGLISH LAW AND THE ENGLISH COURTS

Membership of the European Community has dramatically curtailed the sovereignty of Parliament in the British constitution. It is simply unrealistic to consider the English legal system, or English sources of law, in isolation from the E.C. Year by year, as the ambit of Community power is extended, so the bulk of substantive law accelerates in growth and it is no longer appropriate to consider E.C. law as a single subject. Most of it comes into the United Kingdom "by the back door", through the medium of delegated legislation. Here, I provide a simple and very basic guide to the institutions of the E.C. and the sources of E.C. law. It is essential, however, for every student of English law to understand that they cannot ignore E.C. law. Regrettably, English lawyers suffer an appalling ignorance of E.C. law, which reflects the insularity of the wider British community.

1. INSTITUTIONS

The E.C. was created by the signing of the *Treaty of Rome* in 1957 and the Treaty remains an essential source of E.C. law, as well as the Community's constitution. Incorporation of this and the other E.C. treaties into English law was effected by The European Communities Act 1972. The other major instrument with which we must concern ourselves is the Single European Act of 1986, which created the single European market which was in effect by the end of 1992 and the Treaty on European Union (Maastricht Treaty), ratified in 1993.

The basic four E.C. institutions are the Parliament, the Council, the Commission and the Court of Justice. The other institution which necessitates a brief mention is the Court of First Instance.

2. PARLIAMENT

Members of this large assembly are directly elected by their Member States. It is essential to grasp that, unlike conventional Parliaments on the Westminster model, this is *not* the legislature of the Community, although its powers have been massively enhanced by the 1986 Single European Act and by the Treaty on European Union 1992, as explained below. This has gone some way to remedy the institutional imbalance in the Community and to remedy the "democratic deficit" complained of by critics of the fact that the unelected Council is the primary legislature. Parliament now has a legislative role on several levels:

Advisory

The 1957 E.C. Treaty required that the Council consult the Parliament where legislation was proposed on a number of important areas. The Single European Act 1986 greatly extended the range of matters on which Parliament must be consulted, encompassing most measures relating to the internal market.

The Co-operation procedure

This procedure was introduced by the Single European Act and is now incorporated into Article 189c of the E.C. Treaty. Parliament is given a second opportunity to consider draft legislation. If Parliament then continues to object, the Council may only adopt the proposal if they act unanimously and within three months. Similarly, where Parliament proposes amendments, these must be considered by the Council.

Co-decision

This procedure was introduced by the Treaty on European Union 1992, in a new Article 189b E.C., applying to certain defined areas. The Council must adopt a common position, after consulting Parliament. Parliament may then confirm or reject it, or propose amendments. If the Council does not approve the amendments, the act must be referred to a conciliation committee, composed of members of Parliament and the Council. Council and Parliament may adopt a joint approved text, or Parliament may reject the text. Thus, Parliament has a significant power of veto, under these new procedures.

Informal consultation

Parliament meets members of the Commission in Committees and, in practice, members of Parliament are consulted by the Commission at the pre-legislative stage.

3. COUNCIL ("THE COUNCIL OF THE EUROPEAN UNION")

This body is composed of one representative minister from each Member State. These delegates change according to the nature of the subject under discussion. For instance, on agricultural policy, states will send their agriculture ministers. On economic issues, finance ministers will attend. When the Council is composed of heads of state or government it is known as The European Council. They meet at least twice a year, with the Commission President, assisted by foreign ministers and a Commissioner (Single European Act 1986, Art. 2).

The Council's job is to ensure the Treaty objectives are attained. It has the final say on most Community secondary legislation but, in most cases, can only act on a proposal from the Commission. Since it is not a permanent body, much of the Council's day to day work, initially scrutinising Commission proposals, is delegated to COREPER, the committee of permanent representatives.

4. THE COMMISSION

The Commission's 17 members are drawn from Member States, two from some, one from others, but must act independently of state control. Its functions are these:

The motor

This body has been described as the motor of the Community, in that the Council can only take important decisions following proposals of the Commission but it may request the Commission to undertake studies and submit appropriate proposals.

The watchdog

The Commission enforces the Member States' Treaty obligations and may take an errant Member State to the European Court of Justice, under Article 169, should persuasion fail. It can also impose fines and penalties on those in breach of E.C. competition law. Accordingly, the Commission has extensive investigatory powers.

The executive

The Commission is, effectively, the Community executive. Policies formed by the Council need detailed implementation by the Commission. Much of this is effected by legislation, which requires a final decision by the Council.

Negotiator

In relation to the E.C.'s external policies, the Commission acts as a negotiator, leaving agreements to be concluded by the Council, after consulting the Parliament, where this is required by the Treaty.

5. THE COURT OF JUSTICE

Composition

The Court consists of 15 judges: one for each Member State. Article 167 of the Treaty stipulates that they "shall be chosen from persons whose independence is beyond doubt and they must be qualified to hold highest judicial office in their Member State, or be a jurisconsult of recognised competence (*e.g.* academic lawyer)". They are assisted by nine Advocates General, whose task it is to assist the Court, individually, by making a detailed analysis of all the relevant issues of fact and law in a case before the Court and submitting a report of this, together with recommendations, to the Court. Thus, they can express their personal opinions, which the judges cannot, and they can examine any related question, not brought forward by the parties.

Each judge and Advocate General is appointed for a term of six years.

Procedure

The Court's workload has increased massively since 1970. Then, 79 cases were brought before it and now over 350 cases per year are lodged, with a similar number being lodged before the Court of First Instance. The latter was created to deal with this increased workload but, still, it has proved necessary to devise another coping mechanism. This has been the tendency to hear cases before a chamber of three or five judges, reserving the plenary sessions of seven, nine, 11, or 13 judges for the more important cases. The grand plenum (of, now, 15 judges) is reserved for the most important cases, where issues of fundamental principle are considered, such as the *Faccini Dori* case on horizontal direct effect of directives (see below).

The case for each party is submitted in written pleadings, oral argument being strictly limited to about half an hour per party. The common lawyers appearing before the Court find more difficulty in adjusting to this procedure than do lawyers from continental Europe. The President allocates one of the judges to act as a judge-rapporteur to each case. She prepares a public report after the written procedure, ready for the oral hearing. It contains a summary of the facts and legal argument. She prepares a private report to the judges, containing her view of whether the case should be assigned to a chamber.

Meanwhile, an Advocate General will also have been assigned to the case. They are not assigned to cases brought by or against their native Member State. He prepares an opinion which is delivered orally, at the end of the oral hearing. It contains a full analysis of relevant E.C. law, which may give a more complete and accurate account than that produced in argument by the parties, since the lawyers appearing in the case may appear before the European Court of Justice only once in their legal careers.

The Advocate General also gives his opinion as to how the Court should decide the case. Whilst it is true that the Court follows this opinion in most cases and it is thus a good indicator as to how the Court is likely to decide, as well as providing an essential explanation of the reasoning behind the Court's decision, after the event, this opinion should never be referred to as a "ruling", as is frequently misreported by the British news media.

After this, the Advocate General drops out of the picture and the judges deliberate in secret, without interpreters, in French, the working language of the Court. (Since Finland and Sweden joined the E.C. in 1995, it has been argued that the Court should adopt English as a second official language, since this is the second language of Scandinavians but the cost of double translation would be prohibitive.) After deliberations, the judge-rapporteur will draft and refine the decision.

Function

Under each of the treaties, the task of the Court is prescribed as to "ensure that in the interpretation and application of this Treaty the law is observed". It is the supreme authority on all matters of Community law. In its practices and procedure, it draws on continental models notably French procedure but in substantive law, it borrows principles from all Member States.

The E.C. Treaty is a framework, generally speaking, with few of its provisions spelled out in detail. This gives the Court massive latitude as a court of interpretation, in effect creating E.C. law and jurisprudence. Its boldness has been a matter of controversy but since we are watching the emergence of a whole new legal system and body of law, it is hardly surprising that the Court's decisions contain sweeping statements of principle, especially given that the E.C. Treaty is silent, even on such fundamentals as the relationship between E.C. law and national law (see *Costa v. E.N.E.L.*, 1964, below).

When developing new legal principles, the Court's first reference point is the objectives of the Community and the articles of the Treaty.

Over the years, it has built up a massive body of reported decisions. Like our House of Lords, the Court is not bound by its own previous decisions but usually follows them. The judgment is a single one, rather like that of the Privy Council but without much indication of the reasoning behind it (especially in the older cases). This is where the submission of the Advocate General comes in useful, as an explanation.

Jurisdiction

The Court's work consists mainly of the following:

— determining whether or not a Member State has failed to fulfil a Treaty obligation. Actions may be brought by the Commission or another Member State (Arts. 169, 170);

— exercising unlimited jurisdiction in reviewing penalties (*e.g.* fines imposed by the Commission). Actions may be brought by natural and legal persons (Art. 172);

— reviewing the legality of an act, or failure to act, of the Council or Commission or Parliament. A request for review may be made by a Member State, the Council, the Commission, Parliament or natural or legal persons (Art. 173 EC);

— to grant compensation for damage caused by the institutions. Actions can be brought against the Community by Member States and natural or legal persons (Art. 178, 215(2) EC);

— to act as a court of appeal on points of law from the Court of First Instance;

— to give preliminary rulings at the request of a national court or tribunal (Art. 177 EC).

This last point is most important for our purposes, as this is the mechanism through which E.C. law is developed and interpreted in its domestic context, in English case law. Any case may be referred to the Court from any English court or tribunal, under Article 177, where there is an item of E.C. law to be interpreted. The Court gives its interpretation and then remits the case to the domestic court, leaving them to apply that interpretation and then decide the case accordingly. (See section 6.)

Court of First Instance

The Single European Act (1986) provided for the establishment of a new Court of First Instance and it began its work in 1989. Its 15 judges usually hear cases in chambers of three or five, any of whom, apart from the President, may be called upon to act as Advocate General. Its jurisdiction was limited to disputes between the Community and its servants, cases involving E.C. competition law and applications for judicial review and damages in certain matters under the European Coal and Steel Community. In 1992, however, the TEU amended Article 168a E.C. to provide that the Council, acting on a request from the European Court, could transfer any area of the Court's jurisdiction to the Court of First Instance, except for Article 177 preliminary rulings. Accordingly, a lot of work was transferred down in 1993, to relieve pressure on the Court. By 1996, the Court of First Instance was hearing as many cases as the Court of Justice. There is a right of appeal from this court, on matters of law, to the ECJ.

6. ARTICLE 177 PRELIMINARY RULINGS

Article 177 of the Treaty of Rome enables any court or tribunal in any Member State to refer a point of E.C. law in a pending case to the Court for their interpretation. The Court's ruling on the point is then sent back to the national court to be applied in the case, which will have been suspended in the meantime. These references are a significant volume of the Court's workload and they have proved to be the essential vehicle for the Court to develop its principles and precedent. Article 177, provides:

> "The Court of Justice shall have jurisdiction to give preliminary rulings concerning:
> (a) the interpretation of this Treaty;
> (b) the validity and interpretation of acts of the institutions of the Community and of the ECB;
> Where such a question is raised before any court or tribunal of a Member State, that court or tribunal may, if it considers that a decision on the question is necessary to enable it to give judgment, request the Court of Justice to give a ruling thereon.
>
> Where any such question is raised in a case pending before a court or tribunal of a Member State against whose decision there is no judicial remedy under national law, that court or tribunal shall bring the matter before the Court of Justice."

Paragraph (b) includes all Article 189 legislative acts, described below and the Court has ruled that it also includes non-binding recommendations and opinions. The court cannot rule on questions of national law so cannot rule that a national provision is incompatible with Community law but has said it will provide the national court with all necessary criteria to enable it to answer such a question.

National courts or tribunals that can refer

If parties have contracted to arbitrate, the arbiter is not a court or tribunal within Article 177 but where the law imposes an arbitrator to resolve disputes, then a question can be referred to the ECJ. Even a body exercising functions preliminary to its judicial function may refer. In *Pretore di Salo v. Persons Unknown* (ECJ, 1987), an Italian public prosecutor, who would later act as examining magistrate, was allowed to refer.

Article 177(2): The discretion to refer

The Court originally took a strict view that it was for the national courts and not for them to decide when a reference was necessary for the decision but it has emphasised that it will not answer hypothetical questions or act on references from non-genuine disputes which have been contrived simply to test E.C. law by means of an Article 177 reference.

The Court has specified that, for it to assume jurisdiction, it is essential for the national court to explain why it considers a preliminary ruling to be necessary and the national court must define the factual and legislative context of the question it is asking.

The question of the timing of a reference is left to the national court but the Court has requested that facts and points of national law be established in advance. A national court or tribunal cannot be prevented from making a reference by a national law that it is bound to follow the decision of a higher court on the same question of Community law. In other words, our Court of Appeal could still make a reference, if they considered it necessary, despite the existence of a House of Lords precedent on the same question of Community law.

The approach of the United Kingdom courts to the discretion to refer

In *Bulmer v. Bollinger* [1974] C.A. Lord Denning M.R. set out guidelines for English courts, other than the House of Lords, for deciding when it was necessary to make an Article 177 reference. They were influential in a number of cases but did not meet with uncritical approval. Mr Justice Bingham warned that the European court was in a better position to determine questions of Community law because, for instance, of their expertise, their unique grasp of all the authentic language texts of that law and their familiarity with a purposive construction of Community law. Once he became Master of the Rolls, he set out this important dictum, in *R. v. International Stock Exchange, ex p. Else* [1993] C.A.:

"if the facts have been found and the Community law issue is critical to the court's final decision, the appropriate course is ordinarily to refer the issue to the Court of Justice unless the national court can with complete confidence resolve the issue itself. In considering whether it can with complete confidence resolve the issue itself the national court must be fully mindful of the differences between national and Community legislation, of the pitfalls which face a national court venturing into what may be an unfamiliar field, of the need for uniform interpretation throughout the Community and of the great advantages enjoyed by the Court of Justice in construing Community instruments. If the national court has any real doubt, it should obviously refer."

Commenting on this case, Weatherill and Beaumont, in *EC Law*, praise Sir Thomas for doing a great service in creating a presumption that national courts and tribunals should make a reference if they are not completely confident as to how the issues can be resolved.

"This is a *communautaire* approach consistent with the spirit of judicial cooperation that is needed if the Article 177 system is to do its job of ensuring uniform interpretation of Community law throughout the Community."

It is, nevertheless, a rebuttable presumption so the English law reports have many examples of the courts declining to refer. An example is *R. v. Ministry of Agriculture, Fisheries and Food, ex p. Portman Agrochemicals Ltd* (1994) Brooke, J., in declining to refer, took account of the guidelines in previous case law but was influenced by the fact that neither of the parties wished for the case to be referred and that, given the usual 18 month delay to be expected in receiving the Court's interpretation, the answer would be redundant by the time they would receive it.

Some judges have warned that English courts should exercise great caution in relying on the doctrine of "acte clair" in declining to make a reference. The Court accepts that national courts will apply this doctrine, borrowed from French law, when the interpretation of a provision is clear and free from doubt (see below).

It is possible, in the English legal system, for an appeal to be made against a lower court's decision to refer. Such an appeal was successfully made in *ex p. Else* (above), the Court of Appeal holding that it was not necessary to refer.

Article 177(3): The obligation on national courts of last resort to refer

Although the wording of this paragraph looks mandatory, as if courts like the House of Lords must refer every point of E.C. law to the ECJ, the Court has ruled, in the *Da Costa* case (see below) that this is not necessary where the question raised is materially identical to a question which has already been the subject of a preliminary ruling in an earlier case. In *CILFIT v. Italian Ministry of Health*: (1982, ECJ) the Court spelled out what they consider to be the discretion available to courts of last resort, despite the wording of Article 177(3). They said that courts of last resort have the same discretion as others, to whom paragraph 2 applies, to decide whether a reference is necessary and that there is no obligation to refer if:

— the answer to the question can in no way affect the outcome of the case;

— where the ECJ has already dealt with the point of law in question, even though the questions at issue are not strictly identical; or

— where the question of Community law is relevant to the outcome of the case and there is no previous ruling of the Court on the point of law, if the correct application of Community law is so obvious as to leave no scope for any reasonable doubt as to the manner in which the question raised is to be resolved. (In other words, where the court has the confidence to apply the *acte clair* doctrine.)

Satisfying the conditions for the application of this third criterion will not, however, be easy, as the Court laid down the condition that the national court must be convinced that the matter is equally obvious to the courts of the other Member States and to the ECJ and they reminded courts that, in satisfying themselves of this criterion, they should bear in mind the plurilingual nature of that law and the Court's use of purposive and contextual construction. While many English judges would not shy away from a purposive and contextual approach, I am at pains to see how the House of Lords has the facilities to delve into the domestic law reports of the other 14 Member States to see how a point has been variously interpreted by other national courts, in their many national languages.

There are modern examples of the House of Lords refusing to refer a case to the ECJ, mainly relying on the first *CILFIT* exception, that the Community law point was irrelevant, including a case in which they refused to follow the *Von Colson* principle: *Finnegan v. Clowney Youth Training Programme Ltd* (1990, H.L.) Nevertheless, in recent years, the House seems to have been more prepared to refer to the ECJ and seems more ready to apply European Court case law where it does not refer. A recent example of a reference made by their Lordships and their subsequent application of the Court's interpretation is the case of *Webb v. EMO Air Cargo (No. 2)* (1995, H.L.) The case is illustrative of the fact that, had the House not made a reference, it would have come to the opposite conclusion from that reached by the ECJ and would have refused an appeal which it was ultimately persuaded to allow.

7. SOURCES OF E.C. LAW

The sources of E.C. law are as follows:

— The E.C. Treaty and protocols, as amended by further treaties, such as the Single European Act 1986 and Treaty on European Union 1992.

— E.C. secondary legislation (Regulations, Directives and Decisions).

— International agreements entered into by Community institutions on the Community's behalf, using their powers under the Treaty.

— Decisions of the ECJ and Court of First Instance. This includes the vast body of law and principle established by the ECJ.

Article 5 of the Treaty obliges all Member States to "take all appropriate measures, whether general or particular, to ensure fulfilment" of all these obligations.

8. SECONDARY LEGISLATION (LEGISLATIVE ACTS)

The law-making powers of the Community institutions are laid down in Article 189 of the Treaty (as amended by the TEU). They are set out very clearly and students of English law need to know and understand this Article:

In order to carry out their tasks and in accordance with the provisions of this Treaty, the European Parliament acting jointly with the Council, the Council and the Commission shall make regulations, issue directives, take decisions, make recommendations or deliver opinions.

These measures, described as "acts", are defined as follows:

A regulation shall have general application. It shall be binding in its entirety and directly applicable in all Member States.
A directive shall be binding, as to the result to be achieved, upon each Member State to which it is addressed, but shall leave to the national authorities the choice of form and methods.
A decision shall be binding in its entirety upon those to whom it is addressed.
Recommendations and opinions shall have no binding force.

Distinguish between binding and non-binding acts. Only the first three are binding.

Regulations are generally applicable and designed to apply to all situations in the abstract. Since they are binding in their entirety and directly applicable in all Member States, they may give rise to rights and obligations for states and individuals without further enactment.

227

Directives are binding as to the result to be achieved, upon each Member State to which they are addressed. The state thus fills in the details by enacting domestic law in accordance with the principles it is directed to effect.

Decisions are individual acts, addressed to a specified person or persons or states. They have the force of law and, therefore, have effect without further expansion.

Acts which do not conform with procedural safeguards may be annulled.

Recommendations and Opinions have no binding force in law, although they are of persuasive authority.

9. DIRECT APPLICABILITY AND DIRECT EFFECT

To understand the application of E.C. law, it is necessary to have a basic grasp of the distinction between the principles of *direct applicability and direct effect*. It is also necessary to draw attention to the distinction between *horizontal and vertical direct effect*, that is, between provisions directly effective between individuals, giving rise to rights or obligations enforceable between individuals and provisions giving rise to rights of individuals against the Member States.

When the European Communities Act 1972 took the United Kingdom into the E.C., or Common Market, as it then was, E.C. law became directly applicable, in international law terms, as if it were domestic English law. The terminology becomes confusing, however, because provisions of international law which are found to be capable of application by national courts at the suit of individuals are also termed directly applicable. To spare confusion, therefore, all British writers on E.C. law have adopted the term "directly effective" to express this second meaning, that is, to denote provisions of E.C. law which give rise to rights or obligations which individuals may enforce before the national courts.

Whether a particular provision of E.C. law gives rise to directly effective, individually enforceable rights or obligations is a matter of construction, depending on its language and purpose. Since principles of construction vary from state to state, the same provision may not be construed as directly effective everywhere. For lawyers in the English legal system, whether a provision is directly effective is crucially important because, thanks to the concept of primacy of E.C. law, a directly effective provision must be given priority over any conflicting principle of domestic law.

The E.C. Treaty specifies, in Article 189, that regulations are directly applicable but it has been left to the ECJ to set out, in a group of leading cases, which and when other E.C. provisions can have direct effect.

Treaty Articles

The issues of whether and when a Treaty Article could have direct effect was first considered in the *Van Gend en Loos* case of 1962. The question arose as to whether Article 12 of the Treaty, which prohibited states introducing new import duties, could confer enforceable rights on nationals of Member States. The ECJ held that it could because the text of the Article set out a clear and unconditional duty not to act. The prohibition was, thus, perfectly suited by its nature to produce direct effects in the legal relations between Member States and their citizens. The ECJ clearly thought it desirable that individuals should be allowed to protect their rights in this way, without having to rely on the E.C. Commission or another Member State to take action against an offending Member State.

This case involved a flouted prohibition but ECJ case law soon extended direct effect to positive Treaty obligations, holding that an Article imposing upon a Member State a duty to act would become directly effective once a time-limit for compliance had expired.

The ECJ has found a large number of Treaty provisions to be directly effective, in relation to free movement of goods and persons, competition law and discrimination on the grounds of gender or nationality.

The ECJ applies the following criteria to test whether a provision is amenable to direct effect. It must be:

— clear and precise, especially with regard to scope and application;

— unconditional; and

— leave no room for the exercise of implementation by Member States or community institutions.

The ECJ has, however, applied these conditions fairly liberally, with results as generous as possible to the individual seeking to rely on the Article.

Although the *Van Gend* case involved vertical direct effect, that is, citizen enforcing rights against a state, later case law, notably *Defrenne v. Sabena* (ECJ, 1975) demonstrated that Treaty Articles could also have horizontal direct effect, that is, could be relied on between individuals, such as private employer and employee.

A good recent example of the invocation of vertically directly effective Treaty Articles is the *Factortame* case, discussed below.

Regulations

Regulations are, as stated above, designed to be directly applicable and, thus, directly effective. It is important to understand that this means both vertically and horizontally.

Directives

Directives are an instruction to Member States to enact laws to achieve a certain end result, so it was originally assumed they could not be directly effective. Nevertheless, in *Grad v. Finanzamt Traustein* (ECJ 1970) the ECJ held that no such limitation applied. Here, a German haulier was allowed to rely on a directive and decision on VAT which the German government had ignored.

The conditions for effectiveness are the same as those applied to test Treaty provisions: clarity, precision, being unconditional, leaving no room for discretion in implementation. Once a time limit for implementation has expired, the obligation to implement it becomes absolute but a directive cannot be directly effective before that time limit has expired: *Ratti* (ECJ, 1978).

Where a state has implemented a directive inadequately, it is still possible for it to be declared directly effective, to make up for that inadequacy (*U.N.O.* (ECJ, 1976)).

Horizontal or vertical direct effect?

One of the most significant but difficult issues before the ECJ in recent years has been the issue of whether directives can be declared effective horizontally, that is, to enforce private rights and obligations between private parties. All the case law referred to above relates to the enforcement of private rights against a state, giving *vertical* direct effect to a directive. The ECJ has no problem in declaring vertical direct effect since this is merely enforcing rights and obligations against a state which that state has omitted to effect in its own domestic legislation. It is not so keen, however, to hold private parties bound by a directive which a state has neglected to implement, when the default is clearly the state's.

The leading case on this issue is *Marshall v. Southampton & South West Hampshire Area Health Authority (Teaching)* (ECJ, 1984) but, as we shall see, subsequent case law, in particular the *Marleasing* case and *Foster v. British Gas*, leave the law in a position which is far from clear. The decision in the *Marshall* case is clear enough:

Mrs Marshall was an employee of the Area Health Authority and she challenged their compulsory retirement age of 65 for men and 60 for women as discriminatory and in breach of the E.C. Equal Treatment Directive 76/207. Different retirement ages were permissible in domestic English law, under the Sex Discrimination Act 1975.

On a reference from the Court of Appeal, the ECJ held that the different retirement ages did indeed breach the Directive and that Mrs Marshall could, in the circumstances rely on the Directive against the state (here represented by the Area Health Authority) regardless of whether they were acting in their capacity as a public authority or her employer. The issue of horizontal and vertical effect of directives had been fully argued before the ECJ and they determined that:

> "... a Directive may not of itself impose obligations on an individual and that a provision of a Directive may not be relied upon as such against such an individual."

This looks like a very straightforward refusal to permit directives to have direct effect but problems remain.

1. Here, Mrs Marshall could rely on the Directive against her employers because they were a part of the state so how is "state" to be defined? The wider the definition, the more individuals will be allowed to rely on directives as directly effective.
2. Is the time now ripe for directives to be given horizontal direct effect?
3. Has the ECJ permitted individuals to avoid the harshness of this ruling against horizontal effect by requiring domestic courts to apply directives indirectly, as a matter of interpretation (the *Von Colson principle*)?

What is the state?

In the Marshall case, then, an Area Health Authority was regarded as an arm of the state, as was the Royal Ulster Constabulary in *Johnson v. RUC* (ECJ, 1984), but what of other publicly funded organisations such as universities or publicly run corporations? The House of Lords sought a preliminary ruling from the ECJ on the status of the British Gas Corporation and in their response, in *Foster v. British Gas* (ECJ, 1989), the ECJ took the opportunity to provide a definition, although it is not, I am afraid, definitive.

The Court ruled that a directive may be relied on as having direct effect against:

> "a body, whatever its legal form, which has been made responsible, pursuant to a measure adopted by the state, for providing a public service under the control of the state and has for that purpose special powers beyond those which result from the normal rules applicable in relation between individuals."

The ECJ ruled that:

1. It was up to them to rule which categories of body might be held bound by a directly effective directive.
2. It was up to the domestic court to decide whether a particular body fell within that category.

On the first of these points, it is still unclear which bodies will be classed as part of the state.

On the second point, the refinement of the concept of state is laid open to differences of interpretation by Member States' domestic courts.

The United Kingdom's definition of a state body was addressed in the 1992 case of *Doughty v. Rolls Royce* (C.A. 1992). Here, the Court of Appeal ruled that Rolls Royce did not qualify as part of the state, within the *Foster* definition because they did not provide a public service, nor possess any special powers, despite being wholly owned by the State.

Should horizontal direct effect now be extended to directives?

In three cases in 1993 and 1994, Advocates General separately argued that the court should reverse its decision in *Marshall* and give horizontal direct effect to directives. In the *Faccini Dori* case of 1994, an Italian student sought to rely on a 1985 directive, unimplemented by Italy, to cancel a contract she had entered into with a private company and now regretted. A number of reasons had been put forward by the Advocates General and academic commentators for an extension of the concept. For instance, the court is prepared to give horizontal direct effect to Treaty articles, despite the fact that, like directives, they are addressed to Member States. Secondly, the emergence of the single market in 1993 necessitated enforcing equality of the conditions of competition and the prohibition on discrimination. Thirdly, the TEU had amended the E.C. Treaty to require publication of directives in the Official Journal (so private persons had less excuse not to know their responsibilities under a directive). A full ECJ of 13 judges, nevertheless declined to adopt this reasoning and extend the concept of horizontal direct effect. They reiterated that the distinguishing basis of vertical direct effect was that the state should be barred from taking advantage of its own failure to comply with Community law.

The *Von Colson* principle and Marleasing

Where individuals seeking to rely on a directive cannot show that their opponent is a branch of the state, all may not be lost, because of a principle developed in *Von Colson and Kamann* (ECJ, 1983). Miss Von Colson was claiming that the German prison service had rejected her job application in breach of the Equal Treatment Directive and German law provided inadequate compensation. At the same time, another claimant, Miss Hartz, was making the same claim against a private company. Thus, the issue of horizontal/vertical direct effect and the public/private distinction was openly raised in a reference under Article 177 before the ECJ.

The ECJ avoided opening up these distinctions by relying on Article 5 of the E.C. Treaty. Article 5 requires states to "take all appropriate measures" to ensure fulfilment of their community obligations. This obligation falls on all parts of a state, said the Court, including its courts. Thus, the courts in a Member State must interpret national law in a manner which achieves the results referred to in Article 189, *i.e.* the objectives of a directive. The German courts were obliged, then, to interpret German law in such a way as to enforce the Equal Treatment

Directive. They added, however, an important qualification to this obligation: "it is for the national court to interpret and apply the legislation adopted for the implementation of the Directive in conformity with the requirements of Community Law, in *so far as it is given discretion to do so under national law*." These qualifying words were, however, moderated in *Marleasing* (below) to "as far as possible".

The significance of this case is that it provides horizontal effect in an indirect way. Even though E.C. law is not applied directly, it may still be applied indirectly through the medium of domestic interpretation. As one might expect, the application of the *Von Colson* principle very much depends on the interpretation of the domestic courts.

The principle was extended in a very significant way by the case of *Marleasing SA v. La Comercial Internacional de Alimentacion SA* (ECJ, 1990). The Court held that a national court was required to interpret its domestic legislation, *whether it is legislation adopted prior to or subsequent to the directive*, as far as possible within the light of the wording and purpose of a directive, in order to achieve the result envisaged by it. To extend the principle even to legislation adopted prior to a directive is a large extension and, some would argue, may perhaps have an unfortunate effect in holding parties bound by a directive which was different in scope to the domestic legislation with which they are dutifully complying. Some argue this case is a large step towards accepting the horizontal direct effect of directives. The end result of such interpretation certainly appears to be the same, as far as the individual litigants are concerned.

Further comments on this principle are necessary at this point: First, the Court declined to apply the principle to extend criminal liability (*Pretore di Salo v. Persons Unknown* (ECJ, 1986).

Secondly, it is unclear to what extent national courts are required to depart from national law in order to achieve the result sought by the directive. To achieve such a result may involve the national court departing significantly from the wording of national law. For instance, in the *Von Colson* case, the national law clearly limited the compensation payable to the two women to a nominal amount, whereas the ECJ held that the directive required the amount to be effective. It does seem, however, that the national court is not required to override the clear wording and intent of national law in order to make it comply with the directive which cannot be construed as directly effective.

Thirdly, the ECJ has no jurisdiction to construe national law itself. It can only interpret the directive and must leave it to the national court to construe national law in conformity with that interpretation.

Commentators, such as Weatherill and Beaumont, in *EC Law* (1995) warn, in strong terms, of the dangers of the *Von Colson* principle:

> "it is dangerous to include national courts within the concept of a 'member state' for the purposes of Article 189. It is inappropriate constitutionally to require judges to implement directives into national law; this is a matter for the executive and the legislature."

Damages from a tardy state: The *Francovich* principle

Yet another remedy is available for a citizen who has suffered as a result of the non-implementation of a directive but where the conditions for direct effect are not satisfied. In another case giving a bold interpretation to Article 5, the ECJ held that, in certain conditions, the aggrieved citizen may have a remedy against the state in damages.

In *Francovich v. Italy* (1991), the applicants were employees of businesses which became insolvent, leaving substantial arrears of unpaid salary. They brought proceedings in the Italian courts against Italy, for the recovery of compensation provided by Directive 80/987, which Italy had not implemented. The directive guaranteed payment of unpaid remuneration in the case of insolvency by the employer. The applicants could not rely on the concept of direct effect, however, because the directive's terms were insufficiently precise. The ECJ, nevertheless, held that the applicants were entitled to compensation from the state. Inherent in the Treaty, they said, was the principle that a Member State should be liable for damage to individuals caused by infringements of Community law for which it was responsible. Their interpretation rested, in particular, on Article 5, which places a duty on Member States to take all appropriate measures to ensure the fulfilment of Treaty obligations. The ECJ argued that to disallow damages against the state in these circumstance would weaken the protection of individual rights. The Court laid down three conditions for an individual claiming damages against a Member State for failing to implement or incorrectly implementing a directive:

1. The result laid down by the directive involves the attribution of rights attached to individuals.
2. The content of those rights must be capable of being identified from the provisions of the directive.
3. There must be a causal link between the failure by the Member State to fulfil its obligations and the damage suffered by the individuals.

The ECJ has left it up to each Member State to determine the competent courts and appropriate procedures for legal actions intended to enable individuals to obtain damages from the state. The procedures must be not less favourable than those relating to similar claims under domestic law and must not make it difficult or practically impossible to obtain damages from the state.

Decisions

The *Grad* case, discussed above, confirmed that decisions could be directly effective, provided they meet all the required criteria. This does not pose any of the moral problems of horizontal direct effect of directives, since decisions are, in any event, only binding on the addressee.

International Agreements to which the E.C. is party

The ECJ has shown an inconsistent approach to the question of which international agreements to which the E.C. is a party can be directly effective. The full picture can only be painted by the ECJ on a piecemeal basis, from case to case.

Damages from a State whose legislature flouts E.C. law

In *Factortame 4*, properly known as the joined cases *Brasserie du Pecheur SA v. Federal Republic of Germany* and *R. v. Secretary of State for Transport, ex parte Factortame Ltd and Others (No. 4)* (ECJ, 1996), the Court extended the principle it had developed in *Francovich* to permit a claim of damages against a state, to instances where its national legislature had passed a law which was in serious breach of E.C. law. In the first case, French beer manufacturers were claiming damages against Germany for passing beer purity laws that effectively excluded the import of their beer. In the second case, the United Kingdom Parliament had passed the Merchant Shipping Act 1988, which effectively excluded foreign fishing vessels, notably Spanish, from their right to fish in British coastal waters, by laying down registration conditions of residence, nationality and domicile of vessel owners. Spanish fishermen complained that the Act offended against Art. 52 E.C., which guarantees freedom of establishment. In prior cases, the Court had already ruled the domestic legislation to be in breach of E.C. law. What was now at issue was whether the aggrieved parties could claim damages against the respective states in the national courts. The *Factortame* case had been referred by the Queen's Bench Divisional Court for an Art. 177 preliminary ruling. The ECJ decided the following (paraphrased):

1. The *Francovich* principle, making states liable for loss or damage suffered by individuals and caused by the state's breach of E.C. law, applied to all state authorities, including the legislature;

2. The conditions of a claim of damages in this context were:
   a. that the rule of Community law breached was intended to confer rights on the individuals who had suffered loss or injury;
   b. that the breach was sufficiently serious: the Member State had manifestly and gravely disregarded the limits on its discretion;

c. that there was a direct causal link between the breach and the damage sustained by the individuals.

The state must make good the consequences of the damage, in accordance with its national law on liability but the conditions laid down must not be less favourable than for a domestic claim and must not make it excessively difficult or impossible to make a claim. (Comment: in the context of English law, it was virtually impossible for the Spanish fishing vessel owners to claim damages in the English courts, because we have no substantive or procedural law enabling a claim for damages against Parliament);

3. Such a claim could not be made conditional on establishing a degree of fault going beyond that of a sufficiently serious breach of Community law;

4. Reparation must be commensurate with the damage sustained and this might include exemplary damages, where a public authority had acted oppressively, arbitrarily or unconstitutionally.

It was left to the domestic legal system of each Member State to set the criteria for determining the extent of reparation.

5. Damages could not be limited to those sustained after a judgment finding such an infringement of Community law.

The upshot of these cases, at the time of writing, in 1996, is that the onus is on us to find some procedure, in the English courts, for making a claim against the state for a breach of E.C. law by Parliament. Not only must we find a procedure but we must devise some substantive cause of action in damages. Neither the ground nor the procedure must be too difficult to allow the Spainish claim. For instance, we can forget any idea of limiting damage to the proof of the moribund tort of misfeasance in a public office, which is difficult to establish and was dead all this century until revived, in rare cases, since 1985.

Notice that *Factortame 4* was swiftly followed by a case which clarified how bad the breach of E.C. law had to be before damages could be claimed. In *R. v. H.M. Treasury, ex parte British Telecommunications plc* (ECJ, 1996), the Court ruled that damages could be claimed by individuals who had suffered loss as a consequence of a state's enacting a directive incorrectly (this much was not new). The important point about this case, however, was that they ruled that the breach of E.C. law was not sufficiently serious to merit damages. The United Kingdom had acted in good faith and simply made a mistake in its enactment of the relevant Directive. The wording of the Directive was ambiguous and several other Member States had also misinterpreted it so there was no manifest and grave breach of E.C. law, as required by *Factortame 4*.

10. DIRECT EFFECT OF COMMUNITY LAW IN THE UNITED KINGDOM

The European Communities Act 1972 gave legal effect to E.C. law in the United Kingdom. Pay close attention to the wording of section 2(1):

> "All such rights, powers, liabilities, obligations and restrictions from time to time created or arising by or under the Treaties, and all such remedies and procedures from time to time provided for by or under the Treaties, as in accordance with the Treaties are without further enactment to be given legal effect or used in the United Kingdom shall be recognised and available in law, and be enforced, allowed and followed accordingly; and the expression 'enforceable Community right' and similar expressions shall be read as referring to one to which this subsection applies."

In the *Factortame (No. 1)* case of 1990, the House of Lords interpreted "enforceable Community right" to mean directly effective legal right. This section gives effect to all directly effective Community law, whether made prior to or after the passing of the Act.

Section 3 binds all our courts to interpret matters of E.C. law in accordance with the rulings of the ECJ and requires our courts to take judicial notice of E.C. legislation and the opinions of the ECJ.

Our courts have had no problem in applying directly effective provisions. They seem to have been reluctant, however, to apply the *Von Colson* principle. In *Duke v. Reliance Systems Ltd*, Duke complained that she had been forced to retire at 60, despite her male colleagues' being permitted to work until 65. Equal Treatment Directive 76/207 was not enacted into domestic law until the Sex Discrimination Act 1986. Duke could not rely on the directive as directly effective because her employer was a private company. She argued that the English courts should construe the unamended Sex Discrimination Act 1975 in a manner consistent with the Equal Treatment Directive, treating her enforced retirement as unlawful dismissal. The House of Lords considered the case of *Von Colson* but opined that it did not provide a power to interfere with the method or result of the interpretation of national legislation by national courts. They noted that the Equal Treatment Directive postdated the Sex Discrimination Act 1975 and thought it would be unfair on Reliance to "distort" the construction of the Act to accommodate it. The House of Lords later applied the same objections in relation to the Northern Ireland legislation, despite the fact that it was passed after the Directive (*Finnegan* (1990) H.L.).

Nevertheless, the House is prepared to make a distinction when construing national legislation that has been passed in order to implement a directive. In *Pickstone v. Freemans plc* (1989, H.L.) the House adopted a purposive construction in interpreting an amendment to the Equal Pay Act 1970, in order to make it consistent with the United Kingdom's obligations under the Equal Pay Directive. The same purposive approach was taken in *Litster v. Forth Dry Dock & Engineering Co. Ltd* (1990, H.L.). In this case, Lord Templeman said he thought the *Von Colson* principle imposed a duty on the United Kingdom courts to give a purposive construction to United Kingdom legislation which had been passed to give effect to directives. In *Webb v. EMO Air Cargo (U.K.) Ltd* (1992, H.L.), Lord Keith, giving the opinion of the House, said it was the duty of the United Kingdom court to construe domestic legislation in accordance with the ECJ's interpretation of a relevant Community directive "if that can be done without distorting the meaning of the domestic legislation." He noted that, according to the ECJ, this obligation on the domestic courts only arises where domestic law is open to an interpretation consistent with a directive. In this case the House agreed with the Court of Appeal, the Employment Appeal Tribunal and an industrial tribunal that the applicant had not suffered discrimination under English law. They nevertheless asked the ECJ to construe the relevant directive and the application of the principle of equal treatment to the circumstances of the case. The ECJ sent back its interpretation, flatly disagreeing with the House and ruling that the facts of the case disclosed discrimination. The House applied the ECJ's ruling in October 1995. The report provides an interesting example of how the House had to construe an English statute in accordance with E.C. law in a way which seemed to run contrary to the instincts of domestic courts at all levels.

11. SUPREMACY OF COMMUNITY LAW

Curiously, the founding treaty of the European Community, the Treaty of Rome 1957, did not prescribe the supremacy of Community law over national law. It was left to the embryonic ECJ in developing its limbs, to describe the conception of its supremacy in *Costa v. E.N.E.L.* (ECJ, 1964). This quotation is as oft-cited and as jurisprudentially significant as Lord Atkin's famous neighbour principle, which did so much more than just resolve the problems caused when a snail was left to decompose in a bottle of ginger beer. In addition, the words below are so constitutionally significant, they should be learned and absorbed by every British citizen, let alone every student of English law:

> "By creating a Community of unlimited duration, having its own institutions, its own personality, its own legal capacity and capacity of representation on the international plane and, more particularly, real powers stemming from a limitation of sovereignty or a transfer of powers from the States to the Community, the Member States have limited their sovereignty rights, albeit within limited fields, and have thus created a body of law which binds both their nationals and themselves.
>
> The integration into the laws of each Member State of provisions which derive from the Community, and more generally the terms and the spirit of the Treaty, make it impossible for the States, as a corollary, to accord precedence to a unilateral and subsequent measure over a legal system accepted by them on a basis of reciprocity."

By 1970, the Court had asserted the supremacy of E.C. law, even over Member States' constitutions (the *Internationale Handelsgesellschaft* case, ECJ, 1970). By 1977, in *Simmenthal*, the Court had explained that this meant that every court, however lowly, was under a duty to disapply national law in favour of Community law, where there was a clear conflict. Furthermore, in the *Factortame* case of 1990, the Court added that national courts must be capable of protecting claimed Community law rights in the face of clear contrary provisions in national law, pending the ECJ's final ruling on the precise nature of those rights.

The effects of E.C. sovereignty within the United Kingdom

In the European Communities Act 1972, the British Parliament effectively gave away its legislative sovereignty in matters within the E.C.'s sphere of activity, recognising the principle of supremacy of directly effective E.C. law over domestic legislation. The crucial words of section 2(4) are both retrospective and prospective:

> "... any enactment passed or to be passed ... shall be construed and have effect subject to the foregoing provisions of this section".

This means that, where domestic law conflicts with directly effective E.C. law, the latter must be applied and the only way of altering this position is to repeal this subsection. The House of Lords recognised that this was the effect of this subsection, in *Factortame* (1990), when they disapplied part of the Merchant Shipping Act 1988, the clear words of which flew in the face of established Community law rights, including freedom of establishment and non-discrimination.

In this case, Spanish owners of fishing vessels sought to register as British so that they would have access to the British Fishing quota under the common fisheries policy. The 1988 Act attempted to limit registration to British managed vessels. *Factortame* and others sought a judicial review in the High Court of the legality of the Act. The High Court referred the question of E.C. law to the ECJ but, meanwhile, the procedural question of how to grant interim relief found its way up to the House of Lords. The House declined to grant an interim injunction against the Crown as an injunction cannot, in English law, bind the Crown. Furthermore, they objected, the applicants' Community law rights were "necessarily uncertain" until determined by the ECJ and appeared to run directly contrary to Parliament's sovereign will. They sought a preliminary ruling from the ECJ. The court answered by saying that where the sole obstacle preventing a national court from granting interim relief based on Community law is a rule of national law, that rule of national law must be set aside. Not surprisingly, when the ECJ ruled on the substantive question, they upheld Factortame's complaint that part of the Merchant Shipping Act ran contrary to E.C. law.

In *Equal Opportunities Commission v. Secretary of State for Employment* (1994, H.L.), the House of Lords confirmed that the *Factortame* case had established that a declaration could be obtained in judicial review proceedings that an Act of Parliament is incompatible with Community law. In this case the House accepted the EOC's complaint that part of the Employment Protection (Consolidation) Act 1978 was in breach of Community law. The Act was subsequently amended by Parliament.

A comment on Factortame 4

We have reacted especially badly to the *Factorame 4* ruling, affronted at the thought of having to pay retrospective damages to the Spanish for stopping them coming and raiding "our" fish stocks. What is so ridiculous is that we reacted as if the ruling were a surprise. When we passed this piece of protectionist legislation in 1988, we were warned formally by the Commission, in 1989, acting under their Article 169 powers, that we were in breach of the Treaty so we might have guessed that the ultimate punchline would be that we would have to pay damages to the Spanish. We reacted with the same indignant horror to *Factortame 1*, in 1990, which effectively ruled that a part of the Merchant Shipping Act would have to be suspended, as if we were shocked at this assault on the legislative sovereignty of Parliament. Apparently many of us had not noticed, or worked out that we had given this away, on joining the common market, as it then was, in January 1973. As if to rub salt into the wound made by *Factortame 4*, in March 1996, the beef crisis broke out within days of the judgment. We are now in the hypocritical position of arguing that the Court's powers should be curbed, by the 1996 Intergovernmental Conference (the renegotiation of Maastricht), yet at the same time lodging a claim before the Court against the Commission for losses caused by the export ban on British beef.

CHAPTER 13

HISTORY

1. CONTINUITY

In the foregoing chapters a survey has been attempted of the various elements in the English legal system as it exists in 1996. It is now necessary to complete the picture, for an examination to be made in outline of the history of the system so that the emergence of the present structure can be fully appreciated. The most pertinent factor of this study is that the history is a continuing one; the British system of government, and the legal institutions which form part of it, are only explicable in terms of history. The Inns of Court, the Queen's Bench and Chancery Divisions of the High Court, the Justice of the Peace and the jury—these institutions, like many in the system all have a long history.

One important factor is that whereas most continental legal systems rely heavily on legal principles derived from Roman Law, the English legal system has remained comparatively uninfluenced by this source. The reasons for this would seem to be connected with the unbroken historical development of the system in England, where at no time was it felt necessary to look outside the principles of common law or equity for assistance. Inevitably, through the ecclesiastical courts in particular, some Roman Law influence can be traced but in general terms this is very limited, and especially when comparison is made with systems elsewhere. Indeed, the reason why England resisted the "invasion" of Roman Law, which forms the base of European civil law systems, was that a unified common law system was already growing strength from the period prior to the Norman Conquest.

2. EARLY HISTORY

ANGLO-SAXON LAWS

The earliest English laws of which there is documentary evidence date from the Anglo-Saxon period of English history before the Norman Conquest. These laws are not strictly English laws; more accurately they are the laws relating to a particular tribal area such as Kent, Wessex or Mercia. In practice these laws are based on what seems to have been the original customs of the settlers in question. Not unnaturally there are marked discrepancies in the details of the laws remaining from the different areas. They clearly derive from the time before England emerged as a national unit.

THE NORMAN CONQUEST (1066)

The Anglo-Saxon divisions were just giving way to a national entity when the Norman invasion of England occurred. The result of the Battle of Hastings in 1066 led to William the Conqueror ascending the English throne determined on a process of centralisation. William's tactics were to impose strong national government and this he did by causing his Norman followers to become the major land-owners throughout the country. The system used was "subinfeudation" under which all land belonged to the monarch and was by him granted to his followers on certain conditions. In turn they could grant their land to their tenants. Again subject to conditions, those tenants could make similar grants and so on, down the ladder. This method of granting land created the complete feudal system under which tenants owed duties to their lord, whilst he in turn owed duties to his lord and so on up to the monarch, as the supreme point of the feudal pyramid. However, the system never became as firmly entrenched in this country as it did, for instance, in France.

FEUDAL COURTS

In the development of the feudal system a characteristic benefit to the feudal lord was the right to hold his own court. From the holding of this court he would obtain financial benefits, whilst at the same time it gave him effective power over the locality. So far as the ordinary individual was concerned this local manor court was the one which affected him most. Bearing in mind that the concept of central authority in law and government was still comparatively new, it was to take a long time before the royal courts were able to exercise control over these local courts. Although the passage of centuries did see the transfer of real power from local to national courts, these feudal courts remained in being in many instances down to the property legislation of 1925. Until 1925 there was a tenure of property called "copyhold", which involved the registration of the transaction in the local court roll so that the person held the land by "copy" of the court roll. This was a survival of a feudal court responsibility.

ROYAL COURTS

Following the Norman Conquest, succeeding monarchs soon realised that besides the need for strong national government there was also a need for the development of a system of national law and order. To this end the closest advisers of the monarch—the *"curia regis"*, or "King's council", as it was called—encouraged, over a period of time, the establishment of three separate royal courts which sat at Westminster. These were:

(i) the Court of Exchequer, which as the name applies was mainly concerned with cases affecting the royal revenue, but which also had a limited civil jurisdiction;

(ii) the Court of King's Bench, which taking its name from the original concept of the monarch sitting with his judges *"in banco"*—on the bench—at Westminster, dealt with both civil and criminal cases in which the King had an interest; and

(iii)   the Court of Common Pleas, which was established to hear civil cases brought by one individual against another.

Each of the courts had its own judges. In the Court of Exchequer sat judges called Barons, with a presiding judge known as the Chief Baron. This court appears to be the oldest of the three, emerging in recognisable form in the early thirteenth century having developed out of the financial organisation responsible for the royal revenues. The Court of King's Bench had its own Chief Justice and separate judges, and was closely linked with the monarch and the Great Council for a very long time. This was due, in particular, to the original understanding that this was the court which followed the King's person. The Court of Common Pleas had its own Chief Justice and judges and left records from the early thirteenth century.

All three courts seem to have been required by the monarch—Stow in his survey of London says in 1224—to make their base in Westminster Hall and there arose continuing conflicts between them over jurisdiction. The importance of getting more and more work was largely brought about by the fact that the judges were paid out of the court fees. At any rate these three royal courts, later added to by the introduction of a Court of Chancery, survived five centuries before being reconstructed into the present High Court of Justice in the Judicature Acts 1873–75. The ultimate merger of Exchequer and Common Pleas into the Queen's Bench Division came about in 1880.

3. THE COMMON LAW

ORIGIN

As a centralised system of law and order gradually developed, so it became necessary for the various customary laws of the different regions to give way to national laws. This national law came to be known as the common law. It was called "common" because it was common to the whole country, as opposed to the local customs which had previously predominated in the different regions. Since inevitably the different customs at times turned out to be in conflict, the decisions of the judges, absorbing certain of these customs and rejecting others, came to be of first-rate importance. They were creating "the law of the realm". Consequently, a feature of the original establishment of the common law is that it was derived entirely from case law.

DEVELOPMENT

The Norman Kings, in attempting to weld the country together, made use of royal commissioners to travel the country to deal with governmental matters of one kind and another. The production of the "Domesday Book", as a property and financial survey, is the best known example of this system. The extension of these activities to the judicial field seems to have arisen not long after the Conquest, when the King would appoint judges as royal commissioners, charged with certain royal powers, to travel different parts of the country to deal with civil and criminal matters in the locality in which they arose.

The sending of judges, or, as they were originally called, "itinerant justices in Eyre", around the country, dates from not long after the Conquest; but the assize system, as later developed, really dates from the reign of Henry II (1154–89). The assize system only came to an end with the passing of the Courts Act 1971.

It was an important part of the work of these judges to formulate the common law. A task which over a lengthy period of time they did, by meeting together formally and informally to resolve problems which had arisen in the cases coming before them. The principles of law thus laid down, once accepted and developed, formed the common law. As these judges were linked with the courts meeting in Westminster Hall, the building up of a national system grew apace. However, the common law never completely abolished local custom. In fact, as we have seen in the chapter on Sources, custom has remained a source of law to the present time, even though it rarely applies today.

FORMS OF ACTION

In addition to settling principles of law which were to be followed nationally, the courts also began to establish formal rules relating to the procedure to be adopted in cases coming before them. These rules laid down early that actions were to be begun by the issue of a royal writ, and that the claim made was to be set out in an accepted fashion. This was called a form of action and over a period of time the system took on rigidity in that the judges came to take the view that unless a claimant could find an appropriate form of action their claim was not one known to the law. The court officials responsible for the issue of writs tried initially to satisfy the demands of claimants by drawing up a new form of action, but the judges frowned on this course and the practice was stopped by the Provisions of Oxford 1258. So great was the resulting dissatisfaction that 30 years later by the Statute of Westminster 1285 this strict approach was slightly relaxed, so that the officials could issue a new writ, where the new situation was closely related to that covered by an existing writ. The new writs so issued became known as writs *"in consimili casu"*. The effect which the writ system had on the development of the legal system is seen below in the section concerning Equity.

Common law remains in being today in that the decisions of judges are still adding to it and in theory the legislation produced by Parliament is supplementing it. Every development in the system operates on the basis that its foundation is the common law. Some confusion has arisen because there are several different meanings attaching to the term:

(i) In the historical sense which has already been examined, common law refers to the national law of this country as opposed to local law or custom. It is the law "common" to England and Wales.

(ii) Sometimes the term is used to mean the law as made by the judges, in contrast to the law as made by Parliament. In this context, common law is limited to case decisions or precedents coming from the courts of common law and equity and so does not include legislation. It must not be overlooked that, as a result of the doctrine of parliamentary supremacy, legislation can always change or overrule the common law.

(iii) As the next section will show, there were, for centuries in England and Wales, two parallel systems of law, one known as the common law and the other as equity. In some contexts the term common law does not include the law derived from the courts of equity.

(iv) Finally the term common law may be used to draw a contrast to systems of foreign law. Here common law takes in both equity and legislation in that it means the complete law of England and Wales. When referring to an overseas country which has derived its legal system from England and Wales the term common law system or jurisdiction is used. This explains why sometimes an English judge will find case decisions from such countries contain persuasive arguments.

4. EQUITY

ORIGIN

The difficulty which was experienced in the common law courts in relation to the use of writs and the forms of action led to increasing dissatisfaction with the system. Litigants who were unable to get satisfaction from the courts turned to the monarch and petitioned him to do justice to his subjects and provide them with a remedy. The monarch handed these petitions on to the Lord Chancellor, who, as Keeper of the King's Conscience and an ecclesiastic, seemed to be a suitable person to deal with them. He set up his own Court of Chancery where he, or his representative, would sit to dispose of these petitions. In doing this work the Lord Chancellor would be guided by equity, or fairness, in coming to his decisions. Consequently, the legal decisions which succeeding Lord Chancellors made came to be known collectively as equity. The system seems to have become well established in the course of the fifteenth century.

Because of the rapid increase in the judicial nature of the work, it was soon found necessary to have a lawyer as Lord Chancellor. The discretion vested in early Lord Chancellors gradually gave way to a system of judicial precedent in equity, but it was a long time before the common law joke died, about equity being as long as the Chancellor's foot. In practice both common law and equity came to operate as parallel systems, with each set of courts regarding itself as bound by its own judicial precedents.

DEVELOPMENT

Having once begun to remedy the wrongs brought about by the rigidity and technicality of the common law system, equity soon found itself establishing a jurisdiction over matters where the common law had failed, and continued to fail, to recognise legal rights and duties. The law relating to trusts, for example, was entirely based on decisions of the Court of Chancery. Nonetheless Equity was always a "gloss" on the common law; it always presumed the existence of the common law and simply supplemented it where necessary. That it continued to exist for some five centuries is an indication of the unchanging nature of English legal institutions, as well as of the important contribution which equity made to the development of English law.

(a) Examples of new rights

The whole of the law of trusts, which was to become an important aspect of property law, owed its existence entirely to the willingness of equity to recognise and enforce the obligation of a trustee to a beneficiary.

Equity accepted the use of the mortgage as a method of borrowing money against the security of real property, when the common law took a literal view of the obligation undertaken by the borrower. It introduced the "equity of redemption" to enable a borrower to retain the property which was the security for the loan, even where there was default under the strict terms of the mortgage deed.

(b) Examples of new remedies

At common law the only remedy for breach of contract was damages, a money payment as compensation for the loss suffered. Equity realised that in some cases damages was not an adequate remedy, and therefore proceeded to introduce the equitable remedies of injunction and specific performance. An injunction is used to prevent a party from acting in breach of their legal obligations; a decree of specific performance is used to order a party to carry out their side of a contract. These remedies mean that a party to a contract cannot just decide to break it and pay damages.

Other equitable remedies are the declaratory order or judgment; the right to have a deed corrected by the process known as rectification; and the right to rescind (withdraw from) a contract. The willingness of equity to intervene where fraud was proven and its preparedness to deal with detailed accounts in the law of trusts and the administration of estates, also gained it wide jurisdiction. The appointment of a receiver is another solution to the problem of the management of certain financial matters, and was introduced by equity.

(c) Examples of new procedures

In contrast to the rigid system of common law remedies equity favoured a flexibility of approach. Consequently it was prepared, by a "subpoena", to order witnesses to attend, to have them examined and cross-examined orally, to require relevant documents to be produced, known as Discovery of Documents, to insist on relevant questions being answered, by the use of Interrogatories, and to have the case heard in English, where the common law for centuries used Latin. In the event of a failure to comply with an order, equity was prepared to impose immediate sanctions for this contempt of court.

Another classification sometimes employed is to define the jurisdiction of equity as exclusive, concurrent and auxiliary. In the exclusive jurisdiction sense, equity recognised actions, as in trusts and mortgages, where the common law would provide no remedy; in the concurrent jurisdiction sense equity would add to the remedies provided by the common law, as by the introduction of the injunction and the decree of specific performance; in the auxiliary jurisdiction sense equity employed a more flexible procedure than the common law. It will be seen that these three terms simply emphasise the ways in which equity can be seen to be related to, but to be different from, common law.

MAXIMS OF EQUITY

As a result of its supplemental role, it became possible over the years for an observer to point to certain characteristics of equity. These became so well known as to be called the maxims of equity. Among the most famous are:

He who comes to equity must come with clean hands;
Equity will not suffer a wrong to be without remedy;
Delay defeats equity; and
Equity looks to the intent rather than to the form.

The maxims emphasise that equity, being based in its origins on fairness and natural justice, attempted to maintain this approach throughout its later history. Certainly, the judges retained their personal discretion so that equitable remedies were not, and are not, obtainable as of right. It is very important to understand, for example, that remedies obtainable following judicial review are equitable, and thus discretionary.

RELATIONSHIP BETWEEN COMMON LAW AND EQUITY

Early history

Naturally, as might be presumed, in the early stages of their respective development relations between the two systems were comparatively strained. The common law lawyers regarded equity as an interloper, lacking the firmly-based legal principles with which they were familiar. They were unable, unlike the modern observer with the advantage of hindsight, to see that equity was invaluable in remedying deficiencies in the common law and in encouraging the latter to develop its substantive law and procedure.

As the Court of Chancery built up its jurisdiction and the two systems could be seen to be operating on a parallel basis, inevitably the question arose, what was to happen in the unusual instance when there was a conflict? This problem was solved by James I, in the *Earl of Oxford's case* (1615), by a ruling that where there was such a conflict, the rules of equity were to prevail.

The later history of equity was dogged in the eighteenth and nineteenth centuries by the courts of Chancery becoming overburdened with work, with increasing reliance being placed on judicial precedent and consequent delays. Dickens' attack in his novel, *Bleak House*, on the delays and costs in the system, seems to have been throughly justified, with some examples of cases awaiting judgment dragging on for scores of years until both parties were dead. Parliament in the 1850s endeavoured by legislation—the Common Law Procedure Acts 1852–54 and the Chancery (Amendment) Act 1858—to ease the position, but the dual systems continued in being, to the sometimes substantial detriment of litigants, until the Supreme Court of Judicature Acts 1873–75.

5. NINETEENTH CENTURY DEVELOPMENTS

THE SUPREME COURT OF JUDICATURE ACTS 1873–75

This legislation reorganised the existing court structures completely and, in the process, formally brought together the common law courts and the courts of Chancery. In the Supreme Court of Judicature set up by the Acts, the three original royal courts became three divisions of the new High Court of Justice, the Court of Chancery which administered equity became the fourth division, *i.e.* the Chancery Division of the High Court, and a fifth division, dealing with those matters not within common law or equity, namely Probate, Divorce and Admiralty, completed the new arangements. By Order in Council in 1880, the three royal courts were merged to form the Queen's Bench Division, thus leaving the three Divisions of the High Court—Queen's Bench, Chancery and Probate, Divorce and Admiralty—which were then to remain unchanged for 90 years.

The Judicature Acts 1873–75 placed on a statutory basis the old rule that where common law and equity conflict, equity shall prevail. At the same time, it gave power to all the courts to administer the principles of common law and equity and to grant the remedies of both, as circumstances in a case demanded. Consequently, the old conflict no longer arises, although common law and equity principles still exist.

By bringing the two systems together administratively, and allowing the High Court judge to exercise the principles, procedures and remedies of common law and equity in a single case in the one court, it seemed to many people that the two systems had merged. That this was somewhat superficial is borne out by the exclusive jurisdictions left to the Queen's Bench and Chancery Divisions. In practice the work formerly done by the Court of Chancery is exactly that dealt with in the Chancery Division; equally it has its own judges selected from those barristers practising at the Chancery bar. A Chancery case remains something quite unlike a common law case, and the same can be said of the procedure.

The whole of the legislation has now been consolidated in the Supreme Court Act 1981.

PROBATE, DIVORCE AND ADMIRALTY JURISDICTION

The Supreme Court of Judicature Acts 1873–75 in their reconstruction of the court system established a separate Division of the High Court of Justice called the Probate, Divorce and Admiralty Division. Why was it that these three branches of the law merited a division of their own?

The answer is that these three important legal topics fell neither within the common law nor equity jurisdictions, since Probate (which is concerned with wills) and divorce were, for centuries, treated as ecclesiastical matters, and there was a separate Admiralty Court inevitably influenced by international shipping practices.

Probate and divorce were transferred from the ecclesiastical courts to the ordinary civil courts in 1857 by the setting up of a Court of Probate and a separate Divorce Court.

The High Court of Admiralty although of great age historically gradually lost its widest jurisdiction to the common law courts, but it retained powers over collisions at sea, salvage and prize cases. All other aspects of the law merchant, that is the law affecting traders, had over the centuries been transferred to the common law courts.

APPEAL COURTS

The Supreme Court of Judicature Acts 1873–75, in creating a Court of Appeal alongside the new High Court of Justice, had intended that this court with its specially designated Lords Justices of Appeal should be the final appellate court for civil matters. Political considerations intervened, however and the proposal to remove judicial functions from the House of Lords was shelved. The Appellate Jurisdiction Act 1876 provided for the retention of the House of Lords as the final appeal court in civil cases and for the creation of special judges, Lords of Appeal in Ordinary, as life peers to staff the court.

6. TWENTIETH CENTURY DEVELOPMENTS

CRIMINAL COURTS

In 1907, the Criminal Appeal Act established the Court of Criminal Appeal to provide for the first time a general right of appeal for persons convicted and sentenced in indictable criminal cases. A further appeal in matters of general public importance lay to the House of Lords. The Court of Criminal Appeal became the Court of Appeal (Criminal Division) by the Criminal Appeal Act 1966.

The role of the Queen's Bench Divisional Court in ruling on points of law arising by way of case stated in summary criminal cases was amended by the Administration of Justice Act 1960. This Act enabled an appeal in a case of general public importance to be taken to the House of Lords if the divisional court grants a certificate to that effect and leave is obtained from the divisional court or the appeal committee of the House of Lords.

The court structure for trying indictable criminal cases was substantially changed by the Courts Act 1971 which abolished the historically derived Court of Quarter Sessions and Assizes and replaced them with a court called the Crown Court. The Crown Court was to be organised on a six circuit basis so as to achieve a much needed flexibility to lead to the prompt trial of indictable criminal cases.

CIVIL COURTS

The Administration of Justice Act 1970 created a Family Division of the High Court and amended the jurisdiction of the Queen's Bench and Chancery divisions, redistributing the functions of the former Probate Divorce and Admiralty Division. One novel change in appeal provisions was the introduction by the Administration of Justice Act 1969 of a possible "leap-frog" appeal from the High Court to the House of Lords, by-passing the Court of Appeal. The procedure was, however, made subject to stringent conditions which in practice limit its use.

RECENT HISTORY

The Courts and Legal Services Act 1990, Pt. I, was designed to redistribute civil work by giving almost concurrent jurisdiction to the High Court and county courts. The Children Act 1989 gave concurrent jurisdiction on matters relating to children to the three first instance civil courts. (For details, see elsewhere.)

Chapter 14

LAW REFORM AND THE CHANGING LEGAL SYSTEM

1. THE INEVITABILITY OF CHANGE

The one certainty in the study of any area of law is that it will be characterised by change. Pressure placed by the public on the politicians will lead to the legislature constantly producing new legislation. Every branch of the law, together with the legal system which lies behind it, is constantly undergoing change. Annually, Parliament enacts some 80 new Acts of Parliament whilst substantial changes in existing law are also effected by the 2,000 new statutory instruments which become law every year.

Equally, the decisions of the courts lead to significant changes in the law. There are today more judges and more cases to be tried, than ever before. The judgments pronounced by the judges, and particularly those in the Court of Appeal and the House of Lords, involve the development of the legal principles in every branch of the law. As was seen in Chapter 11, the doctrine of judicial precedent is of particular importance in the English legal system. This is because the decisions of the judges make a continuous contribution to the growth of the various branches of the law. At the same time, the obligation to strive for certainty and consistency causes the judge to ensure that her decision matches, derives from and supports the earlier decisions in that branch of the law.

Inevitably, the more complex the society, the more complex the law and the more complicated the cases which arise. The student of contract will have observed how the nineteenth century leading cases concerned with the sale of horses have given way to involved transactions betwen large commercial corporations. Modern 'cases have found the courts concerned with, for example, the principles of offer and acceptance, when telex, DX and fax machines have been the channels of communication betwen the parties. As such cases are resolved so they add something to the previously accepted law in the law of contract. The same is true of decisions in other branches of the law. When it is recollected that every year many volumes of law reports are published and that even so these contain only a fraction of the total number of cases decided, the scale of change is self-evident.

The result is that in the modern state there can be no lull in legislation nor in case decisions, and the task of the lawyer in keeping pace with change is unenviable, albeit fascinating. It might be thought that changes in the system would be markedly fewer than changes in substantive law but, in practice, there is substantial and constant campaigning by pressure groups like JUSTICE, Liberty, the Statute Law Reform Society and the Legal Action Group, for changes in the legal system. These changes may relate to criminal procedure, to evidence, to the form of legislation or to such matters as legal aid and advice.

2. METHODS OF LAW REFORM

PARLIAMENT

In the realm of change by legislation it is usually the case that the Act in question will have emanated from the government department responsible for the matter, probably at the request of the Minister for the time being. The Minister, in turn, will be under pressure from government colleagues. Education legislation, for example, will be introduced by the Secretary of State for Education and will have been prepared initially by that department. Only a very few private Members of Parliament succeed each year in getting a public Act on to the Statute Book. This is because parliamentary time is so valuable that the government tends to demand almost all of it. If the production of legislation by the government departments is examined, it will be apparent that often the pressure for the legislation has come from interested bodies outside Parliament who wish to see certain changes made. Some of these pressure groups, like the National Farmers' Union or the County Councils' Association, are very powerful organisations with wide national support, but sometimes pressure from a small organisation can have the desired effect.

Very often legislation will be introduced following the report of a Royal Commission or an ad hoc review body. For example, the report of the Civil Justice Review Board (1988) on the distribution of civil business and civil procedure led to Part I of the CLSA 1990 and there are many other recent examples explained earlier in this book.

THE JUDICIARY

As was seen in Chapter 2 above, the judicial function inevitably involves the creation of new law. The scope for the judge effectively to change the law is limited, however, since the judge is presumed to be stating the principle of law which applies to the case, not producing a new principle of law. Equally important is the restraint imposed on the judge by the application of the doctrine of judicial precedent. Today it is rare for a case to arise for determination which involves an issue for which there is no precedent in point. Much more likely is the judicial difficulty of a plethora of conflicting authorities which the judge has to attempt to rationalise in his judgment. Nevertheless, judges can effect quite dramatic changes in the law through the medium of statutory interpretation and reinterpretation of the common law. This happened in 1991 when the lower courts and finally the House of Lords abolished the rule that a husband cannot be guilty of raping his wife.

Ostensibly, judges are not concerned with law reform but it is not uncommon for them to draw attention to anomalies and to call for change. In *President of India v. La Pintada Compania* (1985) Lords Scarman and Roskill called for legislation to amend the law that interest cannot be charged on a debt paid late.

THE LAW COMMISSION

The Labour government, which took office in 1964, passed, as a matter of urgency, the Law Commissions Act 1965, bringing into existence a body made up of five commissioners and a consultant, together with a staff of civil servants. This organisation gives its full time to law reform;

261

in fact the exact terms of reference of the two commissions, one for England and Wales and one for Scotland, are to "keep under review all the law with which [they are respectively] concerned with a view to its systematic development and reform, including in particular the codification of such law, the elimination of anomalies, the repeal of obsolete and unnecessary enactments, the reduction of the number of separate enactments and generally the simplification and modernisation of the law".

The commissioners who have been appointed since 1965 have all been distinguished lawyers seconded from their employment for a five-year period. The chairperson has, in practice, always been a High Court judge. The other commissioners have been either barristers or solicitors, and despite criticism, no lay representatives have been given the opportunity to become commissioners. It is comparatively early to attempt to assess the effect of the Law Commission on its vast task, but a large number of recommendations from its many reports have found their way into legislation. The annual report of the Law Commission contains an appendix which shows whether or not its reports have been given effect. Until recently, implementation by legislation has been quick and effective but the more recent reports have complained of a slowing down in the government's announcement of its policy towards the Commission's and other law reform bodies' recommendations. The Land Registration Act 1986, for instance, implements a 1983 report of the Law Commission.

The 1965 Act, as well as giving the Law Commission major responsibilities for law reform, specified, it will be noted, four separate features which that body is to have regard to in the course of its work. These are codification of law, the repeal of obsolete and unnecessary enactments, the reduction of the number of separate enactments and the elimination of anomalies. Codification is inevitably a long-term plan, since in each case the ultimate objective is a single self-contained code, which will be "the statement of all the relevant law in a logical and coherent form". Good progress has been made in the repeal of obsolete statutory provisions, in particular by the enactment of several Statute Law (Repeals) Acts, the latest being in 1986 and in the passage of many consolidating statutes which contribute to a simplification of the law.

In the white paper published by the Labour government in advance of the introduction of the Law Commissions Bill the point was made that there was an urgent need for a review body. This was substantiated by the fact that there were said to exist some 3,000 Acts of Parliament dating from 1234, many volumes of delegated legislation and some 300,000 reported case decisions. Looked at in this light, the Law Commission deserves to remain a permanent institution in the English legal system and the Labour Party have said that, should they be elected in 1996/7, they will strengthen the Commission's position.

ADVISORY COMMITTEES

For ensuring that improvements are made in the law as circumstances demand, certain standing committees have been set up with responsibility for reporting on particular matters in need of reform.

1. A Law Reform Committee, known originally as the Law Revision Committee, is appointed by the Lord Chancellor with the following terms of reference: "to consider, having regard especially to judicial decisions, what changes are desirable in such legal doctrines as the Lord Chancellor may from time to time refer to the committee". Membership of the committee, which is part-time, is made up of judges and practising and academic lawyers. Being part-time, the meetings of the committee are occasional and although their reports have been very thorough, their total contribution to reform is limited. The committee is limited to civil matters and its reports have led to such legislation as the Occupiers' Liability Act 1957.

2. The Criminal Law Revision Committee is the youngest of the advisory bodies, having been established in 1959 to advise the Home Secretary. Its terms of reference are: "to examine such aspects of the criminal law of England and Wales as the Home Secretary may from time to time refer to the committee to consider whether the law requires revision and to make recommendations". In composition it is very like the Law Reform Committee. It has produced on average one report a year; again it is a part-time body, and these reports have led to such legislation as the Suicide Act 1961 and the Theft Acts of 1968 and 1978. Its reports have sparked considerable controversy, from time to time.

3. Other bodies. The Lord Chancellor, in particular, is advised by several standing and many ad hoc committees. One of the most obvious is the Legal Aid Board. In addition, he currently has working parties considering various topics.

4. Royal Commissions. These are appointed ad hoc, to conduct major reviews of the law or legal system. For instance, the Royal Commission on Assizes and Quarter Sessions (1969) recommended the creation of the Crown Court. The Royal Commission on Criminal Procedure (1980) produced recommendations which led to the passing of PACE. The Royal Commission on Legal Services (1979) was singularly unsuccessful, in that many of its recommendations have been ignored. In 1991, the Home Secretary and Lord Chancellor, established the Royal Commisssion on Criminal Justice, at the height of public concern over famous miscarriages of justice. It reported in 1993 and some of its recommendations have been followed, such as those on appeals, in the Criminal Appeal Act 1995. Others have been ignored, such as those on the right to silence and yet others are still under consideration.

5. Green Papers and White Papers. All government departments may publish green papers setting out their proposals for legislative change. These are open invitations for comment by the interested public at large. Once gathered in, these responses help streamline final legislative proposals which are set out in a white paper. For instance, this was done by the Lord Chancellor's Department, on the subject of legal aid, in 1995 and his proposals, as amended, were published as a white paper in 1996 and are likely to become the Legal Aid Act 1996.

CONSOLIDATION AND CODIFICATION

The work of the Law Commission and other reforming bodies leads on to a consideration of the actual process by which legislation is simplified. Under the Consolidation of Enactments (Procedure) Act 1949, a system was introduced by Parliament under which, where the bringing together of separate statutory provisions, known as "consolidation", was deemed to be desirable, the Lord Chancellor could arrange to have prepared a memorandum showing how these various provisions would take effect in the proposed consolidating Act. Thus, for example, the whole of the legislation concerned with tribunals and inquiries was brought together and updated in the Tribunals and Inquiries Act 1992. The memorandum is duly placed before a joint committee of both Houses of Parliament. If this joint committee approves the proposed consolidating measure, it is virtually certain to be passed by both Houses without the need for lengthy debates. Since the Bill is little more than a simplifying measure, the examination by the joint committee is generally acceptable to the members of both Houses.

This procedure is not possible where the Bill involves changes of substance in the law, known as "codification". A codifying measure brings together the existing statute and case law, in an attempt to produce a full statement as it relates to that particular branch of law. The main examples of successful codification date from the end of the nineteenth century when the following four statutes were passed: the Bills of Exchange Act 1882, the Partnership Act 1890, the Sale of Goods Act 1893 and the Marine Insurance Act 1906. The Bills of Exchange Act 1882, which was prepared by Sir M.D. Chalmers, involved the consideration of 17 existing statutes and some 2,500 decided cases. These were compressed to make a statute 100 sections long. After these Acts were passed, there was no more codifying legislation until the Theft Act 1968.

Today there is considerable talk of the introduction of codifying statutes, so that the coming decade may witness new examples of this type of legislation. The Law Commission has recently published a Draft Criminal Code. A major consideration is the question of parliamentary time. Unlike a consolidating measure, the fact that a codifying Bill proposes to change the law means that members of Parliament will wish to debate it.

3. CHANGE AND THE ENGLISH LEGAL SYSTEM

The 1980s and 1990s may go down in history as producing the most dramatic changes in the English Legal System since the Supreme Court of Judicature Acts of the 1880s merged law and equity and created the Supreme Court.

In the criminal justice system, the decade started with the work of the Royal Commission on Criminal Procedure which resulted in several pieces of legislation. Most notable was the Police and Criminal Evidence Act 1984, strengthening the rights of suspected persons. The Prosecution of Offences Act 1985 created a national prosecution service, The Crown Prosecution Service. The spate of miscarriages of justice which came to light in the late 1980s and early 1990s, notably the Guildford Four and Birmingham Six cases, provoked the establishment of the Royal Commission on Criminal Justice, whose terms of reference charge it with the astonishingly bold task of assessing the desirability of importing inquisitorial elements of procedure from civil law countries. It produced a highly controversial report in 1993 which resulted in some sections of the Criminal Justice and Public Order Act 1994, the Criminal Appeal Act 1995 and, doubtless, further legislation on matters such as mode of trial.

As far as civil procedure is concerned, equally radical changes have taken place. The *Civil Justice Review* of 1988 raised the question of whether a redistribution of civil work and a change in pre-trial procedure and the costs regime could cut out undesirable facets of English civil procedure, notably cost and delay in the High Court. Its recommendations led to Part I of the Courts and Legal Services Act 1990, which gave county courts almost the same jurisdiction as the High Court, allowing for a very significant shift of work down into the county court. The Children Act of 1989 gave parallel jurisdiction, in matters affecting children, to the three first instance courts, the county court, magistrates' court and High Court. The Lord Chancellor said he saw this Act as paving the way towards a family court. The 1980s saw a massive growth in applications for judicial review to the High Court, following a simplification of procedure, and the practice of their being listed in the Crown Office list.

As far as members of the legal profession are concerned, they are still to feel the real impact of the government's attack on their monopolies. The Administration of Justice Act 1985 effectively destroyed the solicitors' conveyancing monoploy by establishing a system of licensed conveyancers. This, however, posed no serious threat, in comparison with the CLSA 1990, which empowered the Lord Chancellor to open up competition to banks and building societies. Neither has the other side of the profession been spared from threat. Again, the CLSA 1990 destroys the barristers' monopoly over rights of audience in the higher courts, effectively allowing anyone to apply to be licensed for rights of audience in the various levels of court. As a corollary of this, judicial and other similar appointments are no longer limited to barristers and the CLSA substitutes rights of audience as the qualification.

The Legal Aid Act 1988 took the administration of civil legal aid out of the hands of the Law Society and gave it to a new Legal Aid Board. It allowed the Lord Chancellor wide and controversial powers to establish a franchising system for the provision of legal advice. At the time of writing, the legal aid scheme is, yet again, under scrutiny, following the Lord Chancellor's 1995 green paper *Legal Aid—Targeting Need* and so is the civil justice system, by Lord Woolf.

THE COURT STRUCTURE

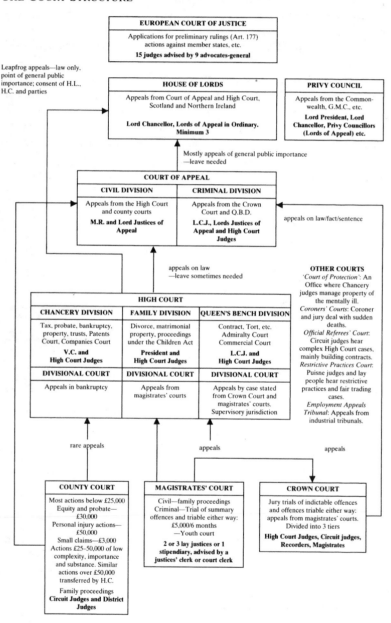

EUROPEAN COURT OF JUSTICE

Applications for preliminary rulings (Art. 177) actions against member states, etc.

15 judges advised by 9 advocates-general

Leapfrog appeals—law only, point of general public importance; consent of H.L., H.C. and parties

HOUSE OF LORDS

Appeals from Court of Appeal and High Court, Scotland and Northern Ireland

Lord Chancellor, Lords of Appeal in Ordinary. Minimum 3

PRIVY COUNCIL

Appeals from the Commonwealth, G.M.C., etc.

Lord President, Lord Chancellor, Privy Councillors (Lords of Appeal) etc.

Mostly appeals of general public importance —leave needed

COURT OF APPEAL

CIVIL DIVISION	**CRIMINAL DIVISION**
Appeals from the High Court and county courts	Appeals from the Crown Court and Q.B.D.
M.R. and Lord Justices of Appeal	**L.C.J., Lords Justices of Appeal and High Court Judges**

appeals on law/fact/sentence

appeals on law —leave sometimes needed

HIGH COURT

CHANCERY DIVISION	**FAMILY DIVISION**	**QUEEN'S BENCH DIVISION**
Tax, probate, bankruptcy, property, trusts, Patents Court, Companies Court	Divorce, matrimonial property, proceedings under the Children Act	Contract, Tort, etc. Admiralty Court Commercial Court
V.C. and High Court Judges	**President and High Court Judges**	**L.C.J. and High Court Judges**
DIVISIONAL COURT	**DIVISIONAL COURT**	**DIVISIONAL COURT**
Appeals in bankruptcy	Appeals from magistrates' courts	Appeals by case stated from Crown Court and magistrates' courts. Supervisory jurisdiction

OTHER COURTS

'*Court of Protection'*: An Office where Chancery judges manage property of the mentally ill.

Coroners' Courts: Coroner and jury deal with sudden deaths.

Official Referees' Court: Circuit judges hear complex High Court cases, mainly building contracts.

Restrictive Practices Court: Puisne judges and lay people hear restrictive practices and fair trading cases.

Employment Appeals Tribunal: Appeals from industrial tribunals.

rare appeals

appeals

appeals

COUNTY COURT

Most actions below £25,000 Equity and probate— £30,000 Personal injury actions— £50,000 Small claims—£3,000 Actions £25–50,000 of low complexity, importance and substance. Similar actions over £50,000 transferred by H.C.

Family proceedings

Circuit Judges and District Judges

MAGISTRATES' COURT

Civil—family proceedings Criminal—Trial of summary offences and triable either way: £5,000/6 months —Youth court

2 or 3 lay justices or 1 stipendiary, advised by a justices' clerk or court clerk

CROWN COURT

Jury trials of indictable offences and offences triable either way: appeals from magistrates' courts. Divided into 3 tiers

High Court Judges, Circuit judges, Recorders, Magistrates

FURTHER READING

General

Zander, *Cases and Materials on the English Legal System* (7th edn., 1996).
Cownie and Bradney, *English Legal System in Context*, forthcoming 1996.
The Law Society's Gazette
The Times law section, every Tuesday.
The Lawyer magazine.
The New Law Journal.

The Legal Profession

The Royal Commission On Legal Services Report, Cmnd. 7648 (1979).
Legal Services; A Framework For the Future, Cm. 740 (1989).
Counsel (magazine).
The Lord Chancellor's Advisory Committee On Legal Education and Conduct, *First Report On Legal Education and Training*, 1996.
Many publications from the Law Society, including their *Annual Statistical Reports*.
The General Council of the Bar Annual Reports.

Judges

Pannick, *Judges* (1987).
The Lord Chancellor's Department, *Judicial Appointments* (1995)

JUSTICE, *The Judiciary In England and Wales* (1992).
Stevens, *The Independence of the Judiciary* (1993).

Magistrates

Burney, *J.P. Magistrate, Court and Community* (1979).
Darbyshire, *The Magistrates' Clerk*, 1984.
Justice of the Peace journal.
The Magistrate magazine.

The Jury

Findlay and Duff, *The Jury Under Attack* (1988).
Lord Devlin, *Trial By Jury* (1966).
Baldwin and McConville, *Jury Trials* (1979).
Cornish, *The Jury* (1968).

The Courts

The Lord Chancellor's Department, annual *Judicial Statistics*.
The Court Service Annual Reports.
The Court's Charter

Civil Procedure and Evidence

Barnard & Houghton, *The New Civil Court In Action* (1993).
Civil Justice Review, *Report of the Review Body on Civil Justice* (1988).

The General Council of the Bar and The Law Society, "Civil Justice On Trial—The Case For Change" (1993).
Lord Woolf, *Access To Justice* (Interim Report, 1995 and final report, forthcoming, 1996).

Criminal Procedure and Evidence

Tapper, *Cross and Tapper on Evidence* (8th edn., 1995).
Padfield, *Text and Materials on the Criminal Process* (1995).
Sanders and Young, *Criminal Justice* (1994).
The Royal Commission on Criminal Justice Report, Cm. 2263 (1993) and research reports listed therein.
The Criminal Law Review

Tribunals and ADR

Council On Tribunals, Annual Reports.
Lord Mackay, *The Administration of Justice* (1994).

E.C. Law

Weatherill & Beaumont, *E.C. Law* (2nd edn., 1995).
Foster, *Blackstone's E.C. Legislation* (6th edn., 1995–6).
Weatherill, *Cases and Materials on E.C. Law* (3rd edn., 1996).
Steiner, *Textbook on E.C. Law* (1994).
Wyatt & Dashwood, *European Community Law* (3rd edn., 1993).
Hartley, *The Foundations of European Community Law* (3rd edn., 1994).

Lasok and Bridge: *Law and Institutions of the European Union* (6th edn., 1994).

Legal Aid and Legal Services

Annual Reports and many special reports of the Legal Aid Board.
Lord Chancellor's Department, *Legal Aid—Targeting Need*, Cm. 2854 (1995).
Responses to the above green paper by the Law Society, The General Council of the Bar, the Legal Action Group and the Legal Aid Board.
Various publications by the Law Centres Federation.

Sources

Manchester, Salter, Moodie & Lynch, *Exploring The Law* (1996).
Zander, *The Law Making Process* (4th edn., 1994).
Bell and Engle, *Cross: Statutory Interpretation* (3rd edn., 1995).
Cross and Harris, *Precedent in English Law*.

History

Baker, *Introduction to English Legal History* (3rd edn., 1990).

Index

279